THE
SEVEN AGES
OF WOMAN

THE
SEVEN AGES
OF WOMAN

A Lifetime Guide to Feeling Good

DR ROSEMARY LEONARD

BANTAM PRESS

LONDON · TORONTO · SYDNEY · AUCKLAND · JOHANNESBURG

TRANSWORLD PUBLISHERS
61–63 Uxbridge Road, London W5 5SA
a division of The Random House Group Ltd
www.booksattransworld.co.uk

First published in Great Britain
in 2007 by Bantam Press
a division of Transworld Publishers

A CIP catalogue record for this book
is available from the British Library

ISBN 9780593055168

Addresses for Random House Group Ltd companies outside the UK
can be found at www.randomhouse.co.uk
The Random House Group Ltd Reg. No. 954009

The Random House Group Ltd makes every effort to ensure that the papers used
in its books are made from trees that have been legally sourced from well-managed
and credibly certified forests. Our paper procurement policy can be found at:
www.randomhouse.co.uk/paper.htm

Typeset in 12/14pt Celeste by
Falcon Oast Graphic Art Ltd

Printed and bound in Great Britain by
CPI Antony Rowe, Chippenham and Eastbourne

2 4 6 8 10 9 7 5 3 1

For Thomas and William, my wonderful sons

CONTENTS

ACKNOWLEDGEMENTS

I can't possibly list all the friends and colleagues who have helped to make this book possible; if I did it would resemble one of those boring speeches at an awards ceremony. So I'm going to stick to the really important ones: thank you to Sheila Molloy, Catherine Best and Rachel Baird for their invaluable contributions to the text; my agent, Jacqueline Burns, and my editor at Bantam Press, Brenda Kimber, for endless patience and encouragement. And last, but not least, huge thanks to Lorraine Gibson, who kept my home clean and tidy while I sat glued to the keyboard.

INTRODUCTION

This book aims to give all the information a woman needs about her own body and her general health right the way through her life, from infancy to maturity. Most women are well aware that good health is important, and know that avoiding disease, or dealing with it so as to lessen its impact, must be a priority. They also know that it's a huge help to be aware of the inevitable changes in their bodies before they happen. Forewarned is forearmed.

I've had a conventional medical training, and what you'll find in this book is up-to-date information based on solid scientific evidence. This isn't a book about alternative remedies, but information about the more popular ones is included where relevant.

There are three main aspects to this book:

● First, you will find descriptions of the normal physical development of women throughout life, from pre-puberty to post-menopause. Knowing what to expect at each stage can play a large part in coping with change.

● Second, in each chapter you will find detailed information on all the common health problems relating specifically, or predominantly, to women of that age. Inevitably there is some overlapping – some diseases can occur at any age, but I've tried to put them in the chapter when they are most likely to be a problem. You will be able to find out about symptoms you or the women in your family are experiencing, and what to do about them.

● Finally, there are sections on diet, skin and hair care, geared to the expectations of each age group and the natural desire of every woman to make the best of herself.

It's impossible, in a book of this size, to cover all illnesses experienced by women, so what I have done is to concentrate on problems that are more common in women, or have a huge impact on a lot of women's lives. Even so, I'm aware that there are some gaping omissions – nothing on asthma, chronic bronchitis, diverticular disease . . . the list goes on. Please let me apologize in advance if you are a woman with a problem that I haven't covered – there just wasn't space.

But whatever your age and family circumstances, I hope you will find something in this book to intrigue and enlighten you. Happy reading.

CHAPTER ONE

CHILDHOOD: BIRTH TO 11

'It's a girl,' says the midwife, handing you a small, red, squealing bundle wrapped in a blanket. At that stage most women won't be thinking about the implications of having a girl rather than a boy; they will be busy counting fingers and toes, and will also be feeling incredibly proud and relieved to have produced this beautiful and healthy infant, however long and hard the labour has been.

Once you've caught your breath, though, your next thoughts may well be, 'What can I expect of my daughter? How will she react to me and the rest of the family? Will we have a special bond? How will she fit in? Most of all, what will she be like?'

So in this chapter I shall try to answer the question 'What is it that makes a girl a girl?' Are female characteristics, which make girls and women so different from boys and men, something we are born with, or are they formed during our childhood?

While a little girl is growing up, it's a mother's job to keep an eye on her physical and emotional development, and to know what to expect in terms of the general health of a daughter.

In this chapter you will find:

● **What makes a girl a girl?**
  ◦ chromosome differences between boys and girls
  ◦ the developing child

- **Staying healthy**
  - medical check-ups
  - growth rates
  - vaccinations
- **Food and nutrition**
  - a healthy diet for life
  - food for babies and toddlers
  - food allergies
  - food for developing girls and school-age children
  - weight problems in growing girls
- **Exercise**
- **Lifestyle and mental health**
  - gender conditioning
  - growing up too fast
  - sex education
  - childhood depression
  - divorce
  - learning difficulties
- **Hormonal issues**
  - the newborn baby girl
  - nappy-changing
  - birth defects
- **Genetic testing**
- **Physical illnesses**
  - common infections
  - other infections
- **Skin care**

WHAT MAKES A GIRL A GIRL?

No matter how much you may have heard about the nature/nurture argument, right from the moment of conception the pattern is set for females to be very different from males. Fascinatingly, these differences can even be detected inside the womb, and they continue throughout life.

THE X FACTOR

Our gender is determined by our chromosomes. There are two 'sex' chromosomes, X and Y, and we inherit one of them from each of our parents. Girls have two Xs; boys have an X and a Y.

All the cells in the human body carry both chromosomes, except, very importantly, eggs and sperm. These have only one. The egg from the mother always carries an X, but the sperm from the father can have either an X or a Y. This means that a baby's gender is determined by the father. If a sperm carrying an X chromosome fertilizes a woman's egg, the baby will be a girl; if one carrying a Y pips it at the post, it will be male.

A female's extra X chromosome helps to prevent clumsiness, hyperactivity, autism and stammer – conditions more prevalent in boys.

The main function of a boy's Y chromosome is to ensure that he gets lots of male hormones, or androgens, most importantly testosterone. Without testosterone all babies would be born as girls – it is testosterone that triggers the baby to develop as a boy, with male genitals and a male brain.

At 6 weeks of pregnancy, boys and girls look the same, but by 12 weeks a girl will have developed fallopian tubes, a womb and a vagina; meanwhile, under the influence of testosterone, boys will have developed a penis, testes and scrotum.

But it's not just the genitalia that are different. At 13 weeks of pregnancy the sense organs have formed slightly differently, and females have a distinct advantage. When a girl is born, her sensitivity to sound, smells and visual images will be sharper.

By 4 months into pregnancy a foetus will have a male or female brain. Although a female has a smaller brain and fewer brain cells, she builds up more complex connections. Experiments have shown that many more sites in her brain swing into motion than in a male's when confronted with facts that have emotional overtones. Research suggests that this is why females tend to be more empathetic than males, even at a very young age.

At 15 months old a girl will also have better language skills and will continue to outstrip her male counterpart verbally. Even at 5 years old she will be on average 2 months ahead of a boy in her speech.

But, yes, the 'women can't read maps' jokes do seem to be borne out by biology. Blame it on testosterone, but men do appear to be endowed with more spatial awareness.

Although boys and girls are wired up differently, there are tremendous variations within each sex. Both sexes produce testosterone, though the amount in girls is much less than in boys, and whether you have a 'girlie girl' or a tomboy with ace spatial skills seems to depend on how much testosterone she produces in the womb and, to some extent, how many maternal androgens cross the placenta.

An infant girl is more mature than a male and generally less fractious, but there will always be those who buck the trend. Each new life is unique.

Initially, most people say that both boys and girls will tend to look more like their father – maybe this is nature's cunning way of ensuring male bonding after a baby is born!

Male/female births

Slightly more males than females are born, but fewer boys survive. Figures from the National Office of Statistics say that in 2003 in the UK, 1,051 males were born for every 1,000 females. Ten years earlier, in 1993, 1,056 males were born for every 1,000 females, so no great gender divide is opening up.

Although infant deaths fell by 3.5 per cent in England and Wales in 2002, stillbirths rose by 6.7 per cent. In that year, 2,028 boys were stillborn compared with 1,744 females.

STAYING HEALTHY

MEDICAL CHECK-UPS

All infants and children should have regular checks with a doctor or health visitor to ensure that they are growing and developing normally. These routine checks also provide a time for any concerns about your daughter's health or general welfare to be addressed. It's the ideal time to bring up the niggling worries or questions that you may not feel warrant a specific doctor's appointment.

These checks are usually done:

- ◆ soon after birth (preferably within 24 hours)
- ◆ at 6 – 8 weeks
- ◆ at 8 months
- ◆ at 2 years
- ◆ pre-school (usually between 3 and 4 years)

Checks are also usually done when a child enters school (by the school nurse) to ensure that immunizations are up to date, and also to measure height, weight, hearing and sight.

DENTAL CHECK-UPS

In addition, dental check-ups should start as soon as your daughter cuts her first tooth – the more she is used to going to a friendly dentist, the less frightening it becomes. Though NHS dental services are thin on the ground, many dentists provide free NHS care for the offspring of their private patients. As with so many aspects of health, with teeth, prevention really is important and regular dental check-ups are vital.

GROWTH RATES

Girls and boys grow at different rates. No two children are the same, and a girl's growth is determined by her genes as well as by her general health and nutrition. If both her parents are taller than average, it's very unlikely that she will be petite.

CHILDHOOD GROWTH/HEIGHT CHART

AGE	GROWTH RATE (PER YEAR)	
	INCHES	CENTIMETRES
Birth to 1 year	7–10	10–25
1 to 2 years	4–5	10–13
2 years to puberty	2–2.5	5–6
Pubertal growth spurt – girls	2.5–4.5	6–11

What matters is the general trend of growth, though some children do grow at a slower (or faster) rate than the norm in early childhood, and then their growth speeds up (or slows down) later on. This often follows a genetic pattern, so if you were the shortest in your class at the age of 4, and then nearly the tallest at 10, your daughter may well be the same.

VACCINATIONS

The other essential part of staying healthy in childhood is vaccinations. It's currently recommended that all children in the UK have vaccinations against ten different diseases:

- diphtheria
- tetanus
- pertussis (whooping cough)
- polio
- hib

- meningitis C
- pneumococcus
- measles
- mumps
- rubella (German measles)

This can seem an awful lot, especially as you watch the loaded needle going into your perfectly healthy baby girl. It's only natural to worry about side effects, and whether all these jabs are really necessary. Many parents also have concerns about potentially overloading a baby's immune system, but in fact the immune system has a huge capacity: you could vaccinate against 10,000 different illnesses safely and effectively.

It's easy to forget that some of the diseases that vaccinations prevent used to be killers in this country, and that they still present a serious threat to someone who has not been immunized.

The bacteria that cause tetanus (lockjaw) are ubiquitous in soil – including your back garden and the local park.

The MMR (measles, mumps, rubella) vaccine, which is given in 2 doses, at about 13 months and prior to starting school, is especially important for girls as it provides protection against rubella, which, although mild in childhood, can cause serious damage to a developing foetus if caught during early pregnancy. In particular, the rubella virus can affect the development of vital organs, and lead to deafness, blindness, and heart and brain damage. In the five years before the MMR vaccine was introduced in this country, rubella seriously damaged about 43 babies a year. The vaccine therefore not only protects your daughter, but also ensures she does not give rubella to a pregnant woman who is not immune to it. The vaccine also gives protection against mumps, which can cause inflammation of the ovaries, leading to fertility problems when she is older. And thirdly, it protects against measles, which can be a nasty, occasionally life-threatening, illness.

I know that many parents are concerned about the safety of MMR, but there really is a huge amount of scientific evidence, gathered both from the UK and from the rest of the world, that it does not cause either autism or inflammatory bowel disease. There is no evidence at all that giving separate vaccines is any safer than giving the combined vaccine – and it involves giving your child six separate injections. Not only that, but none of the separate vaccines is licensed in the UK – they have to be imported from abroad – and there have been concerns about their purity and safety. If you do decide to go down the separate vaccines route, and it's not something I would ever suggest, please check first where the vaccines have come from, and make sure that your daughter completes the full course – many don't, leaving them vulnerable to either one, two or all three infections.

The early pre-school vaccines are usually given at your local GP's surgery, but later boosters are often organized and given in school.

Try to keep a record of your daughter's vaccinations in a safe place. She's likely to be asked about them on numerous occasions as she grows up, so it's helpful to be able to lay your hands quickly on the dates she was given them. This also applies to any additional vaccines she is given if you travel abroad.

FOOD AND NUTRITION

A HEALTHY DIET FOR LIFE

One of the greatest gifts you can bestow on your daughter is a healthy diet. It is never too early to institute good eating habits (and of course that applies to boys as well!). Start as you mean to go on. If you give her the right body fuel, you will not only ensure she reaches optimum growth, develops strong bones, clear skin and shining hair, but you will also protect her from many later-life illnesses.

When it comes to diet, you are a role model, whether you like it or not. If she sees you eating junk food and filling up with crisps or biscuits, she will copy you and – quite rightly – regard your healthy-eating advice as hypocrisy.

FOOD FOR BABIES

Current UK guidelines recommend that for the first six months of their lives babies should get nothing but breast milk. Not only is breast milk the perfect food for their immature digestive systems and a way to continue to receive disease immunity from their mums, but there is also evidence that it will ensure they get fewer respiratory illnesses later. However, despite their best efforts, not all mums can breastfeed. If this happens to you, don't beat yourself up about it – it doesn't mean you're a bad mother!

Because girl foetuses move more quickly in the uterus than boys, and open and shut their mouths more often, the muscles round their mouths are more developed when they are born. This tends to make them easier than boys to feed.

Introducing a baby to solids too early has been linked to increased body fat and weight later, and so it really is best to wait until the baby is 6 months old before you start introducing solids. Of course, some babies are hungrier than others, so it shouldn't be a case of 'Right, she's 6 months old today, so she can have some solids.' Play it by ear – some babies need solids a little bit sooner, some are happy with just milk for another week or two. Weight gain, sleeping patterns and how often she needs to feed can be helpful markers. If she starts needing more frequent feeds, especially at night, and her weight gain is slowing down, then it's time to start weaning.

That said, in many parts of the world a girl will rely on milk alone for the first two years of her life, though this isn't ideal. However, milk (whatever its source) should remain an important part of her diet. It contains a lot of fat, and babies need much more fat than adults because it is a vital ingredient for their rapidly developing brain cells. Parents who decide to replace a small child's full-cream milk with half-fat are therefore not doing them any developmental favours. The only reason to restrict a child's fat intake is on medical advice.

FOOD FOR TODDLERS

Little children can actually thrive on a fairly basic diet. There is a current obsession with diet today but, left to themselves, most children will select healthy food because to do anything else will make them sick and listless.

Small children only need 2 per cent of protein in their diets. Most European children get far too much. They also don't need a vast supply of vegetables, which they will probably hate anyway – though if you have a garden, devoting some space for a child to grow their own veg can reap huge rewards. My sons really didn't take much to carrots till they produced some very misshapen specimens from 'their' own little plot!

Though ideally a child should get as many of her nutrients as possible from fresh food, most of the vitamins and trace elements in vegetables can be found today in cereals, tomato ketchup, fruit juices, yogurt and ice cream – the very things that children love. Just proves that a little of what you fancy can do you good!

If you're worried that your child isn't getting a balanced diet, then supplement it with milk, milk products or vitamin and mineral drops. The most important thing is not to turn food into a major battleground. That's just asking for problems later on, especially as abnormal attitudes to food and eating disorders are becoming so horribly common.

Don't overdo sugar – it will rot teeth, can make children hyperactive and can become an acquired taste, which may lead to later weight problems. As soon as it's feasible, start cleaning your daughter's teeth after meals and encourage her to do it herself as soon as she can, especially after she has had something sweet. There is a surfeit of sugar in fizzy drinks and many ready meals, but plenty of the healthier kind in fruit. However, don't deprive a toddler of sugar either. They burn off most of it and at a time of rapid growth every one of the new cells they create needs sugar.

Salt is an acquired taste, too, so try not to let your child get 'hooked' by over-seasoning her food. I reckon the best thing to do is to leave it out altogether. Too much salt can lead to high blood pressure and heart disease in later life. For any child under 11, daily salt intake should be below 2.5g of sodium (6g of salt). Always read the labels on fast-food packets – though many manufacturers are making efforts to reduce the salt in their products, the amounts that many prepared meals and snacks contain is still frighteningly high.

Many growing children do get hungry in between meals, but rather than letting them have biscuits or crisps, fruit (fresh or dried) and pieces of vegetables are much healthier alternatives.

Try to grill or bake rather than fry food and use vegetable and nut oils – not saturated animal fats which clog arteries – for cooking.

FOOD ALLERGIES

About 2 per cent of children develop a food allergy. The most common triggers are:

- ◆ nuts
- ◆ cow's milk
- ◆ eggs

If other people in the family have food allergies or suffer from eczema, hayfever or asthma, then your child will be at greater risk of developing a problem too. If that's the case, try to breastfeed for as long as possible, avoid eating nuts yourself while you are feeding and keep her away from nuts for her first year of life. If your child develops a rash, wheezes, vomits, feels sick or has diarrhoea after eating a particular food, your GP can carry out a skin test to identify the culprit.

FOOD FOR DEVELOPING GIRLS

After the first year, growth slows down, though a girl will reach half her adult height by the end of her third year.

One way a toddler will exert her growing independence is by choosing what she wants to eat. Unfortunately, this is when some children become fussy eaters. As exasperating as it is, try to keep mealtimes unhurried, relaxed affairs. Anger is counterproductive. The best way to deal with a picky child is to provide her with a wide variety of food with different tastes, colours and textures so she can get the calories she needs. If she refuses to eat what is put in front of her, don't substitute it with her favourite. Just make her wait till the next mealtime. If she gets hungry she will soon learn not to be too faddy.

After the age of 4 a child's energy needs per kilogram of bodyweight are decreasing but, because she is heavier, overall she will need an increasing number of calories to fuel her slow but steady growth. Regular meals and healthy snacks that include carbohydrate-rich foods, fruits and vegetables, dairy products, lean meats, fish, poultry, eggs, legumes and nuts should contribute to proper development without supplying excessive energy to her diet.

Children need to drink plenty of fluids, especially if it is hot or if they are physically active. Water is the best source because it supplies fluid without calories, and also does not encourage a sweet tooth.

However, milk and milk drinks or fruit juices – as long as they have a low sugar content – will keep her hydrated too.

FOOD FOR THE SCHOOL-AGE CHILD

As a girl gets older, becomes more swayed by advertising and then goes on to eat school dinners, her diet is likely to move out of your complete control, but if she has acquired good eating habits there's every chance she will continue to eat healthily. Hopefully by now she won't have developed either a sweet tooth or a liking for salty snacks, but even so, it's worth checking that she doesn't add sugar or salt to foods.

School meals standards have suffered as a result of cost-cutting measures. When cafeterias appeared in schools, a generation of snackers was born. Now that new nutritional guidelines have been introduced, hopefully meals will improve. However, there is only so much schools can provide on a limited budget, so make sure your daughter has a nutritious breakfast before she leaves home.

Children who have bran, porridge or muesli for breakfast (low glycaemic index foods – see page 224) tend to eat less lunch and need fewer snacks than those who start the day with white bread or a sugary cereal (high glycaemic index foods). These cause a quick blood-sugar surge followed by a dip and a need to eat more of the same. Food such as porridge is burnt slowly by the body and provides energy for much longer.

Girls continue to need plenty of milk throughout childhood because it provides the calcium crucial for growing bones, but cheese, yogurt and fish such as sardines, especially if you eat the bones, are excellent sources of calcium too.

WEIGHT PROBLEMS IN GROWING GIRLS

If you are worried that a girl is putting on too much weight or that her body shape is making her unhappy or leading to bullying at school, discuss it with your GP before initiating any DIY diets which may not be in her best interests.

Childhood obesity is increasing alarmingly in Britain and for the first time has been the catalyst for type 2 diabetes in children. It is much better to prevent obesity in the first place than to tackle it when a child's weight has spiralled out of control. A good, balanced diet in early childhood, coupled with exercise, is the best preventative measure.

The Department of Health says there is a 'proven year-on-year rise in obesity among children under 11' and believes the problem should be addressed urgently to prevent children from succumbing to health problems such as heart disease later in life. However, we need to draw a line between obesity and a bit of puppy fat.

There is so much prejudice today about being overweight and so much pressure for girls to conform to an unrealistic idea of stick-thin femininity that even girls of 5 who are merely chubby will now claim they are fat. That's really sad – and unhealthy. Don't be the sort of parent who colludes in this and turns her daughter into a little woman when she is still a child.

To define obesity in children, as in adults, height/weight tables and the Body Mass Index table are regarded as the most reliable benchmarks. However, children's BMIs can fluctuate wildly during normal development, so always discuss this with your GP.

If you know your daughter is eating healthily and gets plenty of exercise, there may be a medical or psychological reason for her weight gain. One cause of obesity in childhood – and it is rare – is sexual abuse, because victims often over-eat to make themselves less desirable.

If your daughter does have a genuine problem she will be asked to keep a record of what she eats so that a dietitian can assess her nutritional intake. In some cases treatment may involve dietary changes for the whole family. It is also likely to include lifestyle adjustments, such as taking more exercise and limiting the amount of time she spends watching TV or sitting at the computer.

EXERCISE

Exercise is vital for a growing child. Alongside eating a healthy, balanced diet, exercise will help to ensure that girls have plenty of credit in the bone-density bank and will be less likely to suffer from osteoporosis (see page 307) later in life. It also promotes general fitness and helps to prevent obesity. Yet only 60 per cent of schoolgirls take the recommended 60 minutes of exercise a day and a worrying number of pre-schoolers today get hardly any exercise at all.

Start as you mean to carry on, and include exercise in your daughter's weekly routine as soon as possible. Babies and toddlers usually love swimming, and special baby gym classes can boost her sense of adventure. Then, as she gets older, try to get into the habit of walking or cycling to school. If you go with her you'll be boosting your own health as well!

Unfortunately, many mid-childhood girls try to avoid exercise altogether because they perceive it as too much of a boy's thing, or they are too self-conscious to step out in shorts. Even if a girl turns her nose up at competitive sport, many schools today provide more imaginative options, such as dance, Pilates, yoga or even kick-boxing.

A toned body is an attractive body, something that becomes more important as girls move out of mid-childhood and approach puberty. Unfortunately, many girls see calorie restriction as the only way to staying slim, but being active is a far better way to a firm body, especially at this age.

Going along with your daughter to a special exercise class might get her moving in the right direction, especially as many of today's celebrities make a big deal out of exercising to stay in shape. Some gyms now welcome under-11s, but this age group should not use weight machines, which can put a dangerous strain on small, growing bodies.

LIFESTYLE AND MENTAL HEALTH

GENDER CONDITIONING

Very few strangers would dare to stick their neck out on an infant's gender if the child was dressed in a yellow sleepsuit. Usually it's the pink or blue clothes, the slide in the hair or the pierced ears that give the game away. It is parents who begin gender conditioning.

At 6 months a baby can tell someone else's gender when viewed from head to toe. At 10 months she can discern gender from face alone, and from 2 to 2½ years she can correctly label pictures of boys and girls. As soon as children know the words 'girl' and 'boy', most will know which camp they are in. At the age of 2 a girl will know she is a girl; by 4 she will understand that she has always been a girl; and by 6 she will appreciate that the condition is permanent.

Because small girls and boys see things in black and white and are groping to understand the idea of gender, their views tend to be simplistic and breathtakingly sexist. As time goes on, parents can encourage more sophisticated views of what it means to be a male or a female.

Treating boys and girls differently is deep-rooted in our culture. Girls are praised for being gentle and kind and are played with less roughly, while a little boy's bloody-mindedness or downright aggression will provoke a 'boys will be boys' tolerance.

A young child's subconscious soaks it all up. Evidence also shows that parents talk more to girls, reinforcing their superior verbal skills in infancy.

Girls are allowed to dress, play and act 'like boys' when they are very small. The reverse is not true for boys. For a girl, being a tomboy is 'cool'; for a boy, being a 'sissy' is not. Girls are allowed to express their emotions, but sadly a lot of boys still learn at an early age that this is a 'girlie thing' to do.

After they start school, girls tend to hang out with two or three best friends while boys form gangs or cliques. The way they interact with their enemies differs too. Boys' bullying is physical. Girls tend to go in for verbal aggression – sarcasm, spreading rumours, ridiculing handicaps, taunting about family, friends, race or weight. Being a bitch can start very early in life! If a girl is being bullied she may be reluctant to go to school and may feign illness. She may start doing badly at school, over-eat or refuse food and become withdrawn or even threaten to harm herself. Every year a number of bullied children commit suicide, so take behaviour changes like this seriously and make sure both the school and your GP know what is going on.

In the cruel world of childhood, peer pressure at school will ensure both genders conform to sexual stereotype or risk ridicule.

Even parents who make a genuine effort to give children of both genders access to all toys – from guns to dolls – will discover that girls tend to choose the dolls and boys the guns. When a group of pre-school boys play together the games tend to be extremely physical – suddenly your house looks far too small for them. Girls' games seem to be a gentler affair, not necessarily based on lots of movement. Generally, age for age, they are more mature than boys and their greater powers of concentration make it easier for them to sit still for longer and to engage in pursuits such as painting or looking at books.

Before she is 4, a girl will often begin to choose to play with her own sex. This will persist until her teenage years, when playing with boys becomes a whole new ball game!

Most educationists accept there are learning and behavioural differences between boys and girls, which is why many experts maintain that they are best educated separately. Others, though, say that being around the opposite sex from an early age leads to better relationships later on.

GROWING UP TOO FAST

Little girls long to be like their mums. They will teeter around on your high heels as soon as they can walk and given half a chance will experiment with your make-up. It's just play, but with the relentless pressure of advertising, dressing girls like little women has spilled out into real life. Today, peer pressure is very powerful, and children as young as 5 now know about designer labels.

Let her have her childhood – it's so brief and precious. Let her wear nail varnish if she really wants to, but only occasionally, as a treat – try not to let it become the norm. But don't give in to her request for heels on her shoes – it will deform growing bones from her feet to her spine.

Whether or not you allow her to pierce her ears has to be a matter of personal choice, but I feel it is better to wait until she is old enough to understand how to look after her ears. If she does wear earrings, make sure they are made of pure gold or silver, to avoid allergic reactions, and make sure they are removed at night. Lying on earring butterflies is not a good way to get a restful night's sleep. They should also be very light, as heavy earrings can stretch the ear lobe permanently. Hooped styles, which can easily become caught and accidentally pulled through the lobe, are also best avoided.

Make-up not only looks unnatural on a little girl but will clog young pores in a complexion that older women would die for. More disturbingly, dressing her like a woman before she is one may attract unwelcome attention from the unsavoury elements in our society. It is one area where parents need to act as a brake, not an accelerator, in the best interests of their daughters.

Girls do seem to be programmed to flirt – as young as 2, most will flutter their eyelashes at their dads. Sometimes they become more overtly sexual, rubbing themselves against furniture or against the thigh of any adult who sits them on their lap. They are doing this because it feels good. It isn't naughty, it's natural, so don't overreact.

When they are young you can easily distract them by offering them something else that feels good – like reading them a story.

By the age of about 4 most children want to explore the genitalia of other children, simply because they are curious.

Don't be afraid to set controls on sexual behaviour if it is becoming too high a priority. If sexual precocity is accompanied by changes in behaviour or genital infections (see sexual abuse, pages 19 and 40) consult your GP.

SEX EDUCATION

As soon as a girl wants to know where babies come from, tell her, but keep it appropriate to her age. 'From mummy's tummy' is a good start. Begin a girl's sex education early and naturally and never blind her with science. Every time she asks, add to her knowledge.

By drip-feeding her the facts and tailoring them to her understanding and maturity, menstruation and the sex act itself will not come as a gigantic shock. It is also a chance to give menstruation a positive spin – talk it up as a badge of womanhood, a sign that she will be able to have babies of her own. Don't let her hear about it from her friends. They might have it all wrong and scare her unnecessarily.

Most girls don't start their periods until the age of 12 – about a year after their peak growth rate starts – but a few unlucky ones will start at the age of 9, so a girl should know the basics by then.

In very rare instances a girl can begin puberty at 6 or 7. Apart from the social and psychological impact this will have on her, it will also affect her height, and in rare cases it is an indication of a serious medical problem such as a tumour. Any girl showing signs of puberty before her ninth birthday should therefore have specialist investigations, which may result in treatment to delay puberty until a more appropriate age.

CHILDHOOD DEPRESSION

About 10 per cent of under-12s in England and Wales experience a psychological disorder such as depression, obsessive thoughts or anxiety. Sadly, emotional and behavioural disorders among children are increasing.

Bouts of depression can be triggered by sad or stressful events, which means that young children are especially vulnerable when their family experiences a major upheaval, such as a divorce, or when their single mum or dad finds a new partner. Children particularly at risk of taking a mental tumble are those with low self-esteem, a pessimistic view of life or an unusual sensitivity to stress. Some children can also be particularly vulnerable to the feeling that they are not up to the challenge of today's competitive society. Depression also tends to run in families.

Like toothache, if depression is not addressed it will get worse, because depressive thinking can become an integral part of a child's developing personality. Although there is plenty of help available and the issue is better understood today, many parents are reluctant to admit that their children have problems because of the stigma attached to mental illness. It means that in this country an estimated 40 per cent of depressed children do not get the professional help they need.

But there are warning signs . . . To begin with it will affect her performance at school and her relationships with friends and family. Later, it can lead to substance abuse, disruptive behaviour, violence and even suicide.

Unlike an adult, a child is unlikely to say she is depressed or sad, and the symptoms can be so vague that it can be difficult to spot that something serious is wrong. She may use words such as 'bored' or 'angry' or tell you she is not happy, but often it is behaviour changes that are the giveaway. Signs to watch out for are persistent melancholy, inability to feel pleasure, irritability, fatigue, insomnia, lack of self-esteem and social withdrawal.

Depressed children often suffer from physical symptoms, too, such as stomach aches, headaches or failure to gain weight normally. They may feign illness and make negative comments such as 'I'm just stupid', 'Everyone hates me' or 'I wish I was dead'. A girl may also get over-anxious about her own safety.

But the good news is that, even in the young, depression is treatable. If the behaviour persists, your GP, and in some cases your child's teacher, can refer you to experts who can help. There are plenty of options available besides prescribed drugs, such as cognitive or family therapy.

DIVORCE

Children experience grief when their parents decide to part or divorce, but in the ensuing emotional adult turmoil their feelings are often overlooked. It is better to make children aware in advance that Mum and Dad are having problems than to hit them with 'We're getting a divorce'. They don't need to be part of the discussions but they do need to know what is going on. They will pick up on the mood anyway and may be imagining something even worse.

Pre-school children may become confused, irritable or worried and may regress. Children between the ages of 6 and 9 are still not mature enough to know exactly what is happening, but they will know something unpleasant is afoot and will find it difficult to express their emotions. They may react with anger or their schoolwork may suffer.

Many children will blame themselves for the divorce and it is crucial to let them know that the break-up is not their fault. A child deserves honest answers to her questions, appropriate to her age, during this fraught time. As uncomfortable as this is for adults, especially when they feel guilty themselves, children must be free to express their feelings. They may tell you they hate you – and mean it – but if they are not encouraged to say what they are feeling, they may become depressed later.

Children will also suffer from divided loyalty and you can do much to minimize this. A mother who is genuinely trying to help her children during this stressful time will not give vent to anger about their father in front of them. You may think your soon-to-be ex is a vicious, adulterous, lying, penny-pinching swine, but it will not help your children if you share this with them.

Look at the endgame: children fare much better when they can go and happily spend some time with one parent without feeling guilty about 'betraying' the other one. You may no longer need their father – they always will. There is plenty of evidence that children who lose touch with a parent – and very many do – are more likely to be disturbed by the divorce. Most kids eventually adapt but are slower to do so when there is continuing conflict between parents.

The same rules apply when a woman brings a new man into the family home. Again, prepare children before the event and try to assess and respect their feelings. Don't force a new partner on them, even though you are desperate for everyone to get on. It's also important to sit down with your new partner and do some very straight talking about parental responsibilities. Flag up potential pitfalls, such as a clash of personalities, jealousies and discipline. You can't hope to second-guess all the problems that you might face, but all too often this kind of talking only happens when major problems have already set in and the relationship is strained to breaking point.

He and your children need time to forge their own relationship independent of you. Don't try to pass him off as their dad either, because this will exacerbate the whole divided-loyalty issue. Although he will never replace their dad, in time he could become a valued and much-loved father-figure and a great friend if he is willing to tread carefully at the outset.

LEARNING DIFFICULTIES

As well as depression and family trauma, there are other conditions that can affect a girl's school performance, especially if they remain undiagnosed.

Although dyslexia, which affects three times as many boys as girls, is widely recognized, and there is plenty of literature on Attention Deficit Hyperactivity Disorder (ADHD), which affects nine times more boys than girls, very little research has been carried out on dyscalculia – or maths blindness. And guess what? This affects far more girls than boys.

This condition severely impairs a girl's ability to acquire mathematical skills. She may have difficulty understanding simple number concepts, lack a grasp of statistics and find it hard to learn number facts. Ironically, sufferers tend to have normal or advanced language skills and a good memory for the printed word.

Girls with dyscalculia have difficulty visualizing numbers and often mix them up, resulting in what appear to be silly mistakes. However, there are plenty of teaching strategies that can help, once the problem is diagnosed, such as providing visual aids and giving her extra time to memorize mathematical facts. Some girls find their work improves if they read a maths problem out loud or get someone else to do it so they can employ their auditory, instead of visual, skills. Providing graph paper to work with also helps them keep their numbers lined up.

Even in this age of computers and calculators, poor numeracy is more of a handicap in getting and keeping a job than poor literacy, according to a recent report from the Basic Skills Agency. So if a girl does have a problem with maths, speak to her teachers and see the Special Educational Needs Coordinator (SENCO) at her school. The SENCO will create an individual education plan for your daughter, which will enable the school to provide appropriate support for her.

HORMONAL ISSUES

THE NEWBORN BABY GIRL

A newborn girl's genitals – including her uterus – are likely to be swollen because of the effect of her mother's oestrogen. There is often a vaginal discharge, which is occasionally blood-stained. It is, in fact, a tiny menstrual period. It's usually painless, lasts less than a day and no treatment is needed. When a girl infant's body responds like this to a drop in hormone levels it is a sign that her body is working normally. However, after infancy and before she reaches puberty, vaginal bleeding should not occur. If it does, the cause – often either a minor infection or a foreign body inside the vagina – should be investigated.

Very rarely a newborn girl's labia may appear to be fused at birth, but in most cases are easily separated. Her breasts may also be swollen due to residual maternal hormones but should become normal within 6 weeks.

NAPPY-CHANGING

New mums with baby boys often make comments about how difficult it is to clean around all their 'bits', but, if anything, cleaning little girls is even more difficult. After all, at least with boys it's a sealed unit, whereas little girls have lots of folds, nooks and crannies, which can, and do, get dirty. Baby poo can irritate skin quite easily, so it is important to be quite thorough and to remove all traces of it from around the genitalia.

However, the vagina itself is largely sealed off by the hymen, so there is no need to go poking inside it. Despite the fact that your daughter is just like you, it can be difficult to know what is what, and if you are unsure what to do and just where to go when you clean her, ask your midwife or health visitor.

BIRTH DEFECTS AFFECTING THE FEMALE GENITALIA

The female reproductive system develops in the womb from two identical 'tube' systems on the left and right. The upper parts of these remain separate as the fallopian tubes, while the lower portions fuse together to form the uterus and the upper two-thirds of the vagina. The lower third of the vagina forms as an ingrowth from skin of the vulva. The hymen, a thin membrane with a central small opening, marks the level where the two systems join together. However, as with other organs in the body, faults can occur in the development of the genital tract, resulting in a range of defects.

About 1 in 1,500 to 1 in 2,000 baby girls is born with some form of genital abnormality. Some of these are immediately obvious; others do not become apparent till a girl either fails to go into puberty or, despite other signs of puberty, fails to menstruate. The most common is an imperforate hymen, where the hymen remains intact. This becomes apparent when a young girl, who otherwise has developed normally, fails to have any obvious periods. In fact, menstruation does occur, but the blood that is shed collects in the vagina above the hymen. Once detected, this can be easily corrected with simple surgery.

The other relatively common problem that occurs is that two duct systems fail to fuse properly at the level of the womb. Sometimes just a small septum remains in the upper part of the womb, or there may be a division extending nearly to the cervix – a 'bicornuate' uterus. This type of defect often does not cause any symptoms, but in some can cause heavy periods and also recurrent miscarriages. It can be detected on an ultrasound scan. Small septums can often be removed surgically, but treatment of a bicornuate uterus is much more difficult. More rarely, there are two wombs, each with its own cervix (so yes, women with this need to have two cervical smears!) and sometimes even with a double upper vagina as well.

There are also some more serious defects that can occur in girls as a result either of hormonal problems or of chromosome abnormalities.

TURNER'S SYNDROME

This random syndrome affects 1 out of every 2,000 female births. It is caused by a missing or defective X chromosome, so affected girls have cells that contain only one X, rather than two.

Symptoms include reduced height, webbed neck, lack of secondary sex characteristics, hollow chest, low hairline, low-set ears, soft fingernails and toenails and droopy eyelids. Symptoms are more obvious the greater the chromosome abnormality, and are most obvious in those with the full-blown syndrome. They may be only minor in those who have part of a chromosome missing.

The lack of two normal X chromosomes affects the development of the ovaries, and this means that they do not start to produce oestrogen at the normal age. In some, the condition is diagnosed only when breast development and the other signs of puberty fail to occur. Girls with Turner's syndrome also fail to have the normal growth spurt that occurs in puberty, and are therefore usually of short stature.

Treatment with oestrogen allows an affected girl to mature sexually, and ideally should be started in the early teens, when puberty normally occurs. Oestrogen treatment is also important in helping to prevent osteoporosis.

Women with Turner's syndrome can live long and healthy lives but unfortunately the lack of ovarian tissue means that they are infertile.

CONGENITAL ADRENAL HYPERPLASIA (CAH)

This condition is caused by excessive production of testosterone from the adrenal glands, resulting in a baby girl being born with an enlarged clitoris that resembles a small phallus. In more severe cases the external genitalia are even more masculinized, to the extent that the urethra, the tube from the bladder, comes out through a small penis, while the labia are enlarged and fused together so that they look like a small scrotum. However, inside she will have a uterus, fallopian tubes, ovaries and vagina.

CAH is genetic, inherited from parents who carry an abnormal gene. In order for the condition to occur, the gene must be inherited from both parents. Those who inherit the gene from just one parent will have normal genitalia but, because they carry the gene, could possibly have an affected child in the future. A woman who has had one child with CAH can request a pre-natal diagnostic test in future pregnancies (see page 37).

CAH is treated by taking medication to correct abnormal hormone levels; it usually has to be taken for life. Plastic surgery can correct the abnormal genitalia. But apart from this girls with CAH can have a completely normal life and will be capable of getting pregnant and having babies.

ANDROGEN INSENSITIVITY SYNDROME

This is the opposite of CAH, and can lead to a genetic boy (carrying XY genes) being born with female genitalia and being mistaken for a girl at birth. It is caused by a fault in the way the body tissues respond to androgens, which can occur to a varying degree. It is an 'X-linked recessive disorder' (see page 36), which means it is inherited from a carrier mother.

An affected child has a small vagina, but no uterus, and instead of ovaries there are two small testes inside the abdomen. The syndrome is often only discovered when the child fails to go into puberty as normal and does not start having periods. Once the diagnosis has been made, oestrogen treatment can stimulate normal pubertal development, at least in appearance.

Inevitably, girls with androgen insensitivity syndrome are infertile but, interestingly, because they are brought up as girls, those with the syndrome are as likely as those in the general population to feel a normal female gender identity and to be sexually attracted to men.

GENETIC TESTING

Our genes contain a unique set of instructions that can have a huge influence on our health and well-being. The most common effect is to make a person more susceptible to a certain illness, for example heart disease or thyroid problems. Slightly defective genes can also make you more at risk of some cancers, for example the BRCA1 and 2 genes that increase the risk of breast cancer. In these cases, though your genes may put you at increased risk of a health problem, taking action – changing your lifestyle, taking medication or even having preventative surgery – means that illness is not inevitable.

Sometimes, however, the effects of genes are more profound and cause illness, such as cystic fibrosis or haemophilia, which cannot be avoided.

Our genes are coded into our DNA, which is found in the nucleus of every cell in our body. The DNA is arranged on to 22 pairs of chromosomes, and we all inherit one of each pair, with its unique set of genes, from each of our parents. As a result, we all have two sets of genes. In addition, as we have seen, we all have two 'sex' chromosomes, XX in women, XY in men.

This means that diseases can be inherited in several ways.

♦ 'Dominant' conditions are caused by inheriting just one abnormal gene, which then overrides the other copy. Examples of this include Huntington's disease and familial hypercholesterolaemia.

♦ Sometimes, though, a disease does not occur unless an abnormal gene is inherited from both parents – 'recessive' conditions. If you have just one copy of it, the normal copy inherited from the other parent keeps you perfectly well. However, because you carry the abnormal gene, there is a chance of passing it on to your children, and if your partner also carries the abnormal gene, there is a 1 in 4 chance that your children will have the condition concerned. The most common example of this is cystic fibrosis, where 1 in 25 of the population is a carrier.

♦ A third possibility is 'X-linked recessive conditions', which have particular importance for women, who can, often unknowingly, act as carriers. In these, the abnormal gene is on the X chromosome. If a woman has a normal gene on her other X chromosome, she will be a healthy carrier, but if a man inherits the abnormal gene then he will be affected because he only has one X chromosome. If a woman is a carrier, there is a 50 per cent chance that any son she has will be affected by the condition (as he may inherit the healthy X). Examples of this are red–green colour blindness and haemophilia.

An increasing range of genetic tests can be done which can reveal if a person is carrying the genes or chromosomes that will either cause disease in their children, or put them at increased risk of disease themselves in later life.

Tests can be done at any time in a person's life, even, occasionally, before a fertilized egg has implanted in the womb – pre-implantation testing. Testing amniotic fluid or a tiny sample of the placenta can detect whether an unborn baby is carrying a defective gene. After-birth tests are done with an ordinary blood sample; occasionally samples of saliva or skin tissue are required.

There are three main types of test:

♦ Pre-symptom tests. These are done on people who, though currently healthy, may be at increased risk of developing a particular inherited illness in the future. Examples include testing for the breast cancer genes BRCA1 or 2.

♦ Carrier tests. These are for people who carry altered genes which, although harmless, may be passed on and cause illness in their children. An example is cystic fibrosis.

♦ Diagnostic tests. These are used to try to discover the cause of a person's medical problem. An example is testing a woman who has had recurrent miscarriages for a hidden gene defect, or to check whether a teenager with a late puberty has Turner's syndrome (see page 32).

Genetic tests can cause a huge amount of anxiety, and anyone having them done should be fully counselled by a genetics expert beforehand. You need to be fully prepared for the implications of a positive test.

I do not think anyone should ever do a DIY genetic test (they are available from some shops and from the internet). If you are concerned about a possible genetic problem in your family, then see your doctor.

Though some gene tests can be useful, the results of others, particularly predictive tests, are not always a good indicator of your future health. At present the results of genetic tests do not have to be disclosed to life insurance companies (unless you are taking out a very large policy), but this situation may change in the future. I hope it doesn't.

Paternity testing is slightly different. This compares the genetic patterns of DNA (the substance that holds genes in each cell) of the mother, a man and a child to determine, with a high degree of accuracy, whether or not the man is the father of the child in question. In the past, blood samples were required, but now DNA from a swab taken from inside the mouth, a hair follicle or even just a fingerprick of blood is all that is required. Paternity-testing kits are widely available on the internet, but not all are reliable. Check for the ISO/IEC 17025 quality-assurance standard.

PHYSICAL ILLNESSES

COMMON INFECTIONS

You cannot stop children getting common infectious illnesses – and neither should you want to. There is good evidence that minor infections – coughs, colds and the odd tummy bug – can help to boost the immune system and help to stop allergic diseases developing in the years to come. And for a girl, catching some infections in childhood can be especially beneficial, as the lifelong immunity she will acquire will mean that the infections will not pose a risk when she becomes pregnant.

Rubella (German measles) used to be top of the list, but that can now be prevented by immunization (see page 9). If a girl has not had the MMR vaccine, then make sure she knows she may not be immune to rubella well before she starts having sexual relationships. She can then choose to be immunized before she decides to start a family. Odd sporadic cases of rubella do still occur, and if caught during the first 4 months of a pregnancy, there can be devastating effects on the developing foetus.

Chickenpox can also cause severe birth defects if caught during the first 5 months of pregnancy. Not only that, but the illness tends to be much more severe in adults, with more complications, so there is a lot to be said for letting your young daughter play with a pox-ridden friend! Though the illness causes discomfort and misery, and the spots look pretty awful, most girls are over the worst within a week, and then have lifelong immunity.

Slapped cheek disease is another common childhood infection that can be dangerous if caught in pregnancy. This is caused by a parvovirus and, as its name suggests, causes a bright red rash on both cheeks, just as if they have been slapped, along with a slight fever. It usually only lasts a few days, and is most common between the ages of 4 and 12. Infection in the first half of a pregnancy can cause miscarriage, and can also cause foetal abnormalities.

It's easy to forget about common childhood illnesses once your daughter is older, but it will be incredibly useful for her to have a written record. Keep it in a safe place – maybe along with her childhood photos or school reports. If she knows she's definitely had chickenpox, she won't need to be concerned if she comes into contact with it when she is pregnant – and you won't be on the receiving end of a worried phone call.

OTHER INFECTIONS

It's not just grown women who suffer from vaginal discharge or soreness. Though much less common, it can occur in the pre-pubertal years as well.

Vaginal discharge in older girls is sometimes caused by poor hygiene or by thrush. It can also be due to infection with other organisms more usually found near the anus. Wiping forwards after going to the toilet is often to blame, and all girls should be taught, right from the start, always to wipe front to back. This can help to prevent urinary-tract infections (UTIs) as well.

Occasionally, in younger girls, a vaginal infection can be due to something being in the vagina that shouldn't be there – a small toy, or even a piece of food! This isn't as odd as it might sound – young girls do put things in their vaginas out of curiosity or because they have spied an older sibling or their mother inserting a tampon.

Sometimes a sore vulva can be due to irritation from chemicals, such as perfumed soaps or bubble baths, or residues from biological detergents or fabric conditioners. If you have a girl with sensitive skin, always wash her clothes in non-biological detergent, and if you must use fabric conditioner make sure it is a brand that is suitable for sensitive skin.

It's sad, but occasionally a sore vulva or a vaginal discharge can be a sign of sexual abuse, so it is important that it's never ignored, especially if it's a recurring problem.

Because of the arrangement of female plumbing – the close proximity of the urethra, vagina and rectum – girls and women, no matter what their age, are more prone than men to urinary-tract infections. Surveys have shown that 1 per cent of girls aged between 5 and 14 have bacteria in their urine. Though small numbers of bacteria may not cause any symptoms, larger quantities, as in adults, can cause inflammation of the bladder, with a need to pee more often, and pain on passing urine. In toddlers still in nappies there may be a noticeable change in the smell of the urine, and those who are potty trained may suddenly start wetting their pants. The diagnosis can be confirmed by a simple urine culture, and a short course of antibiotics is all that is required.

Repeated urinary-tract infections in young girls can be a sign of a slight bladder abnormality, notable reflux of urine from the bladder up towards the kidneys on each side. For this reason, it is usual practice for young girls who have had two confirmed urine infections to have an ultrasound scan of their kidneys and bladder, just to check that all is normal.

SKIN CARE

One of the best things you can do for your daughter is to protect her skin from the sun. Letting her play outside without any sunblock isn't just putting her at risk of painful sunburn; it's also a quick way to premature ageing, and will increase her risk of skin cancer. There is now increasing evidence that many cases of malignant melanoma – the most dangerous form of skin cancer (see page 388) – can be traced back to excess sun exposure in childhood.

Though boys should be protected just as much, at the risk of sounding very sexist, girls are generally much more conscious of the appearance of their complexion and your 30-year-old daughter is more likely to notice wrinkles around her eyes than her twin brother! Teaching her good sun habits at a young age will set a good pattern for later life. If she learns early on that a suntan is bad news, she won't be tempted to 'lie and fry' when she is older.

Though staying out of the sun, especially between 11a.m. and 3p.m., is the best way of protecting young skins, clothing is important too. The more dense the fabric, the better the protection it is likely to give – some swimwear is now especially designed to block out UV light.

Wet clothing stretches, and can lose up to half its UV protection, so put her in dry clothing after she has been playing in water.

All children, whatever their skin type, should also wear a wide-brimmed hat (preferably with a neck protector as well) whenever they are outside, along with sunglasses – sunshine is the major cause of cataracts.

Sunscreens are useful for protecting the skin, but no matter how strong they are, they can never provide complete protection against sunlight and should never be used just to allow a child to spend longer in the sun. Children play outside at school, so if she can't put sunscreen on there, get into the routine of putting it on before she leaves in the morning.

The sun protection factor is a measure of the sunscreen's ability to filter out dangerous UV light. Factor 15 gives 93 per cent protection, and though higher factors are available, they are generally much more expensive and only give a fraction better protection. They can also give a false sense of security. It is still possible to burn wearing factor 60. Most sunscreens have a shelf life of only 2 to 3 years, so if you can't remember when you bought that bottle at the back of the bathroom cupboard, chuck it out!

UVA rays can also cause burning – some sunscreens rate this with a star system, while others say they offer 'broad spectrum' protection. Water-resistant brands are generally preferable, especially for children running in and out of paddling pools, but even these wash off and should be re-applied frequently, every 2 hours.

To sum up, make sure you:

♦ apply sunscreen frequently

♦ give her a wide-brimmed hat with neck protector . . .

♦ . . . and sunglasses

♦ put on dry clothes after swimming

♦ if possible, keep her out of the sun in the middle of the day

Later on, she may even thank you for looking after her skin in childhood.

IN SUMMARY

Baby girls need a lot of care. From birth until the age of 11 it is the job of family members, usually the mother in particular, to supply this care. With the help of this chapter, I hope you will find it all a bit easier, and be reassured that you are doing the right thing in looking after her physical and mental health as far as you can, checking on her development, taking her for vaccinations and keeping an eye out for problems. Many conditions are easier to deal with in the early stages, so don't be afraid to ask to see your doctor if there is anything you are worried about.

Obviously a child's diet is crucial in the early stages, so I have tried to emphasize how you can help by supplying the best-quality nutrition for your growing girl and encouraging her to take regular exercise.

However, other factors do come into play right from the beginning of a child's life, both in her genetic predisposition and in her ability (and yours) to cope with upheavals such as childhood infections, divorce or bereavement.

You are giving a baby girl the best possible care if you not only look after her physical health, but also play with her, give her love and attention and anticipate changes, as described in Chapter 2.

CHAPTER TWO

TEENAGE YEARS: 11–19

B etween the ages of 11 and 19, girls undergo tremendous mental and physical changes. The dependent schoolgirl of 11 gradually becomes the increasingly independent young woman of 19, learning to make her own choices, lead her own life, and step away from the influence of her parents. It can be a bewildering time, not just for the girl, but also for her mother, as she watches a young woman appear within a matter of years.

At this time, hormones take centre stage. Oestrogen, in particular, will have a major influence on a woman's physical and emotional well-being for the next 40 years.

In this chapter you will find:

- **Staying healthy**
- **Food and nutrition**
  - key nutrients for a growing teenager
  - the adolescent diet
  - vegetarian and other diets
- **Lifestyle and mental health**
  - eating disorders
  - smoking
  - alcohol
  - drugs

- stress and mood swings
- depression
- teenage crushes
- **Raging hormones**
  - puberty
  - periods and period pains
- **Physical illnesses**
  - glandular fever and post-viral fatigue
- **Becoming sexually active**
  - common sexually transmitted infections
  - HIV, hepatitis, syphilis
  - thrush, bacterial vaginosis, pelvic inflammatory disease
- **Skin and hair**
  - acne
  - tanning
  - hair care

STAYING HEALTHY

There are no specific tests that an average teenager requires, but it does make sense to keep an eye on growth, particularly if your child seems too small, or too large. (See page 8.)

All girls should have a booster immunization for tetanus, pertussis (whooping cough) and polio at the age of 14, and TB vaccination is also recommended for young teenagers who live in areas with a high incidence of the disease. In some areas these jabs are arranged by schools; check with your school or GP's surgery.

This is an important time for laying down solid foundations for a healthy life to come: learning and practising sensible eating, the importance of exercise, and avoiding slipping into bad habits, particularly with alcohol, drugs and sexual behaviour.

FOOD AND NUTRITION

Teenagers need lots of energy and nutrients to fuel their growth. On average, girls between 11 and 14 need 1,850 calories a day, while those between 15 and 18 need 2,100 calories. These amounts need to be increased for those doing a lot of exercise.

But sadly, even though their bodies are screaming out for plenty of nutrients, obsessing about their weight means that far too many teenage girls don't eat as healthily as they should. More than 50 per cent have been on a diet at some time or another, and 10 per cent admit to *always* being on a diet. Skipping meals, especially breakfast, eating unhealthy snacks and fizzy drinks, and not eating enough fruit and veg are the most common bad habits.

At this age, food intake can vary enormously from day to day, but by and large the required nutrients tend to balance out. However, there are two key nutrients that are often lacking in a girl's diet at this time but which are crucial to her development: iron and calcium.

IRON

The recommended daily allowance for iron is 15mg. Iron-deficiency anaemia among adolescent girls is one of the most common diet-related deficiency diseases. Not only are girls changing shape and gaining weight, but blood lost during menstruation also robs them of iron, which is needed to build up haemoglobin, the red pigment in blood that carries oxygen, and the related protein myoglobin in muscle.

Common symptoms of iron deficiency are tiredness, lethargy, difficulty concentrating and a reduced attention span – not good news if you are working for important exams. Low iron levels can also affect your sporting performance, making you short of breath more quickly.

The body absorbs some sources of iron more efficiently than others. The best sources are the iron found in red meat, meat products and offal. These are much better absorbed than the iron found in cereals, pulses such as baked beans, dark green leafy vegetables and fruit. It means girls who are vegetarian need to take special care (see page 53).

To increase the amount of iron your body will actually use from your food, avoid drinking tea or coffee with meals – leave at least a 30-minute gap – because the tannins interfere with absorption. Don't add lots of bran to food because the phytates it contains have a similar effect. The oxalates in spinach and rhubarb do not make them great sources of iron, either.

But having food rich in vitamin C at the same time as eating iron-rich pulses, cereals and vegetables will increase the take-up rate – a glass of orange juice with your breakfast cereal, for example.

To sum up:

- iron is best absorbed from meat – vegetarians need to take extra care
- don't drink tea or coffee with meals
- drink a glass of orange juice with breakfast

CALCIUM

The speed of bone growth doubles during adolescence, and 90–95 per cent of peak bone mass is achieved by the age of 20. Teenagers need 1,200mg of calcium a day to fuel their rapid bone growth and to prevent them from getting osteoporosis in later life (see page 307).

There are plenty of sources of calcium. As well as milk and dairy products, it's found in tofu and soya, pulses such as chickpeas, green vegetables, dried fruit, nuts and seeds. No problem with being a vegetarian here.

OTHER KEY NUTRIENTS

Vitamin D. Calcium is only one half of a partnership: to absorb it properly it's important to have enough vitamin D, which we get from sunshine on our skin, margarine, spreads, breakfast cereals and oily fish.

Magnesium. More than half Britain's teenage girls do not get their

300mg recommended daily allowance (RDA) of magnesium. Crucial for energy production, magnesium plays a key role in the metabolism of blood sugars and in the formation of DNA and RNA. There is also some evidence that it can help to lift the mood of youngsters suffering from depression or chronic fatigue.

The best sources are:

♦ grains and nuts (especially cashews and almonds)

♦ bananas

♦ cocoa

♦ parsnips

♦ avocados

♦ dark green leafy vegetables (although it is more difficult to absorb magnesium from this source)

Refining flour, rice and sugar removes magnesium. Wholemeal flour, rice and natural sugars (from fruit) are better. Menstruation, and too much alcohol or coffee, also rob the body of this essential mineral.

Because most magnesium is stored in tissues, the first sign of a deficiency is likely to be leg cramps or foot pain. A magnesium deficiency has also been implicated in pre-menstrual syndrome (PMS; see page 258). So if there's a moody, pre-menstrual teenager in the house, hooked on junk food and secretly binge-drinking, she may be missing out on magnesium. You can try fighting back by feeding her a daily banana – this may be acceptable!

Potassium There's also evidence that two out of five girls between the ages of 15 and 18 do not get their 2mg RDA (recommended daily allowance) of potassium. Potassium regulates the body's water balance and helps maintain the heart, nervous system, muscles and kidneys.

Alcohol and sugar deplete supplies. Potassium is abundant in:

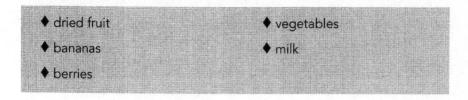

- ◆ dried fruit
- ◆ bananas
- ◆ berries
- ◆ vegetables
- ◆ milk

Signs of a deficiency include muscle fatigue and, more rarely, irregular heartbeat.

THE ADOLESCENT DIET

Whatever they eat during the day, and whether they are carnivores or vegetarians, teenagers should try to get into the habit of eating regular meals – it's the best way of ensuring a healthy, well-balanced diet.

Breakfast A nutritious breakfast is especially important – it's not only good for the body but it sharpens the mind, and going to school on an empty tummy has been proven to affect academic performance. Eating breakfast also reduces the risk of filling up on unhealthy snacks mid-morning. The best breakfast contains plenty of low glycaemic index (GI) foods, which give slow-release energy for several hours. For more information on GI foods, see page 224.

Junk food. One of the biggest challenges for teenagers is limiting the amount of processed junk food that they eat. Convenience foods might be the quickest way to fill a hungry teenager's empty stomach, but they are loaded with lots of unhealthy salt, sugar and hydrogenated vegetable oils. These are far more unhealthy and artery-clogging than animal fats, and are found in most fast foods, hard margarines, doughnuts and biscuits, and in some vegetarian and vegan sausages and burgers.

Unfortunately, when teenagers acquire a taste for too much salt and sugar, normal, more healthy food will taste bland and they won't want it. Even if you have policed their diets as children, those good habits can be totally undermined by peer pressure and slick advertising now.

Salt and sugar. Adolescent diets continue to be overloaded by too much salt (RDA 6g a day, 2.5g sodium) and sugar. Eating too much salt has become a national habit. Fast food is full of it because it is a cheap way for manufacturers to add bulk and flavour to food. You might find it surprising that there is approximately 329mg of sodium in McDonald's chocolate shake and 456mg in their cherry pie, for example. About 75 per cent of daily intake of salt comes from food products such as breakfast cereals, soups, sauces, ready meals, crisps and savoury snacks. It is important always to read the labels to check salt content.

The concentrated calories in refined sugar must take the blame for a lot of teenage obesity and dental problems – and there are always plenty in the fast food they love. Due to its simple construction, sugar provides a quick energy high, followed by a crash in blood-sugar levels and a longing for more of the same. The more sugar you eat, the more you want. Like salt, sugar is an addiction.

Snacks. Teenagers do get hungry between meals, but try to encourage healthy snacks, especially fruit – fewer than 15 per cent of girls between the ages of 13 and 25 eat the recommended 5 portions of fruit and vegetables a day. Having a piece of fruit will also not ruin her appetite for a healthy meal that is to follow in an hour or so. Nibbles of dried fruit and nuts are a good alternative for the girl who doesn't fancy carrying a bruised apple or banana in her schoolbag and can't be bothered to peel a small orange!

VEGGIES

During adolescence, many young women decide to adopt a vegetarian diet. Though it is often claimed that a vegetarian diet is 'better' than one containing meat, some vegetarian diets are very unhealthy – as with any diet, a well-balanced mix of foods is essential.

What you should eat

The key to a good vegetarian diet is to eat as wide a variety of plant foods as possible – the fewer types you eat, the less your nutritional needs are likely to be met. As a general rule of thumb, the stronger the colour, the greater the benefit.

The amino acids found in protein are vital for growth, and the best sources of these are meat and fish. However, cow's milk, low-fat cheese, beans, breads, cereals, nuts, peanut butter, tofu and soy milk are good sources too. Don't rely on one source though – to get a good balance of amino acids, aim to eat a mixture of plant proteins throughout the day.

What you might miss

The main risk of a vegetarian diet in teenagers is a lack of iron and vitamin B12 (as these are mainly found in meat). Foods high in iron include broccoli, raisins, watermelon, spinach, black-eyed peas, blackstrap molasses, chickpeas and pinto beans, plus fortified breakfast cereals. To increase absorption, eat a food containing vitamin C with your iron-rich food. Vitamin B12 is found in yeast extract (such as marmite), fortified bread and fortified breakfast cereals.

Include three or more good sources of calcium in your diet every day. Get it from cow's milk and dairy products, tofu processed with calcium sulphate, green leafy vegetables, calcium-fortified soy milk and orange juice.

Another potential problem is selenium, which is required for a healthy immune system and is mainly found in meat and fish. It's also found in nuts, though, especially brazil nuts, and in smaller amounts in bread and eggs.

VEGANS AND OTHER RESTRICTED DIETS

Some teenagers decide to adopt more extreme restricted diets, and while these rarely do harm if followed for a week or two, they can soon lead to problems at a time when nutrient requirements are so high. Vegan diets especially (which exclude foods of all animal origin, including dairy products and eggs) can lead to shortages of protein, iron and vitamin B12. If you have an obstinate teenager who insists on eating a very restricted diet, some expert nutritional advice may be advisable.

LIFESTYLE AND MENTAL HEALTH

EATING DISORDERS

In the UK, at least 60,000 people have been diagnosed with an eating disorder. However, this is probably an underestimate, and experts reckon the true figure is likely to be around 1.1 million – around 2 per cent of the total population – and 90 per cent of them are women.

The onset of puberty and the desire to control body shape is a powerful trigger, especially when young girls' role models look as if they have not eaten a decent meal in weeks. Even the British Medical Association (BMA) has said the media's obsession with unhealthily skinny fashion models has contributed to a growth in eating disorders among young girls.

Some believe that the seeds of eating disorders are sown in early childhood: mealtimes may have been accompanied by pressure to eat, coupled with lavish praise if a child complied and anger if she did not. This emotional overload associated with food can resurface in teenage years, triggered by peer pressure or a cruel comment about a girl's body.

If a teenager does develop an eating disorder, her parents need to arm themselves with as much information as they can about her condition, seek professional help as soon as possible and remain loving and supportive.

The key to tackling an eating disorder is to spot it, and do something about it, as early as possible. The longer it continues, the more the abnormal behaviour becomes ingrained in a girl's personality and the more difficult it is to stop.

If the illness is mild and the reasons for it straightforward, a girl may be able to regain normal eating patterns with support from a good GP and practice nurse. More usually, though, expert help is required from a specialist eating disorders unit, though unfortunately these often have long waiting lists.

ANOREXIA NERVOSA

Although this mainly affects adolescents, in today's weight-obsessed world little girls as young as 5 have become anorexic because they have got the idea that they are 'fat'.

Anorexia usually starts when a girl goes on a normal weight-reducing diet to lose puppy fat – but then takes it to extremes. It's very tricky for parents to confront her about her diet or make her see her GP because she's likely to react with hostility or try to hide her problem. Tolerance, tact and gentle persuasion are vital to give her the help she needs. This is a battle you must win for her sake.

There'll be behaviour change, too. She'll become more serious and introverted, lose contact with friends and show little interest in anything except food and schoolwork. Often she will become obsessive about cleanliness and tidiness. She may offer to cook family meals and encourage everyone else to over-eat. Ironically, the more she loses confidence, the more she will attempt to control those around her.

Anorexia can occur on its own, but more commonly sufferers also have some signs of bulimia (see page 58), which include vomiting after meals and abusing laxatives.

Tell-tale signs

- ♦ ongoing weight loss to a clearly abnormally low level
- ♦ intense fear of weight gain
- ♦ perceiving herself as overweight, despite being underweight
- ♦ over-exercising
- ♦ restricting food or food types that contain a lot of calories, especially fat
- ♦ stopping or never getting periods
- ♦ secrecy and lying about what she eats
- ♦ denial of an eating problem

Why does this happen?

We do not know precisely why some girls become anorexic, but sufferers tend to be conformist and hard-working, with a tendency to perfectionism. Often they come from families with high expectations of them.

There seems to be an increased risk if other family members have suffered with eating disorders. Sometimes in the year or two before the anorexia starts there has been an escalation of problems or pressures – such as exams – that create anxiety.

Physical symptoms

When someone starves themselves, their body tries to conserve energy by cutting out non-essentials. A girl's periods will stop as her weight drops to around 44kg (7 stone); circulation to extremities such as hands and feet diminishes (making them feel and look very cold); heart rate slows and blood pressure falls. If a girl's weight drops to around 32kg (5 stone) there is a real risk of heart failure. Prolonged weight loss in adolescence may stop a girl growing properly and leave her vulnerable to osteoporosis in later life (see page 307).

Treatment

Initially treatment has to be based on getting an anorexic to eat more, though this can be incredibly difficult due to her abnormal thoughts, especially about her body image. All anorexics are terrified of being what they consider 'fat', and the thinner she is, the worse her mental instability. Psychotherapy (see page 237) can help to sort out the underlying mental illness, but this is unlikely to be successful until a girl is somewhere approaching a normal body weight.

As well as helping a girl to eat properly again, doctors at an eating disorders unit will explore psychological issues that may have triggered the illness. Because sufferers have a characteristic profound loss of confidence, getting them back to normal can be slow.

Treatment of anorexia is difficult and isn't always successful; tragically, a few girls die from this condition, despite the best expert treatment.

BULIMIA NERVOSA

About 4 women in 100 will become bulimic at some point, and the teenage years are usually the time when this eating disorder surfaces. Girls with bulimia may go on to develop anorexia, and vice versa. Bulimia is a relentless binge–purge cycle. A girl will gorge uncontrollably on vast amounts of food in a short space of time, often in secret. This will probably happen a couple of times a week. Then she will feel shame and try to rid herself of the thousands of calories she has consumed. She may do this by fasting, making herself sick, taking laxatives or diuretics, or exercising excessively.

Tell-tale signs

These vary more than with anorexia – but the cardinal sign is lack of control over eating.

Other symptoms can include:

- eating vast amounts of food, often in secret, then disappearing to the loo to vomit
- being preoccupied with weight, but size is not a good guide – bulimics come in all sizes, fat, thin and average
- frequent weight fluctuations
- cravings and preoccupation with food
- self-harm
- obsessive exercising
- self-image unduly based on body shape

Because girls with bulimia are secretive and can remain the normal weight for their height, the illness can be difficult to spot until other health problems emerge.

Long term, bulimia can lead to tooth decay, gum disease and bad breath because of stomach acid in the mouth. She may have a sore throat and rough skin on her knuckles and fingers from manually induced vomiting. Other signs are:

- ◆ heartburn
- ◆ swollen salivary glands, which will make her face puffy
- ◆ severe dehydration, which at its worst can damage kidneys
- ◆ inflammation of stomach and oesophagus
- ◆ constipation, diarrhoea, abdominal pain
- ◆ swollen hands and feet
- ◆ sleep problems

Bulimia can also cause long-term health problems such as infertility, due to periods stopping, and heart damage.

Why does this happen?

The cause of bulimia is not fully understood, but girls most at risk are those with low self-esteem and who evaluate their worth primarily by the shape of their bodies. They may suffer from depression or other mental-health problems. Girls who have tried several weight-loss diets seem to be more at risk, and the disease also occurs more than average in type 1 diabetics (often with disastrous consequences; see page 355).

Binge-eating may be a way to block out unhappy feelings, so over-critical parents, emotional upsets such as bereavement, divorce or abusive relationships may also trigger the condition.

Treatment

One of the biggest challenges with bulimia is admitting the problem and seeking help. Treatment is with psychotherapy (see page 237), and sometimes with antidepressant medication. The outlook for bulimia is generally better than that for anorexia, and though some people do continue to have problems for many years, many others do overcome the disorder.

SMOKING

Teenage girls are the nicotine industry's best friends. Two major studies have concluded that girls of this age are twice as likely to start smoking as boys. The 'quit smoking' message may be getting through to adults, but it is cutting no ice with adolescent girls. They may not doubt that smoking will damage their lungs and heart, but continue to kid themselves that the health warnings apply only to older people.

It has been widely suggested that teenage girls smoke to control weight, but far more powerful reasons seem to be bound up with self-image. Girls see smoking as desirably rebellious, a badge of sexual maturity and a way to attract boys. Despite all the evidence to the contrary, they perceive it as a cool thing to do, especially if all the rest of their gang are puffing away too.

Yet nicotine addiction not only destroys health, it ruins looks. Perhaps this is where we can best target the anti-smoking message to teenagers. Tobacco smoke dries skin and restricts blood flow and oxygen to its surface, making the skin look grey and tired. Squinting to avoid the smoke and puckering your mouth to take a drag leads to deep lines and wrinkles forming round your eyes and mouth. Smokers in their forties are as wrinkled as non-smokers in their sixties.

Smoking stains fingers and nails, turns teeth yellow, causes bad breath and gum disease and will ultimately make teeth fall out. As for 'pulling boys', a lad who does not smoke will find the stink of nicotine on a girl's breath, hair and clothes revolting, no matter how attractive she is.

Although smokers do tend to gain weight when they quit, a few dietary tweaks and increased exercise can make this a temporary situation.

Parents who smoke will probably get nowhere if they try to get their daughter to quit – it is a case of leading by example and doing all you can to discourage her and help her stop.

While a girl lives at home it is reasonable to demand that she does not smoke in the house. Also, cigarettes are expensive and, until she gets a job, you hold the purse strings. Make sure you are not subsidizing the nicotine addiction that will destroy her health.

There are several ways to help both girls and women to stop smoking, and many GP surgeries run special clinics. NHS cessation services are free and if they recommend the use of nicotine replacement therapies, such as gum or patches, they will be available on prescription. There is also an NHS telephone helpline to support quitters who are struggling.

Some people have stopped successfully after hypnosis, acupuncture, taking Chinese herbs or attending private – and expensive – clinics. If you fall by the wayside after one attempt at quitting, try again – and again. The benefits of stopping smoking are enormous and many people also feel a great source of pride at being free of the drug that once controlled their lives.

ALCOHOL

Though many parents worry about drugs, in reality the bigger threat, especially to young women, is alcohol. It is widely available and tends to be an accepted part of many people's social life; most parents think that getting drunk now and then is a normal part of growing up. So it's easy to forget that alcohol is a very powerful drug. Yes, it is true that small amounts of alcohol can actually be good for your health, in particular reducing the risk of heart disease. But the negatives about booze are far more important, especially for women – no matter what your age.

For young women, a major danger is the effect it can have on the brain. Alcohol makes you less inhibited and impairs your judgement so you are more likely to hop into bed with someone you wouldn't look at twice if you were sober. You may then fail to use contraception that will protect you from an unwanted pregnancy or a sexually transmitted infection (see pages 85–109).

And when it comes to pregnancy, just small amounts of alcohol can harm a developing baby. More long-term use can cause permanent damage to the liver, heart and nervous system, and increase the risk of breast cancer. Yet despite all this, women in Britain drink twice as much alcohol as they did ten years ago. More women than men now die from cirrhosis of the liver, permanent damage from alcohol that has no symptoms until the liver has been virtually destroyed. Alcohol is a very dangerous drug but 'going out for a drink' – youthspeak for getting hammered – is very much part of the pub culture in Britain.

There's no sexual equality when it comes to alcohol consumption. It is a simple fact that women's bodies can't process booze as well as men's. If a woman drinks the same amount as a man, she will get twice as drunk as he does.

Alcohol consists largely of ethanol, which the body regards as poison. Both sexes have an enzyme in their stomachs called dehydrogenase which turns ethanol into a safe substance before releasing it into the bloodstream. However, dehydrogenase works 70–80 per cent more efficiently in men, so more of the poisonous ethanol gets into a woman's bloodstream. Eventually alcohol ends up in the liver for final processing. A man's liver can break down one alcoholic drink in an hour – a woman's liver will take longer. Not only this, but women generally weigh less than men, and their bodies have a higher fat content, which means there is less water to dilute alcohol. This results in, drink for drink, a higher blood-alcohol concentration.

It all adds up to one sorry fact: a woman will have a shorter drinking career than a man before the onset of serious medical problems caused by alcohol.

The current government guidelines are 14 units a week for a woman. A unit is a half-pint of average-strength beer, a single shot of spirits or a small glass of wine. But many experts believe that if a woman wants to reduce her risks of alcohol-related illnesses she should limit her consumption to one drink a day, four times a week.

The driving limit in this country is 80mg of alcohol per 100ml of blood. Many people believe this needs revising downwards, too, because driving becomes reckless and judgement is impaired at the 60mg level.

Heavy drinkers tend not to eat properly because they get most of their calories from alcohol. This means they are often short of vital amino acids and vitamins. A severe deficiency of thiamine (vitamin B1), which goes hand in hand with alcoholism, leads to Wernicke's encephalopathy, which causes paralysis of eye movements, loss of balance and confusion.

No matter what your age, even if you think you have your drinking under control, if you can answer yes to any of the following questions you should think very seriously about cutting down your alcohol consumption.

♦ Do you drink alcohol every day?

♦ Has drinking become a central part of your life?

♦ Do you drink regularly at lunchtime?

♦ Do you need a drink if you haven't had one for 10 hours?

♦ Do you always have a drink to relax after you arrive home from work?

♦ Do you ever drink more than 6 units in one session?

♦ Do you have regular morning hangovers?

♦ Do you have black-outs?

If you want to curtail your drinking:

♦ Choose a limit when you go out and stick to it.

♦ Never drink alone.

♦ Drink spritzers rather than neat wine – they last longer and are not so damaging.

♦ If you drink spirits, top up with tonic water instead of more alcohol.

♦ Have at least two alcohol-free days a week.

♦ Drink slowly.

If you are planning to get pregnant, try to lay off alcohol completely or just have an occasional glass of wine. Alcohol crosses the placenta and has been linked with a higher risk of miscarriage, stillbirth and premature births. Heavy drinking is especially dangerous for a foetus in the first 3 months when its organs and limbs are forming.

Babies affected by their mother's drinking may grow more slowly, both before and after birth, have facial or organ defects or mental disabilities. In their most severe form, these problems are known as the foetal alcohol syndrome.

The law and alcohol

Under-5s. It is illegal to give an alcohol drink to a child under the age of 5 except under medical supervision.

Under-14s. Under-14s cannot go into a bar or pub that doesn't have a 'children's certificate', unless it is to an area where alcohol is drunk but not sold, for example a garden or family room.

Under-15s. 14- and 15-year-olds can go anywhere in a pub, but cannot drink alcohol.

Under-18s. It is against the law for anyone under 18 to buy alcohol, but they can drink (and buy) beer or cider as an accompaniment to a meal, but only in areas set aside specifically for eating – so not in bars, off-licences or supermarkets.

DRUGS

Nearly all young people are aware that drugs are dangerous. But that doesn't stop them experimenting with them, either because they are curious or because they just want to 'break the rules'. Thankfully, only a very small proportion of teenagers who use drugs develop an addiction – most young people who use illegal drugs only do so occasionally and do not continue to use them in the long term. However, any drug use can have serious consequences, and just one dose of the wrong drug can be enough either to get a person hooked or to cause permanent health damage.

I'm constantly asked about the signs that parents should look out for that might indicate that their offspring is using drugs, but in the early stages especially this can be very difficult, as any behaviour changes that could be caused by drugs are much more likely to be due to normal teenage behaviour. Drugs affect everyone differently, according to the drug itself, its purity, the amount taken, and whether they are an habitual user. But in general, warning signs include:

♦ sudden changes in mood – happy one minute, down the next

♦ irritable, short-tempered

♦ a personality change

♦ restlessness, and surges in energy; being able to keep dancing or awake for hours into the night without getting tired

♦ extreme tiredness; being unable to wake up in the morning; sleeping through loud alarms

The giveaway that a teenager is using drugs is often the simple fact that they cost money, which leads to stealing, often from a parent's purse, credit card or bank. If you are concerned that your teenager is using drugs, much as you may be tempted to lose your rag, this will only lead to an almighty row which is likely to make the situation worse. Difficult as it may be, keep cool and have a calm discussion – but only when they are not under the influence of either drugs or alcohol. Explain that you are concerned about their health and well-being, offer support, but also lay down clear boundaries of what is acceptable and what is not. Guidance on tackling the problem from experts can also be invaluable – see the list on page 447.

STRESS AND MOOD SWINGS

These may be 'the best years of your life' but they are also a time of enormous transition, from dependence on others to independence, and from girl to woman. Any change brings stress, so change of this magnitude brings it in bucketloads.

Society today places far more pressure on adolescents to conform to unrealistic ideals. They are bombarded with images telling them how they should look, sound and behave – hammering home the message that their appearance or possessions are more important than what they do. Money, or rather lack of it, becomes a major issue. And for some there is the pressure to conform with their peers, which can be very strong and can lead to depression in any teenage girl who feels different or inadequate. Then there are the additional pressures, which girls often feel very keenly, of doing well in important exams and living up to parental expectations.

Some teenage girls exhibit the classic symptoms of stress, such as tension, frustration, worry, sadness and withdrawal that can last from a few hours to several days. Some try to ignore the problem by embarking on a wild social life, blotting it out further with alcohol or drugs.

Girls are much more likely than boys to talk things over with their friends. This is a big plus, unless it is their friends who are causing the stress, particularly if they are competing with each other over looks and boys!

And when you combine all these stresses with the fact that teenage girls are also at the mercy of rapidly changing hormone levels, it's no wonder that the result can be violent mood swings and a young woman who is very difficult to live with. As well as the monthly oestrogen/progesterone see-saw, they may get bad PMS (see page 258). This causes mild depression and irritability even in adult women – teenage girls are mere novices at coping with it.

A girl is also coming to terms with her rapidly changing body. This hinterland between girlhood and womanhood can be very confusing. She may look like a woman but her parents still treat her like a child. She often behaves like one.

It is very difficult for parents to cope with a stressed-out teenage girl who will often scapegoat her mother for everything going wrong in her life. It is hard to be on the receiving end of so much animosity and to turn the other cheek; no mother can manage it all the time. However, there will be lulls in the emotional storms and it is important to keep the lines of communication open and assure her that you are still there as her emotional safety net. Let her know she can always talk to you about her feelings and problems.

During exam time, parents can support their angst-ridden teenagers by making sure they have a healthy diet and enough sleep. Making sure they are not glued to the TV or an internet chatroom late into the night is important, along with providing support and a sympathetic ear. Girls should also take regular breaks from studying and get outside in the fresh air. Playing sport is not only good for their growing bodies but is a great protector against stress and depression because it releases feel-good hormones in the brain.

DEPRESSION

Sometimes there is something more than 'teenage stress' going on. Depression is a more severe and long-lasting problem, but in this age group it can be difficult to spot because all teenagers express negativity, withdrawal, sulkiness, irritability and anti-social behaviour as part of normal growing up. Unfortunately, depression in teenagers does appear to be becoming more common. It needs to be taken seriously – left untreated it can blight young lives, and leave emotional scars for years.

Tell-tale signs
Besides many of the symptoms of adult depression, there are some other clues that should ring warning bells:

♦ deterioration in school performance

♦ change in personal hygiene and appearance

♦ destructive and/or defiant behaviour

♦ hallucinations or unusual beliefs

♦ drastic appetite or weight change

- ◆ agitation or restlessness or, conversely, inability to move
- ◆ energy loss and tiredness
- ◆ feelings of guilt or worthlessness
- ◆ a belief that life is not worth living

There are plenty of 'talking cures' which can help depressed teenagers and your GP can provide referrals to specialists, usually in an adolescent mental-health unit. As family issues are often bound up with teenage depression, doctors often ask for parents and siblings to take part in therapy sessions. Averse as you may well be to this, seeing a psychiatrist does not mean you are to blame – remember, you are doing this to help your daughter.

Drug treatment of teenage depression is a controversial topic. Only fluoxetine (Prozac) is officially licensed for use in under-18s in the UK, though this is mainly because its manufacturers have done the relevant trials and have proved that it can be of some use.

Chemical changes in the brain of a depressed teenager are different from those in the adult brain. Moreover, the brain is still developing up to the age of 20. There are real concerns about whether antidepressants are really safe in teenagers, or whether they can increase the risk of suicide. For this reason they are best prescribed by a specialist, and someone should be around, 24 hours a day, to watch over the person to whom they have been given, especially in the first week of treatment.

TEENAGE CRUSHES

Most teenage girls' bedrooms are festooned with posters of unattainable love objects – handsome hunks with six-packs – usually pop or soap stars. Sometimes a girl will develop a crush on someone nearer home, typically an authority figure: a teacher (sometimes female) or youth-club leader. In most cases it is harmless fantasy and passes when a girl has her first real romantic relationship.

If the love object is someone you know and the crush is getting out. of hand, a word in their ear may be necessary. Any mentally mature adult on the receiving end of attention from an adoring teenage girl will feel uncomfortable with it and may have to let her down gently if the situation becomes too extreme. It's the other sort of love object who poses the problem – the man or woman who enjoys the ego trip and encourages the inappropriate attention. However, if you share your fears and concerns with the person concerned, they will know you are on the case and looking out for the best interests of your daughter. It is still against the law to have sex with a girl who is under the age of 16.

Crushes are normal in teenage girls, but in rare and extreme cases they may make her vulnerable to depression or alcohol or drug abuse. She may be suffering the humiliating pain of unrequited love, real feelings of distress accompanied by loss of appetite and self-worth. Parents need to employ tact, resist the temptation to trivialize or mock, and bear in mind that puppy love can hurt just as much as 'the real thing'.

RAGING HORMONES

The biggest physical change in a young girl's life – until she hits the menopause some 30 or 40 years later – is the onset of puberty.

Puberty usually starts between the ages of 10 and 12, but any time between the ages of 9 and 15 is regarded as normal. Though this phase in a young person's development is given a name, it's not really a distinct event; it is actually just part of the very gradual process of growing up. But the changes that occur at this time of life certainly do have dramatic physical and mental effects.

Deep inside the brain, the pituitary gland starts secreting two hormones, FSH (follicle stimulating hormone) and LH (luteinizing hormone). Together, these two hormones trigger the ovaries into action to start producing eggs, and also hormones. The most important hormone is oestrogen, but progesterone and small quantities of testosterone are produced as well.

THE FIRST SIGNS OF PUBERTY

It is the action of the hormone oestrogen that is mainly responsible for the physical body changes that girls undergo at this time. The first sign of puberty is usually the appearance of breasts, and some sign of breast development often occurs well before puberty really begins. This means that in some girls the breasts start to change as young as 8, but because the process is so gradual the other signs of puberty are not visible for at least a year. The tissue underneath the nipple gradually enlarges, together with the pink area of skin around the nipple (the areola). Initially, the nipple stays flat, but as puberty progresses it becomes more prominent.

Pubic hair starts to develop about a year after the breasts noticeably start to grow. At first, it is usually fine and straight, but gradually becomes darker, coarser and more curly. It is usually a slightly darker shade than the hair on your head.

It's when the pubic hair starts appearing that a girl will suddenly begin to shoot up in height. At their fastest, girls can grow at this time as much as 8cm (3 inches) a year. The growth spurt usually lasts about 2½ years, progressing in an 'outside-in' fashion. So hands and feet are the first to expand, followed by the arms and lower legs. Then it's the turn of the spine, and finally the hips and pelvis widen, giving a girl a womanly shape.

All this growth can occur so fast that the bones hurt – growing pains really do exist, and tend to occur especially in the legs. The skin sometimes can't keep up with what is going on underneath, and stretch marks often appear, especially on the breasts, thighs and hips. Though this can be alarming, they do gradually fade over the next year or so.

Oestrogen also stimulates an increase in muscle and body fat – it's normal for a girl to acquire curves at this age – and for the oil and sweat glands to become more active, leading to increased body odour and a tendency to greasy skin and acne (see page 109).

The genital area changes too. The outer folds of skin – the labia – enlarge slightly and darken, and the glands around the entrance to the vagina become active, leading to small amounts of secretion. This means it's normal for the genital area to feel slightly moist, but there should be no noticeable smell or staining on underwear.

The most significant event of puberty for girls, the start of periods, happens fairly late in the overall process, usually towards the end of the growth spurt. The average age for periods to begin in the UK is 13, but anything between 11 and 15 is normal.

Why does this happen?

It's only natural that when a girl sees her best friend in a pretty new bra, she wants one too, and not changing at the same time as your friends can cause huge anxiety (and envy). Sadly, the fact is that puberty is a very individual event, and there are huge variations between girls. Quite why one should start having periods at 11 while another has to wait till she is 15 is often unclear, but the timing can run in families – if your mother started her periods early, then the chances are you will too. Timing of puberty is also dependent on body weight – the growth spurt does not start till a girl weighs 30kg (nearly 5 stone), and periods are unlikely to start until a girl weighs at least 47kg (7½ stone).

The improved nutrition we have now is the main reason why puberty occurs much earlier than it did 150 years ago, but for the last 50 years the age of puberty has remained pretty constant – contrary to what you may have read, it's not getting any earlier. Though there have been reports of 7-year-olds growing breasts, these are mainly in girls who are overweight – it's fat, not breast tissue, that's appeared. Sadly, eating disorders, with girls keeping themselves underweight, mean that the opposite problem of periods occurring later is also becoming more common (see pages 56–7).

However, occasionally the puberty process can go wrong. The pituitary gland misbehaves, starting up too soon or too late, and sometimes there is a problem with the ovaries. Very rarely, lack of periods can be due to an underdeveloped womb, or to a minor structural problem in the vagina, which means the menstrual blood cannot escape (see page 31).

Any girl who has signs of puberty (other than tiny breasts) before the age of 9, or has none by the age of 15, should see their doctor.

PERIODS – THE MONTHLY CURSE

Some girls do go straight into a nice pattern of regular monthly release of an egg (ovulation), followed by a regular bleed, but often ovulation and periods are very erratic to begin with, occurring at completely unpredictable times. Two periods in a month, then a 2–3-month gap, is quite common. Continued erratic periods after the first couple of years should not be blamed on age alone, though, and checks should be done for an underlying cause.

What is happening?

A period is actually the shedding of the womb lining, together with a small amount of blood. Timings of periods are always based on the first day of bleeding, and the average cycle is 28 days – that is, the first day of a period to the first day of the next (not the end of one to the beginning of the next). Anything between 25 and 33 days is regarded as normal.

The thing that governs the length of a woman's cycle is the time it takes for an egg to mature; after it has been released a period always occurs 14 days later (unless you get pregnant).

During the first half of the cycle, oestrogen levels rise very gradually, but then there is a sudden big rise in the level a couple of days before ovulation. This is followed by a sudden surge in the amount of LH (luteinizing hormone) produced by the pituitary gland, and it is this surge that triggers ovulation – the release of the egg from the ovary. Throughout the first half of the cycle, the oestrogen stimulates gradual thickening in the lining of the womb.

After ovulation, the ovaries continue to produce oestrogen and, in addition, a second hormone, progesterone. Levels of both hormones continue to rise until around 1 week before a period, when (unless the egg has been fertilized) the levels fall. Once they go below a critical level, the womb lining is shed as a period.

Oestrogen and progesterone don't just act on the womb lining though – they have effects on just about every part of a woman's body. Once puberty starts, these two hormones will have a profound influence on a woman's life for the next 40 years, playing a major role not just in fertility, but also in physical and emotional well-being.

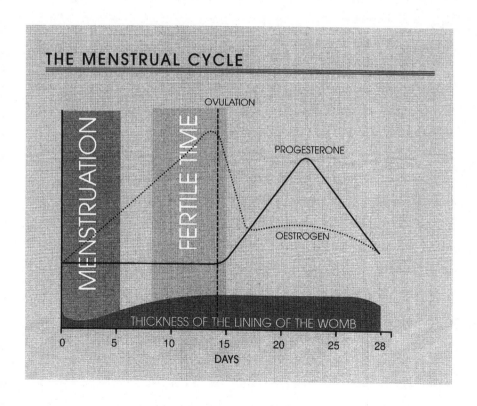

What's normal?

The average amount of blood lost during a period is 6oml – that's about a small coffee cupful. That may not seem much, but when it comes to blood a little can go a long way, particularly on white linen trousers! Judging whether or not you have normal, light or heavy periods is very difficult – after all, women don't go in for examining each other's sanitary towels – but as a general rule, during the second and third days, which are usually the heaviest, a woman having an average period will need to change a sanitary towel every 4 hours or so. If you have to change a heavy-duty towel after 2 hours, or regularly soak through a tampon and a towel quickly, or if you pass large clots, then your periods are heavier than normal.

Types of sanitary protection

The type of sanitary towel you use is largely one of personal preference, and tampons are suitable for women of all ages, including young teenagers who have just started their periods. It can take a while to get used to them, though, so don't leave it till you are on your summer holiday and desperate to wear your bikini before you start using them for the first time. If you have not had sex, inserting a tampon does involve stretching the hymen, and this can be quite painful. Very small, non-applicator tampons are good for starters, and once you are used to these you can work your way up to larger tampons which have greater absorbency.

Tampons are not dangerous, but it is important they are used with care, as leaving in tampons for longer than necessary has been linked with toxic shock syndrome, a very rare but potentially lethal infection.

For this reason, if you use tampons you should:

- Always use one with the lowest absorbency suitable for your period flow, and if possible, don't use tampons for days on end – use a sanitary towel from time to time during your period.

- Change tampons regularly, and never insert more than one at a time. Wash your hands before and afterwards.

- For nighttime use, insert a fresh tampon before going to bed and remove it on waking.

- Always remember to remove your tampon at the end of a period. Check if you can't remember!

- Never use a tampon for a vaginal discharge.

PERIOD PAINS

I have yet to find a woman who has not experienced period pains. They are an inevitable part of menstruation, but they do, of course, vary enormously from woman to woman, from just an occasional twinge to severe cramps that mean you can do nothing other than lie curled up in a ball in bed.

Period pain – or dysmenorrhoea as the medics call it – is a very distinct type of pain, deep in the pelvis, that can spread to the back and down the front of the legs. These pains can occur at any time in a woman's reproductive life, but tend to be particularly bad in the teenage years, easing off with increasing age, especially after having a baby.

The pain is linked with the production of prostaglandins, powerful chemicals that can trigger contractions of the womb muscle and can also cause the nausea, vomiting and diarrhoea that some women experience at the beginning of a period. In young women it's thought that pain may be increased by a very tight cervix, but often there is no obvious underlying reason why some women have their lives wrecked for 2 days each month, while others are completely untroubled by their monthly bleeds.

Occasionally, however, bad period pains can be a signal that something is amiss, especially if they suddenly become much worse than previously. Common reasons for bad period pains are pelvic inflammatory disease (PID) and endometriosis (see pages 105 and 181). Fibroids can be to blame, especially in older women, along with IUDs (see pages 257 and 172).

Self-help

◆ Painkillers available from chemists can ease mild pains. Ibuprofen, which reduces prostaglandin levels, is generally more effective than paracetamol. Codeine is stronger still, but can make nausea worse.

◆ Relaxing in a hot bath can help to ease cramps. Try adding a few drops of lavender, chamomile or sweet marjoram essential oil. Massaging your lower tummy or back with these oils (diluted in a carrier oil) can also be soothing.

◆ Getting uptight always makes period pains worse. Practise relaxation exercises in between periods, then put them to good use when pain strikes.

◆ Some women find that exercise helps. A brisk walk, a swim or an exercise class may help to take your mind off the pain.

Help from your doctor

Yes, you really can go to your doctor with period pains. You will not be wasting anyone's time. Period pains are a genuine medical problem, and there's a lot your doctor can do to help. Neither need you be scared that you are going to have an internal examination – this is rarely necessary unless you have suddenly developed really bad pains.

Your doctor may prescribe:

♦ Stronger and more effective anti-prostaglandins, such as mefenamic acid, together with drugs that can relax the womb muscle, such as hyoscine. Anti-sickness pills can help to relieve nausea.

♦ If these don't work, the combined pill can have a dramatic effect in relieving period pain. If you are not keen on taking the pill all the time, you can take it for just a few months, to get you through important exams, for instance, or the start of a new term at college or a new job.

♦ Very severe cases warrant investigations to check for an underlying cause. The starting point is usually a pelvic ultrasound scan (most accurately done via the vagina), followed, if necessary, by a laparoscopy (see page 185).

PHYSICAL ILLNESSES

Most teenagers have rude health – the immune system is so efficient at this age that the minor infections that they do get, such as coughs and colds, are usually shaken off in a few days. However, this is the time when glandular fever and post-viral fatigue can lead to months of illness.

Once they become sexually active, other dangers rear their heads –
sexually transmitted infections, and the chance of pregnancy (see pages
85–109).

GLANDULAR FEVER AND POST-VIRAL FATIGUE

Anyone can get glandular fever, but it is most common in teenagers
and young adults, and has a horrible habit of striking when important
exams are looming. It is caused by the Epstein Barr virus, which is
transmitted by being in close contact with an infected person – but
despite its nickname as the 'kissing disease', just having the person next
to you at school cough over you is enough for the infection to spread.

It usually starts with a really nasty sore throat, which can be so bad
that it makes swallowing difficult. Then severe flu-like symptoms start,
with aching muscles, a high fever and extreme tiredness. As the body's
immune system fights off the infection, lymph glands swell, most often
in the neck, but also in the armpits and groin. The eyes may become
puffy and, in some, the liver becomes inflamed, leading to mild
jaundice.

There is no specific treatment for glandular fever – antibiotics don't
help, because it is caused by a viral infection. The best way of tackling
the illness is to take paracetamol, drink plenty of water and rest. The
worst is usually over in a couple of weeks, but the illness is notorious
for causing tiredness and extreme exhaustion after just minor exertion
– one late night can leave its effect for days afterwards. It's best to build
up energy levels slowly and avoid strenuous sports or activity for at
least 6 weeks.

Most youngsters are back to normal in a couple of months, but about 3 in 20 sufferers still have fatigue 6 months after the initial illness, and some (but not all) of these go on to develop more persistent tiredness – 'post-viral fatigue'.

Also known as Myalgic encephalomyelitis (ME) or chronic fatigue syndrome (CFS), this can affect people of any age, but is most common in young women. It's not just triggered by glandular fever – it can follow on from any illness, and in some it seems to occur out of the blue. Stress and environment toxins have also been suggested as a possible cause in some sufferers. It is very poorly understood and its exact cause isn't known.

It is generally accepted that to be diagnosed with CFS you must have had severe tiredness which has severely affected your day-to-day life for at least 6 months, along with at least four other symptoms, such as headaches, aching muscles, joint pain, memory problems, and exhaustion after any physical exertion that lasts for more than 24 hours. Many sufferers have other symptoms, including digestive upsets, dizziness, night sweats, chest pain, coughing, and pins and needles in various parts of the body. Psychological symptoms, such as depression, anxiety, irritability and panic attacks, may also occur, but whether these are part of the original illness or as a result of it is not known.

There is no specific treatment for CFS, but graduated exercise – very slowly increasing the amount done – does seem to be helpful in many, along with physiotherapy to increase muscle strength. Tackling any underlying stress and depression, counselling and cognitive behaviour therapy (CBT) to tackle negative thinking (which is, not surprisingly, very common in people with CFS) can also be beneficial (see page 237).

BECOMING SEXUALLY ACTIVE

Much as mothers may want to protect their daughters from men, there comes a time when hormones, lust and the urge for sexual exploration take over. The average age of loss of virginity in women in the UK is 17, and though some wait much longer than this, it is not unusual for girls to become sexually active in their early teens. Though it is illegal for a girl to have sex before the age of 16, in practice this only becomes an issue for the police when there is lack of consent. Unfortunately, far too many young women learn the hard way that 'once is enough', and the rates of abortion and unplanned pregnancy in teenagers are horrifyingly high.

Doctors can prescribe the pill and arrange abortions for girls under 16 as long as they feel the girl has the maturity to understand the decisions she is making. Most doctors do try to encourage young girls to include at least one parent in the decision-making process, but if the girl is adamant that she wants to keep things confidential, and away from her parents, then that is what the doctor must do. I can understand why many parents deplore this (and feel they should know if their 14-year-old is taking the pill) but better a teenager who takes proper precautions than one who ends up going through the trauma of an abortion.

Contraception is covered fully in the next chapter.

SEXUALLY TRANSMITTED INFECTIONS

Who can catch a sexually transmitted infection?

Absolutely anyone can get a sexually transmitted infection, or STI. It doesn't matter who you are: if you have intimate contact with another person any bugs they may have can be passed on to you. You can catch STIs via your mouth, and orally transmitted infections are on the rise, but the biggest risk comes from sexual intercourse.

STIs are a huge problem, everywhere – the UK, Europe and the rest of the world. The statistics are frightening: 1 million people around the world will catch an STI today, and at least 1 in 10 young people in the UK has an STI, right now. Worse still, many are unaware of it, so are potentially passing on their infection to someone else.

You don't need to be promiscuous to catch an STI – just one partner is enough – but the more people you have contact with, the bigger your risk. To protect yourself, it's vital you practise safe sex (see page 86).

Where to go for help

Anyone who thinks they may have an STI should have a check-up as soon as possible. And even if you think you are probably OK, it's still a good idea to have a check-up if you've had sex with a new partner recently – or, better still, *before* you start having sex with them.

The best place to go is the Genito-Urinary Medicine (GUM) clinic of your local hospital, also sometimes known as the sexual health clinic. They can diagnose most STIs immediately, and treatment is free. Many offer a walk-in service as well as appointments, though waiting times can be long.

Young people under the age of 25 can get help at Brook Advisory

Centres, and you can also go to NHS walk-in centres. You could go to your GP, though frankly many aren't very good at diagnosing STIs.

SAFE SEX

Unfortunately it's true that practising safe sex can mean that mad moments of spontaneous passion just don't happen any more. But the payback, and it's huge, is that you will be protecting your health. And remember, catching an infection can be the biggest passion-killer of all.

To help protect yourself:

- During foreplay cover cuts, sores and other skin lesions with waterproof plasters (that means your partner as well as you). Don't let anyone with anything that even might be a cold sore kiss you – anywhere.

- Have a look at your partner, particularly his penis. I'm not suggesting you go in for a full anatomical examination, but there are ways you can do this without it being obvious what you are doing. Any secretions should be clear, not cloudy or coloured. Check for ulcers or sores. If there is anything that you're not sure about, then don't go near him.

- Always get your partner to put a condom on before any genital contact. It's not just ejaculate that can be infectious – the secretions at the end of an erect penis can be full of bugs, and some viruses can be passed on just from skin-to-skin contact.

- You can't get pregnant from anal sex, but it's a very efficient way of transmitting infections. Get your partner to use an extra strong condom, and use plenty of lubrication to stop it tearing.

- Infections can be transmitted via sex toys. Wash them thoroughly between partners.

COMMON SEXUALLY TRANSMITTED INFECTIONS

CHLAMYDIA

Chlamydia is now the most common STI in the UK. It's caused by a tiny bacterium, and though it usually affects the genitals, it can also infect the throat, rectum and eyes.

It is very infectious, being easily spread from one person to another, usually through sexual activity. It can also be spread to a mother from her baby at birth. But you can't get chlamydia from kissing, hugging, sharing baths, towels or cutlery, or from toilet seats or swimming pools. In other words, if he's given you chlamydia, it's because he got it from being intimate with someone else. However, this doesn't mean he's been unfaithful because . . .

Tell-tale signs

Often there aren't any. Around 70 per cent of women and 50 per cent of men who have chlamydia have no symptoms at all. That means that someone can have it for ages (months or maybe even years) without knowing it. Others have symptoms that are so mild they go unnoticed, and this means that if you are diagnosed with chlamydia, it can be difficult to pinpoint exactly when you caught it.

A few women may get an unusual vaginal discharge or pain when passing urine (which may get mistaken for cystitis – see page 196). However, all too often chlamydia doesn't cause any symptoms until it has spread up to the womb and fallopian tubes, where it can wreak havoc.

Chlamydia is the commonest cause of pelvic inflammatory disease (PID; see page 105). It causes inflammation, which may be mild and just cause a little bleeding in between periods or after sex. It can also cause pain, which may just start as a dull ache, or there may be some unusual discomfort during sex or afterwards. But sometimes there may be no symptoms at all that it has spread – 'silent' PID.

It's been estimated that up to 40 per cent of women who have chlamydia will develop PID of some sort, and as a result have permanently damaged fallopian tubes and fertility problems. However, many women are unaware they have been infected with chlamydia until they have investigations to find the cause of their infertility. The damage caused by chlamydia can also increase the risk of having an ectopic pregnancy (see page 155).

Diagnosis and treatment

Chlamydia can be detected via a swab (which looks like an elongated cotton bud) taken from either the cervix or the urethra (the bladder opening). It can also be detected via a special urine test, which is now available at many chemists. Very importantly though, it cannot be detected by the ordinary swabs or standard urine tests that most GPs use, so just because you have had a swab or urine test done does not mean you have been tested for chlamydia.

Chlamydia can be treated with antibiotics, either as a large single dose or as a course lasting up to 2 weeks, depending on the severity of the infection. It's important to have a check-up afterwards, to be sure the infection has cleared, and that your partner is treated at the same time.

GONORRHOEA

After chlamydia, this is the second most common STI in the UK, and in many ways it is very similar to chlamydia: it's often a silent infection that goes undetected, and one that can have serious consequences for your long-term health.

Gonorrhoea is caused by a small bacterium that can infect the genitals, the rectum and the throat. It is spread in exactly the same way as chlamydia (see page 87).

Tell-tale signs

Around 50 per cent of women with gonorrhoea (but only 10 per cent of men) don't have any symptoms. Any symptoms that do occur tend to appear between one and 10 days after infection, and can include a strong-smelling vaginal discharge that may be thin/watery or yellow/green. There may also be pain when passing urine, but in many women the first signs of infection are when the symptoms of PID appear – pain in the pelvis, pain during or after sex, and abnormal bleeding (see page 106).

Diagnosis and treatment

Gonorrhoea can be detected on a swab taken from either the cervix or the urethra, or, if indicated, from the throat or rectum. But it may be missed on a swab just taken from the vagina (which is unfortunately what many GPs do).

It is usually treated with a large single dose of antibiotics, though a longer course is required for PID. It's important to have more swabs done 2 weeks later to be sure the infection has cleared, and, as always, your partner should be checked and treated at the same time.

HERPES

This probably causes more angst amongst women than any other STI, mainly because some people get recurrent attacks. But getting herpes should not mean a life sentence of chastity, and you can enjoy a good sex life after you have had it. It's caused by the herpes simplex virus. There are two types, and though traditionally type 1 causes cold sores around the mouth and type 2 causes genital herpes, either type can affect either area.

It is passed on by direct skin-to-skin contact; that means you can get it even if you don't have intercourse. Though it is often spread by close genital contact, you can also get herpes from kissing or having oral sex with someone who has a cold sore. And it can be spread by sharing sex toys.

Condoms don't offer complete protection against herpes, as they only cover the penis and the virus can be spread from sores on other parts of the genitals. Rather worryingly, it is possible to get herpes from someone who has never noticed any signs or symptoms, though this is fairly rare. Most people get herpes from someone who knows they have had an attack.

Tell-tale signs

The first symptoms usually occur within 2–7 days of being infected. These symptoms are:

♦ usually tingling of the affected area of skin

♦ this is followed in the next 24 hours by a collection of blisters

♦ these break down, again usually within a day, to form acutely painful ulcers

- over the next week to 10 days these gradually scab over and heal

- during the first attack more general flu-like symptoms may also occur, with a mild fever, tiredness and muscle aches

During an attack of genital herpes, passing urine can be agonizingly painful. Drinking plenty of water, which dilutes the urine, can be helpful, and if necessary pee in the bath.

Diagnosis and treatment

An experienced doctor will be able to diagnose herpes just by seeing the characteristic sores, but a special swab taken from a visible sore can give confirmation.

The sores will heal up on their own, but prompt treatment with anti-virals really can speed up the process. Creams containing acidovir are available directly from chemists (they are marketed for cold sores, but they work just as well on genital herpes), but tablets, taken by mouth, are far more effective, and they are available only on prescription. They also work best the sooner they are started, so if you think you may have herpes, see a doctor as soon as you can.

The lesions of herpes are full of virus and are highly infectious. But once the skin has completely healed over it is no longer infectious in the vast majority of people, and it is safe to resume normal sexual activities.

Occasionally, people who get recurrences shed the virus from seemingly normal skin for a week or so before and after an attack, and so inadvertently infect another person, but this is fairly unusual; if it does happen, it's most likely in the year after the first attack.

Recurrences

What makes herpes the subject of so many scary stories is the fact that once you have been infected with it, the virus stays inside your body. It lives inside the nerve cells of the spine and occasionally it can become active, travelling down the nerve to the skin, where it causes a recurrent attack.

This does not happen to everyone – many people only ever have one attack. Quite why some have recurrences and others don't is a mystery. We also don't know why some people only ever have one recurrence, while a few unlucky people have frequent attacks.

Recurrences may be linked to stress, being over-tired, and also exposure to sunlight, so simple lifestyle changes may be helpful. Eating a sensible, balanced diet and avoiding chafing the skin with tight underwear can also help reduce the impact of recurrences.

Taking anti-viral tablets can definitely help reduce the severity of recurrent attacks. These are best started as soon as the skin starts to tingle, and if you have had one attack, make sure you keep a supply of tablets in your first aid kit. Don't wait until you get an attack and then can't get an appointment at the surgery – your doctor should be happy to supply you with a 'spare' set of tablets.

If you get frequent recurrences, say more than once a month, then it's worth taking a long course of anti-virals for several months to try to suppress the activity of the virus.

Having herpes does not increase your risk of cervical cancer (see page 121), and neither does it affect your fertility, though it is possible to infect the baby during delivery if you have any active sores present. If you have an attack when you go into labour you should be offered a Caesarian section.

WARTS

Genital warts are incredibly common, and are caused by the human papilloma virus (HPV). There are more than 100 different types of wart virus. Some cause warts on the hands, or verrucas on the feet; only a few types cause visible genital warts. They are spread by direct skin-to-skin contact, and this means that condoms offer only partial protection.

Tell-tale signs

You can be infected with HPV and not know it; only a small proportion of people infected actually develop visible warts. If they do appear, it's usually at least 2 weeks after being infected, and may be several months later.

Warts can vary a lot between different people. Some get just one tiny lump, while others develop larger rough lumps, which look a bit like a miniature cauliflower. They can occur anywhere around the genitals, including inside the vagina and on the cervix. They are usually painless, but can be irritating.

Diagnosis and treatment

In most cases the diagnosis is obvious, but if there is any uncertainty painting the warts with a mild vinegar solution turns them white.

Visible warts should be treated to stop them growing any bigger, and to stop the virus being passed on to someone else. This involves physically destroying them, either with freezing or with caustic chemicals. These have to be used with care as they can easily damage the surrounding delicate skin. A paint is available, but is so strong that it's generally used only by health professionals. However, a cream that you can use at home (Imiquimod) is available on prescription.

Sadly, you can't get rid of warts instantly – several treatments are usually required over a period of a few weeks. Never try to use wart remedies from chemists for genital warts – they are designed for warts on the hands and feet, and they are far too strong for use on the genital area.

Having warts does not mean you are at increased risk of cancer of the cervix (see page 121) – that is caused by different strains of HPV that do not cause visible wart-like lesions. Unfortunately, having the strains that cause visible warts does not offer you protection against any other strains, and it's quite possible to have been infected with more than one strain at the same time. The moral here – just make sure you have regular smear tests (see page 121).

TRICHOMONAS VAGINALIS

Also known as TV, this is caused by a tiny parasite (like an amoeba) that can infect the vagina and urethra. It can be passed on during vaginal sex and while sharing sex toys. It can also, rarely, be passed from a mother to her baby during delivery.

Tell-tale signs

Up to 50 per cent of affected women have no symptoms, but if they do appear it will be between 3 and 21 days after infection.

TV classically causes a profuse creamy/green frothy vaginal discharge, which has a musty or fishy smell, though some women just notice a thin, slightly yellow discharge. It also causes soreness and itching in and around the vagina, which may be particularly noticeable after sex, and may cause slight pain on passing urine.

Diagnosis and treatment

TV can be diagnosed by a straightforward vaginal swab, and treatment is usually with a large single dose of the antibiotic metronidazole. Unlike most other STIs, TV may also be diagnosed from a cervical smear test (see page 121). As always, have a check-up afterwards to be sure the infection has cleared.

TV isn't a serious infection, but if you've caught that, you could have caught something else. If your GP picks it up with a standard swab or a smear, it's a good idea to have special swabs done to check for chlamydia or gonorrhoea (see pages 87 and 88), which the first test won't have detected.

VERY SERIOUS INFECTIONS

The most serious STIs are HIV, hepatitis and syphilis. Not so long ago, I wouldn't have had to include these in a book on women's health, as they were generally only found in men. Sadly, though, they can affect and are affecting increasing numbers of women.

HIV

Human immuno-deficiency virus (HIV) is a virus that affects the body's immune system, gradually destroying a person's natural defence against infections. At the moment (and sadly, also for the foreseeable future) there is no cure for HIV – once you've been infected with it, you've got it for life. However, it is no longer a death sentence, as modern treatments mean that many people are surviving for a long time with the virus. But it certainly affects your quality of life, and most people with HIV are destined to be taking large quantities of medication every day, which can cause unpleasant side effects.

HIV can only be passed on through the transfer of blood, semen, vaginal fluids and breast milk. The two main ways people are infected are via vaginal or anal intercourse with an infected person, or by using infected needles when taking illegal drugs. An infected woman can also pass the virus to her unborn baby before or during the birth.

Occasionally HIV is also passed on through oral sex, but only if a person has cuts or sores in their mouth. There are very few proven instances of this, as generally saliva contains only a very small concentration of the virus. This is why kissing is generally safe.

Drug addicts, bisexual men and those who have recently come from Africa are more likely to have HIV, and many cases in women can be traced to sexual contact with a high-risk person. However, some women have caught HIV from a man who is not in a high-risk group, and the number of new cases of HIV in the UK in heterosexuals now exceeds those in homosexuals. You can never be too careful.

Tell-tale signs

There are no immediate signs or symptoms after infection – how much better it would be if there were! Though a few people may develop a flu-like illness after a few weeks, this usually goes unnoticed. The only way to know if you are HIV positive is to have a test.

Diagnosis and treatment

The HIV test checks for antibodies to the virus in the blood. It normally takes 3 months for these to develop, so a test done soon after you've been infected may give an inaccurate result.

You can get free HIV tests at GUM clinics and at your GP's surgery. Pregnant women are also routinely tested for the virus. Regardless of where you have the test done, you'll have to wait several days for the result, and it won't be given to you over the phone; you'll have to go back and get it personally.

Treatment is free to anyone in the UK, and is organized by HIV specialists, not your GP.

HEPATITIS

This is the result of a virus that causes inflammation of the liver. There are several types; the two that can be sexually transmitted are types B and C (type A is usually caught from contaminated food). Both hepatitis B and C can cause short- and long-term damage to the liver, and can increase the risk of getting liver cancer. Both can be contracted in the same way as HIV.

SYPHILIS

Syphilis is probably the oldest STI of all, and Henry VIII probably gave it to all of his wives. Sadly, though it did become much less common in the mid part of the twentieth century, it hasn't gone away and is now staging a twenty-first-century comeback.

Syphilis is caused by a bacterial infection, which can be passed on through vaginal, oral or anal sex, and also from intimate body contact with syphilis sores or rashes. It can be passed from a mother to her unborn baby.

The infection goes through several stages:

- First, one or more painless sores appear; in women these are usually on the vulva or at the entrance to the womb. These occur 3–4 weeks after infection and take around 6 weeks to heal.

- 3–6 weeks later, a non-itchy rash appears, which may cover the whole body; it is accompanied by a flu-like illness with a sore throat and headache. This may last for several weeks or months, and this stage is very infectious.

- There may then be no symptoms for years, but then third-stage syphilis may appear, causing serious damage to the internal organs, especially the heart, brain and nervous system, which can be fatal.

Syphilis can be detected via a blood test, which is offered routinely to everyone attending a GUM clinic, and also to pregnant women. Treatment with a 2-week course of antibiotics can eradicate the infection during the first and second stages, but organ damage in the third stage may be irreversible.

OTHER GENITAL INFECTIONS

Thrush and bacterial vaginosis are two other genital infections that commonly affect women, and are the most common causes of a vaginal discharge; however, they are not usually sexually transmitted.

THRUSH

This is caused by the yeast candida. It mainly affects the vagina and surrounding genital area, but can also occasionally occur in the mouth, and around the nipples of breastfeeding mums.

Small amounts of candida commonly live in the vagina, but the immune system and the other bacteria that live in the vagina keep it in check. The most important of these bacteria are lactobacilli, which help to keep the vagina slightly acidic, which in turn prevents the growth of yeasts. It's a good case of nature working in harmony, but if something happens that upsets this natural balancing act, the yeasts may multiply, causing symptoms.

This is likely to happen:

- when the area becomes very moist and warm (conditions ideal for yeasts to grow)
- at times of hormonal change (particularly pregnancy)
- when taking antibiotics (which often destroy lactobacilli as well as other more harmful bacteria)
- if the sugar level inside the vagina increases, which is why diabetics can get frequent attacks

Tell-tale signs

The main symptom of thrush is soreness and itching, which is usually worse after sex. There may be vaginal discharge, which is usually creamy and may be quite thick, with a slight musty smell. The whole genital area can become very red and swollen.

Thrush isn't dangerous – it doesn't invade the rest of the body – but it can make your life a bit miserable. It's no fun wanting to scratch yourself all the time, and not being able to have sex because it's just too sore.

Diagnosis and treatment

If you think you've got thrush you can buy effective treatment from the chemist. There is no need to go to your doctor, though some treatments are cheaper on prescription. Options include creams, pessaries and fluconazole, a single capsule that's taken by mouth. It's important not to rely on using a cream just on the outside genital area; the infection is nearly always focused inside the vagina and this must be treated too.

If the treatment you choose doesn't work, then you should see your doctor to have the diagnosis confirmed and to check that there isn't another cause for your symptoms. However, it may be simply that you need a different type of anti-fungal, as unfortunately some strains are becoming resistant to standard treatments.

Alternative remedies

♦ Tea-tree oil has anti-fungal properties and can be used to clear mild attacks of thrush. However, it can be very irritant, so must be used with care. Test a tiny drop on your genital skin first. If there is no reaction, then apply 2 drops to a damp tampon and insert it into the vagina for a couple of hours. Repeat twice daily for 3 days.

♦ Natural yogurt contains large quantities of lactobacilli, and can be used both to prevent thrush and to treat mild attacks. The easiest way to do this is again by using a tampon. Dunk it in natural yogurt, then leave it in the vagina for a few hours.

Prevention

Thrush is very common, and most women have at least one attack during their life. Some, though, get it repeatedly, often for no apparent reason.

You can help keep thrush at bay by:

- always wearing cotton underwear, which allows sweat to evaporate, and helps to prevent a build-up of moisture; lycra and polyester are not the thrush-prone girl's best friend
- opt for stockings rather than tights
- never douche – it never does any good, and merely washes away those all-important protective bacteria
- it's also a good idea to avoid using perfumed products in the bath, as these can irritate the vaginal surface and again upset nature's delicate balancing act
- if recurrent attacks become a real problem, using a special gel that helps to keep the vagina acidic, such as BIO-FEM Actigel, can be helpful

Very occasionally, thrush can be sexually transmitted. Affected men get a red itchy rash on the tip of the penis, together with a white discharge that collects under the foreskin. It can be treated with standard anti-fungal creams, applied twice a day, but if your partner is affected you should avoid having sex till both of you are clear.

BACTERIAL VAGINOSIS

Often known as BV, this is not caused by a single bacterium, but rather is an overgrowth of the normal harmless bacteria that usually live in the vagina. Like thrush, it's a case of an upset in nature's delicate balancing act.

About 10 per cent of women get BV at some time, and often there is no obvious reason why it has happened. It cannot be caught from anyone, but it may be linked to an increase in sexual activity, which may alter the balance of organisms in the vagina.

It is not caused by poor hygiene; if anything, it's due to the opposite problem, as over-washing and douching can remove protective natural secretions. Some women who have a copper IUCD (see page 172) seem more at risk from BV.

Tell-tale signs

BV may not cause any symptoms – some women find they have it only when they have a swab taken for other reasons. However, it often causes a watery/creamy discharge that has a characteristic fishy smell. The smell may be particularly noticeable after sex (which can be alarming for both of you). The smell is also particularly strong if an alkali solution is added to a sample, and this is how the diagnosis is often made by doctors. It can also be diagnosed by a swab test.

Diagnosis and treatment

Treatment is necessary only if there are troublesome symptoms. In many cases, the balance of bacteria may correct itself. The options for those requiring treatment are metronidazole or tinidazole, given either by mouth or via a vaginal gel.

Unfortunately, BV has a habit of recurring; half the women who are treated are likely to find they have symptoms again within 3 months. However, a second course of treatment is likely to be successful. If you are prone to recurrent attacks of BV, follow the advice for preventing thrush (see page 101) – the same tactics work for BV too.

Metronidazole

This antibiotic deserves special mention as it is so frequently used to treat gynaecological infections in women. This is because it is effective at eradicating not only trichomonas (see page 94) and the bugs that cause bacterial vaginosis (see above), but also organisms that flourish in low-oxygen environments – anaerobes. Anaerobes thrive inside the womb and fallopian tubes, and can often contribute to PID (see page 105).

Metronidazole is not nice stuff. It can cause nausea and digestive upsets, and leaves a nasty metallic taste in the back of the mouth. It is also the one and only antibiotic that cannot be mixed with alcohol. This isn't because booze stops it working – it doesn't – but rather because the combination can cause really severe nausea, often to the point of vomiting.

Unfortunately, if you need metronidazole, there is usually no alternative – you just have to grin and bear it.

Vaginal discharge – a quick guide

Discharge	Likely cause	Action
Clear, sticky, no smell.	Increased oestrogen. Normal for a few days before ovulation Also common in pill users. May also be due to a cervical erosion (see page 250).	None needed unless persistent and a nuisance. Changing pill may help.
Creamy white, thick, musty smell, soreness and itching.	Thrush.	Anti-fungal cream, pessaries or oral capsule. See a doctor if it persists.
Slightly creamy, fishy smell.	Bacterial vaginosis.	May get better on its own. If not, see a doctor for treatment.
Green, frothy, itchy and sore.	Trichomonas.	See a doctor for antibiotics.
Slightly green or cream, no noticeable smell.	Could be chlamydia or gonorrhoea.	See a doctor for test and treatment.
Brown staining.	Old blood.	See a doctor to identify the cause.
Foul smell, watery, slightly coloured.	Retained tampon or contraceptive.	Check! See a doctor if you can't find the cause or if it's stuck.

In older women: slightly watery, creamy or yellow, soreness or irritation.	Infalmmation due to lack of oestrogen.	See a doctor for proper diagnosis. Oestrogen cream may help.

PELVIC INFLAMMATORY DISEASE – PID

Pelvic inflammatory disease – often known as PID – is an increasingly common cause of both pelvic pain and infertility. About 1 in 50 sexually active women develop PID each year, and it's most common between the ages of 15 and 24. Imagine a hall full of 100 sixth-form girls sitting an exam. It's likely that one or two of these girls will have had PID and put their fertility at risk for the rest of their lives.

As its name suggests, the symptoms it causes are due to inflammation of the pelvic organs, notably the womb and fallopian tubes.

Why does this happen?

In most cases PID is due to an infection that has been sexually transmitted into the vagina, travelling up via the cervix. That means you are more at risk of PID if you have unsafe sex. The more partners you have, the greater the risk.

Women who have a copper IUCD (see page 172) are more at risk of getting PID if they get an infection in the vagina, but the same increased risk does not appear to apply to women with a Mirena coil (see page 167), as the progestogen thickens the cervical mucus and helps to prevent invasion of the womb by bacteria.

Occasionally PID can occur after gynae operations, especially termination of pregnancy, and less commonly after a miscarriage.

The most common cause of PID is chlamydia, but gonorrhoea and anaerobes, or a mixture of these, are often implicated too (see pages 87, 88 and 103). Sometimes the infecting organisms produce a vaginal discharge, but in many women there are no signs of infection until the symptoms of PID appear. This means that you can get PID weeks or months after you were initially infected.

Tell-tale signs

These vary according to the severity of the infection, and the inflammation it causes. They include:

♦ Pelvic pain. This varies from a dull ache to really severe pain. The pain may be felt deep in the pelvis, and also in the back. It may be continuous or intermittent.

♦ Pain on intercourse, especially deep penetration. It may make having sex impossible.

♦ Heavier, more painful periods, or bleeding in between periods.

♦ In more severe cases, it may also cause a fever and make you feel very unwell.

In some women the symptoms come on suddenly and are so obvious that they can tell something is wrong. But more commonly, the symptoms appear slowly and may continue for several weeks before the woman seeks medical help.

Diagnosis and treatment

If you think you may have PID you should see a doctor as soon as you can, as prompt treatment could save your fertility.

PID is usually diagnosed in a rather old-fashioned way, according to the symptoms and by examining the patient, as there is no specific diagnostic test. If your doctor suspects you have PID, she should do a proper pelvic examination, which needs to be done with two hands – one in the vagina, one on the tummy. Pain when the doctor touches or moves the cervix is highly suggestive that the womb is inflamed. Beware any doctor who makes the diagnosis by just feeling the tummy or, worse still, without doing an examination at all.

It is good practice for swabs to be taken from the cervix to check for chlamydia and other infections, but these aren't always very useful, as they only give information about what is going on in the cervix, which may be different from the situation in the womb and the fallopian tubes. It's quite common for these tests to come back clear, when a woman obviously has PID. A pelvic ultrasound may reveal very swollen fallopian tubes, but in many cases this too is normal.

The only way that the diagnosis can be made with certainty is by laparoscopy (see page 185), but this is only necessary in women with persistent symptoms and is rarely done in the first instance.

PID may not be diagnosed immediately, especially if it is not severe. The symptoms may be mistaken for other gynaecological problems, or for a urine infection. This is very unfortunate, because PID can cause permanent damage, especially if it is left untreated.

Treatment is usually with a combination of 2 antibiotics and should be continued for at least 10 days, often longer. As the exact type of bacteria responsible is rarely known, the idea is to use drugs that will kill off the most likely culprits.

Is it dangerous?

Most cases of PID aren't that serious, in the sense that it's not life-threatening, but occasionally it can cause such severe pain and fever that hospital treatment with intravenous antibiotics is required.

However, it is serious in the sense that it can result in infertility. The inflammation it causes can lead to scarring of the fallopian tubes, which may then become blocked. This also increases the risk of having an ectopic pregnancy (see page 155). After just one episode of PID at least 1 in 5 women will have permanently damaged tubes; the more severe the attack, and the more attacks a women has, the greater the chance of tubal damage.

Afterwards

Though some women do make a good recovery from PID, in others the tubes remain inflamed, which can cause chronic pelvic pain and increase the risk of them becoming infected again very easily. Sometimes recurrent attacks of PID are triggered by a new infection, but sometimes just the mechanical action of having sex may be enough to cause another bout of inflammation. Sometimes recurrent bouts of pain are due to adhesions that have developed between the pelvic organs during the acute infection. These can be surgically divided via a laparoscopy.

Unfortunately, a few women continue to have chronic pelvic pain after they have had PID, and sometimes the only cure is to remove the affected organs – sometimes just the fallopian tubes, but occasionally the womb and ovaries as well (see Hysterectomy, page 253). Although this sounds drastic, it can give welcome relief to women whose pain has caused them years of misery.

SKIN AND HAIR

ACNE

Just why is it that at a time in your life when you really want to be attractive, your face erupts in spots? And your hair is a lanky mess, which needs a daily wash – and even then, it's greasy at the roots by the end of the day?

Acne can occur at any age, but it is far more common between the ages of 12 and 25. If it's any consolation, though, it's more common and often worse in blokes; but even so, at least 80 per cent of girls will develop spots. It's the most common reason why young girls visit their doctor. In some, there are just a few pimples, but in others it can be so bad that the whole face and upper back is covered with large red pustules. No wonder that it can cause social isolation and depression.

The skin is lubricated by oil, or sebum. Sebum is produced by the sebaceous glands, which lie alongside hair follicles. The entrances to these glands are visible as tiny pores. During the teenage years, the raised hormone levels, particularly of testosterone, stimulate the sebaceous glands to produce larger quantities of sebum, which makes the skin more greasy. In addition, the layer of cells on the surface of the skin thickens, and there is also an increase in the number of bacteria that live on the skin.

Together, these can block the pores, which become visible as whiteheads or blackheads (the black colour is caused by skin pigment, not by dirt) and the swollen sebaceous glands underneath may become infected, leading to spots.

Sometimes the surrounding skin becomes inflamed and the result is hard red lumps, which can be tender to touch. In more serious cases, small abcesses may develop and, as these heal, they can cause scarring.

Why does this happen?

In general, it's a complete lottery as to who gets bad acne and who has a lovely clear complexion. However, there are some things that can make acne worse, such as:

♦ Stress. This drives up testosterone levels, and high testosterone is the main reason why boys tend to have much more severe acne than girls.

♦ Some types of contraceptive pill can make acne worse. Check with your doctor.

♦ It can be a sign of the hormone imbalance in polycystic ovarian syndrome (PCOS; see page 186).

♦ Picking or squeezing at spots can definitely make matters worse.

♦ Very thick, heavy make-up can block pores more. If you want to cover your skin, make sure you use a brand that is labelled 'non-comogenic'.

♦ Getting hot and sweaty can make a tendency to blocked pores worse. If you are prone to spots on your chest or back, try to wear clothing made of natural fibres.

♦ Some medicines, such as strong steroid creams for eczema, and tablets used to treat epilepsy, can make acne worse. Again, check with your doctor if you are on any medication.

But to dispel a few myths:

♦ You can't catch acne. It's not infectious.

♦ It's not caused by poor hygiene, but it does help to keep your skin reasonably clean.

♦ It's not inherited either. Just because your mother had bad acne doesn't mean you will too.

♦ Eating greasy food, too many burgers or chips, or too much chocolate cannot give you acne. But that said, you are more likely to have a clear skin if you eat a healthy diet.

♦ You can't cure acne by drinking lots of water.

Treatment

The comment 'Oh, it's just a few spots' is not what teenagers want to hear. They want to be rid of them and not to have any scarring – and with the right treatment, that is possible. But it won't happen instantly; it takes time, and it usually means continuing with treatment for several years.

Treatments can work by:

♦ reducing sebum production

♦ unblocking pores

♦ killing off excess bacteria

♦ reducing inflammation

Self-help

There is a lot you can do yourself to help to clear your complexion, but that doesn't mean you have to spend a small fortune on umpteen different products from the chemist. Most of them contain very similar ingredients, just in a slightly different formulation, so get in the habit of reading the contents label. Buying three will usually do the job just as well as thirteen.

♦ First, wash twice a day, either with ordinary soap or with an antibacterial skin wash.

♦ Then wipe your face with an antibacterial toning lotion to remove final traces of excess oil and dirt.

♦ Thirdly, apply a cream containing benzyl peroxide either once or twice a day, depending on the state of your skin.

Acne often gets worse just before a period, and you may have to step up your treatment regime during this time. Benzyl peroxide reduces sebum production and has an antibacterial action, but it can make the skin feel quite dry, so start with a low strength (2.5 or 5 per cent) and work up to 10 per cent slowly, if need be.

Blackheads can be squeezed, and this will unblock the pore to release trapped sebum, but you must do it carefully. After a bath is best, when the skin is warm. Wash your hands and cover your fingers with a tissue. Never have a go at your face with dirty fingernails, and don't squeeze spots unless they have come to a yellow head; even then, do it very gently and stop if the spot starts bleeding. Never, ever squeeze hard red lumps; you'll only spread the infection beneath the skin's surface and end up with a worse mess than before.

Help from your doctor

If your spots persist despite using stuff from the chemist, then do see your doctor – there is a lot she can do and you won't be wasting her time.

◆ Stronger creams for drying excess sebum and unplugging pores are available, such as those containing tretinoin or adapalene. They can cause dryness and irritation, so need to be used carefully, especially at first.

◆ Antibiotics, especially tetracyclines and erythromycin, can reduce numbers of bacteria in the skin and are particularly effective if you have a lot of yellow spots or hard, sore, red lumps in the skin. They can be used either in the form of a cream or lotion applied directly to the skin, or taken by mouth.

◆ The contraceptive pill Dianette contains cyproterone acetate, which lowers testosterone levels. It can be a particularly good choice for women with acne who also need contraception.

All the treatments described so far are available on prescription from GPs and they can be very effective for the vast majority of women with acne. However, a small number of people with severe acne will benefit from seeing a specialist dermatologist, who can prescribe roaccutane. This is a very effective drug for acne, but it can have nasty, and potentially serious, side effects, including depression and very dry, uncomfortable skin. It can also affect the development of an unborn child, so any woman using it must avoid getting pregnant for the time she is using the drug and for 3 months afterwards.

It's common to have to use acne treatment for 5 years to keep the skin clear. Most women do grow out of it by their early twenties, but occasionally it persists for years and years, and some people find that after their skin has been clear for a decade or more, their spots return. Sorry – there's no way really of predicting what will happen: you just have to wait and see.

SKIN CARE

The average teenage skin does not require a daily moisturizer – generally it produces quite enough moisture of its own (though of course the cosmetics industry would love us to believe otherwise!). Dry skins do need moisturizer, usually not just on the face, but everywhere. The only exception to this is when the face is exposed to a lot of sun, wind or cold weather, and if this is the case then there's no need to spend a fortune on special face creams – a simple general moisturizer will do. The one place you shouldn't put these is round the eyes – the moisturizer can be too heavy and lead to puffiness, no matter what your age.

Tanning and sunbeds

I know pale is supposed to be interesting, but it can look dull, and I can understand why many women feel they are more attractive with a touch of colour. But sadly, sunshine is generally very bad for your skin. It accelerates ageing, gives you lines and wrinkles, and, worse still, it gives you skin cancer (see page 388).

The younger you are, the worse the damage, and though you may not realize it, getting a tan now could add ten years to the look of your face by the time you are 40. The bottom line is that any tan acquired from UV light – whether from the sun itself or from a sunbed – is a sign of skin damage.

I'd be the first to admit that a light tan can give you a glow, but sadly, it's anything but healthy. If you want to look tanned, no matter what your age, get into the habit of reaching for a bottle of fake tan.

Teenage skins do require protection; however, I don't agree with the purists who say that you should never go out in the sun. A little sunshine can be good for you – it can lift your mood, and it can also boost the production in the skin of vitamin D.

So be sensible. If you are going outside for more than half an hour – 15 minutes in the peak summer months – always wear sunscreen, especially on skin that gets a lot of sun, such as your face, shoulders and legs. And never, ever lie on a sunbed, especially if you have fair, freckly skin.

HAIR CARE

There is nothing wrong with washing your hair every day – it doesn't stimulate oil production, or make your hair more lank or greasy. Choose a shampoo that's suitable for your hair type. Hair that is prone to greasiness doesn't usually require a conditioner either, as long as it's going to be dried naturally. However, using a dryer or especially straightening tongs can strip the ends of moisture, so some added protection from a conditioner (but only on the ends) can help to prevent split, dry ends.

IN SUMMARY

The teenage years see the beginning of the process that turns a dependent little girl into an independent woman, capable of bearing children of her own. This transformation is governed, as we have seen in this chapter, by physical changes related to hormones. Not until she reaches the peri-menopause, at 40 or over, will she be subject to quite such a massive change in her body in such a short space of time. With any luck the woman of 40-plus will be more mentally capable of coping with the next change; a girl needs a lot of help to sail through the teenage years unperturbed, and this is where the information I have given in this chapter can be vital to her and to her family.

This transition phase can be fraught with difficulties. It's still up to a girl's family members to help her to cope with the ups and downs of physical changes, and yet she should be learning how to manage on her own. At 19 many girls will have left home, even if only for a term at a time at college. They will be learning to look after themselves, cook (and tidy up!), handle their own money, develop relationships with new people and generally feel capable of standing on their own feet, even if they return home for economic reasons later on.

Before the age of 19, however, a girl must face the increasing demands of schoolwork, peer pressure, social life and home life. No wonder many girls take refuge in eating disorders at this age – this is something they can control themselves. Parents should be watchful and get help for their daughter, whether she wants it or not, at the earliest possible stage. Generally, the topic of food is a controversial one at this age – many girls are dieting or bingeing, many have access to 'naughty' foods such as sweets, chocolate and fizzy drinks for the first time without having to ask their parents' permission. All the parents can do is to encourage an interest in healthy eating, and provide good-quality food at home whenever possible.

This chapter contains a long section on the dangers of sexually transmitted infections. It cannot be overemphasized how important it is to avoid and/or deal with these quickly for the sake of a girl's future health and the chance to have a family of her own.

However, once past the upheavals of the teenage years, and often at an earlier age than boys, girls will find themselves maturing into responsible women, ready to face the challenges of the next part of this book – the reproductive years.

CHAPTER THREE

REPRODUCTIVE YEARS: 20–39

W omen in their twenties and early thirties are often at their physical peak. The hormonal upheaval of puberty is over and menstruation has usually settled into a regular pattern. If you've had a difficult time as a teenager, or if your daughter has had a tough time, then by now you (or she) will have developed into a responsible, independent adult.

However, many important life choices are made at this age. You may have embarked upon a serious, long-lasting relationship. How can you tell when it's time to settle down with your partner? When should you think about starting a family? Should all this nest-building be put on one side while you push your way to the top of your chosen career?

Many young women find themselves juggling the responsibilities of career and motherhood, almost without knowing how this came about. It's always a difficult balancing act. Even if you decide it's a good time to start a family, you may then find you can't get pregnant easily or quickly. On the other hand, those who don't want to have children need foolproof contraception. There are so many choices to be made that will influence a woman's life and health for many years to come.

In this chapter you will find:

- **Staying healthy**
  - cervical smears and cervical cancer
- **The reproductive years**
  - conception
  - when to start a family
  - pregnancy
- **Motherhood**
  - coping with babies
  - your rights
  - the juggling act
- **Food and nutrition**
  - ingredients for a healthy diet
  - diet for PMS, conception and pregnancy
  - supplements
  - detoxing
- **Hormone issues**
  - fertility
  - miscarriage
  - ectopic pregnancy
- **Contraception**
  - termination of pregnancy
  - physical health
  - endometriosis
  - polycystic ovarian syndrome
  - pelvic pain
  - cystitis and urinary-tract infections

- irritable bowel syndrome
- piles
- allergies and food intolerance

STAYING HEALTHY

This is a time in your life when you should be in glowing health. But to stay that way, and to look after yourself for the future, you should have a few routine health checks. These include:

♦ regular cervical smears, once every 3 years

♦ checks for sexually transmitted infection if you think you may be at risk (see pages 85–109)

♦ a blood pressure check, once every 5 years

You should also be breast aware (see page 314) and check your skin all over, once every 6 months, for changes to any moles (see page 390). Get a loved one to check your back.

If you are thinking of starting a family you should also have checks for:

♦ your immunity to rubella (German measles) and chickenpox (see page 38)

♦ your iron level if you are vegetarian or eat very little red meat

CERVICAL SMEARS AND CERVICAL CANCER

The whole point of having regular smear tests is to prevent cervical cancer. There is no need for any woman to get cervical cancer, but it still happens and, unfortunately, it can still kill.

A cervical smear is not a test for cancer, but rather a test for detecting abnormal cells which, if left untreated, could turn cancerous. It involves taking a sample of cells from the cervix using either a wooden spatula or a plastic brush. The sample is then sent to a hospital laboratory for analysis. The traditional way of scraping the cells on to a microscope slide is now gradually being replaced by placing the cells in a tiny bottle of special preservative liquid (liquid-based cytology), which leads to fewer errors in analysis.

Under current NHS guidelines, all women between the ages of 25 and 49 are eligible for a free cervical smear test every 3 years, and those between 50 and 64 can have a test every 5 years. More frequent tests are offered to women who have had an abnormal smear in the past 3 years. Women over 65 need to have a test only if they have not had one since the age of 50, or have had a recent abnormal test.

Though experts agree that frequent smear tests on older women are generally unnecessary, there is concern that starting smear tests at 25 may be too late, especially for young women who started having sex in their early or mid teens. The 3-yearly interval is also longer than ideal, but it must be remembered that all NHS screening programmes have to take cost into account. If you can afford it, pay to have a smear test done privately between your NHS tests, and, if you are sexually active, have your first one done once you've entered your twenties.

Though smear tests used to be done on teenagers, this is now not advisable, as not only is cervical cancer incredibly rare in teenagers, but the results are unreliable as the cervix is still developing and changing at this age.

HPV – an important virus

It's reckoned that regular smears leading to early detection and treatment of abnormal cells can prevent 75 per cent of cervical cancers. That's good, but it's not perfect, and prevention of cervical cancer could be improved by testing for HPV.

It's now firmly been established that cervical cancer is caused by the human papilloma virus – HPV for short. There are more than 200 different strains of HPV. Many are harmless, while others cause visible warts on the body, particularly the hands and feet (where they appear as verrucas). Around forty strains of HPV are spread through sexual contact. Some cause visible warts (see page 93), and it is now known that fifteen strains (which generally don't cause obvious warts) can cause changes in the cells that eventually lead to cancer.

Testing for infection with 'high-risk' HPV strains can be done, and many experts feel this is a better way of identifying women at increased risk of cervical cancer. However, at present it is not generally available on the NHS, and, like smear tests, HPV testing has drawbacks.

Between 50 and 80 per cent of women who have been sexually active will be infected with HPV, but in many the infection is transient – the virus is cleared from the body. So having a positive test could cause a lot of unnecessary anxiety. Not only that, but if you are found to have HPV there is nothing you can do about it, as there is no treatment. It's just an indication that you should have more frequent smear tests to check what, if anything, is happening to your cervix. Thankfully, only a small number of those infected will develop abnormal cells. Smoking can put you more at risk of this – it seems that the toxic chemicals in smoke make the cervix more susceptible to damage from HPV. Starting sex at a young age, and exposing the immature cervix to the virus, is also a risk factor.

The good news is that vaccines against HPV have been developed and one is now available in the UK. It will prevent infection with the two strains that most commonly cause cervical cancer, and could offer the next generation of women really good protection against this potentially lethal disease. At the time of writing it is not available on the NHS, only privately, so for now we have to rely on smear tests. Make sure you know when you last had one done and when the next one is due.

What if the result is abnormal?

Don't panic! Sometimes there are insufficient cells present for analysis, or those that are there cannot be analysed properly because they are obscured by either blood or inflammatory cells caused by an infection. In these cases the smear just needs to be repeated. Sometimes, very occasional abnormal cells are seen – not enough to classify the smear as abnormal. These are labelled 'borderline' and a repeat smear in 6 months is usually recommended.

Abnormal smears are graded as CIN (Cervical Intraepithelial Neoplasia) 1, 2 and 3. Many grade 1s revert back to normal of their own accord and, again, the recommendation is usually for a repeat smear in 6 months. But if the repeat is abnormal, or if CIN 2 or 3 is present, then a colposcopy should be done. This is an examination of the cervix using a special microscope. A tiny biopsy of any abnormal-looking areas is taken, to confirm the diagnosis. The abnormal cells are then destroyed, either with heat (diathermy), freezing or laser. If the abnormal cells extend up into the cervical canal, they are removed surgically by cutting away a cone of tissue – a cone biopsy.

Any of these procedures can cause scarring, but they should not affect your fertility.

THE REPRODUCTIVE YEARS

When to have a baby is one of the most difficult decisions a woman ever has to make and one that will change her life irrevocably. Whatever your age, there are pros and cons. It's important to remember that motherhood is hard work – possibly the most exhausting task you will ever undertake – and, to varying degrees, a job for life. It's not a question of being tied to a baby for a couple of years, then gradually regaining your independence. How many friends do you have whose grown-up children are still living at home for one reason or another, or who drop everything to sort out some crisis or another that has occurred in their offspring's life? It's rare to find a woman who ever completely 'lets go' of her children!

CONCEPTION

From a biological point of view, the best time to conceive is between the ages of 20 and 35. A woman is born with a finite number of eggs; once she is in her late thirties, not only are there fewer left, but their poorer quality can in some cases increase the risk of Down's Syndrome and other abnormalities, and also of miscarriage. There is also a higher incidence of pre-eclampsia and ectopic pregnancies (see page 155) in over-35s.

A woman aged between 20 and 25 has a 25 per cent (1 in 4) chance of conceiving per menstrual cycle. It takes a couple in their early twenties an average five cycles before they are successful. A woman aged between 30 and 35 has a 15 per cent chance of successfully conceiving and it will take her an average nine cycles.

Women's fertility is only half the picture. As men age, their testes become smaller and softer and sperm quality declines. When a man is under 25 the probability that a couple will take longer than a year to conceive is only about 8 per cent, while it almost doubles to 15 per cent when the man is over 35. The older a man is, the more likely he is to have a problem fathering a child. There is growing evidence, too, that older fathers have more sperm with DNA mutations because the natural 'weeding out of the weakest' process (apoptosis) does not work so efficiently.

WHEN TO START A FAMILY

There is now a clear trend for women to have their babies at a slightly older age. Over the past twenty years the average age for a woman to have a first baby has risen from 26 to 29 and, for the first time, the rate of pregnancies for women in their thirties has overtaken that for younger women. Not only that: we are in an age of late baby boomers and increasing numbers of women now delay motherhood until their late thirties or even their forties. Many assume that if their natural fertility does let them down, they can turn to IVF. However, IVF treatment is by no means a dead cert for having a family. It has a high failure rate, especially in older women, can cost a lot of money and can carry an extra risk of multiple pregnancy when it is successful. If you try for a baby in your early twenties and discover there is a problem with your fertility, you have more time to seek help than if you leave it until your late thirties. And the harsh reality is that if medical reasons rule out pregnancy, younger women are the preferred choice of adoption agencies.

Biologically then, you do stand a better chance of conceiving at 20 than at 35, but if that sounds negative, it is true that many women in their late thirties and early forties have healthy babies with no difficulty.

In terms of social implications, later motherhood can have distinct advantages. For a woman of 20, having a child can mean a time of financial difficulty and disadvantage, especially if she is a single parent. At this age, you're unlikely to be a high earner or to have the necessary qualifications to return to a well-paid career. As a result, you may find yourself frustrated – and poor – when the child is tiny, and you also need to consider that when you do decide to return to work or to study for a qualification or degree, you will have the added burden of caring for a child at the same time. The very high cost of childcare if you are in a poorly paid job may make these options impossible before your child starts school. All mothers make plenty of sacrifices for their children – you are less likely to resent this when you have enjoyed some time, freedom and money as an independent woman.

PREGNANCY

Women have the unique privilege of nurturing a new life from conception through to birth. And despite all the many other roles that we take on, having babies and raising a family is still, for many, the most important rite of passage in their lives. Maternal instincts can be very strong!

At least half of all babies born in the UK are from unplanned pregnancies, but this does not mean they are unwanted. In fact, nearly all of these are very much wanted by the time of their birth. I suspect this is because an awful lot of women (and men!) just can't make up their minds one way or the other whether they definitely want a child, and so don't use an ultra-reliable method of contraception. There's nothing wrong with that, as long as you are fit to have a healthy baby; sometimes we are presented with just too many choices, so nature takes over.

There isn't space in this book to go into all the details about pregnancy, so I'm going to just stick to some of the basics, especially those that can arise early on – often before you've really got your head around the idea that you are going to have a baby.

Very early stages

Most women do have an inkling that they are pregnant within a few weeks of conception – sometimes even before they have missed a period. I know that you hear stories of women who seemingly go into labour without any idea that they are about to have a baby, but, · honestly, they are rare.

The first signs are usually tender, full breasts – overnight your bra is a cup size too small – and a need to pee more often. And many women say they just feel different. They just know.

Pregnancy tests

You can find out for sure by doing a pregnancy test, using a sample of urine, from the day your period is due – anything earlier can be inaccurate. You can buy a DIY test (they are widely available), ask the chemist to do a test for you (for a small charge) or get a free test done by your GP or family planning clinic. Timing of testing for women with erratic periods can be difficult, but for a positive test the egg must have been fertilized for at least 2 weeks, so think back to when you might have conceived.

In pregnancy, everything is counted from the first day of the last period. The average pregnancy lasts 40 weeks, but anything from 38 to 42 weeks is regarded as normal.

How will I feel?

Pregnancy is not an illness – it's a very natural state of affairs for a woman and, for many, it's very enjoyable. Many women say that during pregnancy they feel more feminine than at any other stage in their life. And though a lot of women are concerned about how on earth they will cope with the huge change in body shape, it's important to remember it happens very gradually. By the time you do have a noticeable bulge, you are probably already admiring your new rounded contour and wishing it bigger!

Similarly, though it's normal in the beginning to be very worried about labour and the birth itself, by the time it happens, 9 months on, it's often not such a major deal. It's just something that you have to get through. And the fact that so many women go on to have at least one other child is proof that it's really not so bad!

What to expect

Pregnancy is usually divided into 3 stages – or trimesters.

The First Trimester: up to 12 weeks

Rather surprisingly, for many women the first 12 weeks are by far the worst. Even though outwardly you look the same (apart from your boobs) you can feel very different. The main problems are:

♦ Tiredness, verging on exhaustion – getting through a normal day can leave you shattered by 8 p.m., and fit for nothing but bed.

♦ Morning sickness – around 50 per cent of women get morning sickness, though in some it can be really bad, and last all day. However, most women do have episodes when they feel light-headed or nauseous in the first 12 weeks.

♦ Watching what you eat and drink. Vital development of the internal organs – heart, lungs, brain – spine and limbs, takes place during the first 12 weeks. This is the time when the baby is incredibly vulnerable to damage from infections and also from alcohol and medicines. Never take pills (including herbal medicines) unless you have checked that it is safe to do so, and be careful to avoid foods that might carry infections that could be dangerous to either you or the baby (see pages 143–6).

TESTS AND CHECK-UPS

Once you know you are pregnant, you should make an appointment to see your GP, but there's no rush – around 6–7 weeks is fine. You are entitled to free prescriptions and dental care during pregnancy and for a year afterwards. Ask your doctor for the relevant form to get the exemption certificate.

The first test you'll need is an ultrasound scan to check the baby's early development (and also to see how many babies there are!). This is usually done at around 11–12 weeks, but if you have had any bleeding, or if you have had a previous miscarriage, it may be done earlier.

Chorionic Villus Biopsy (CVS) checks for Downs Syndrome and other chromosome abnormalities, and is carried out at around 11 weeks. This (or amniocentesis, see page 131) is routinely offered to women over 36, and those thought to be at above average risk. It involves removing a tiny sample of placental tissue, and carries about a 1 per cent risk of miscarriage.

Second Trimester: 13–28 weeks

This is a time when most women really enjoy their pregnancy. If you've been feeling tired your energy levels will improve, and there is no reason why you can't carry on leading an active life, though you should avoid doing hard contact sports. Your 'bump' will gradually become more obvious, and by 16 weeks the chances are you'll have to swap your favourite clothes for ones with a larger, stretchy waistline.

During this time the baby grows from around 85mm to 30cm. Most women feel the first movement betwen 17 and 19 weeks, and by 22 weeks the kicks are much more distinct.

Though your appetite may increase, remember you don't need to eat for two! Just have slightly larger portions of healthy food, and if you feel hungry, have fruit between meals.

TESTS AND CHECK UPS

You should have your first full ante-natal appointment around 14–16 weeks, when you will also have blood tests, and a chance to talk through any queries you may have. After that you should be seen every 4–6 weeks. Most checks are done by midwives, but if any problems are suspected, you should be seen by a doctor. At each appointment you should have your blood pressure measured, along with the size of your bump, and the midwife will listen to the baby's heartbeat. You'll also need to give a sample of your urine to be checked for sugar (for diabetes) and protein (a check for possible infection and also for kidney problems).

You should have a scan to check on the baby's growth around 20 to 22 weeks.

If you are 36 or over, or the baby is thought to be at increased risk of abnormalities (for instance because of your family history) you may be offered an amniocentesis. This involves taking a small sample of the fluid that surrounds the baby, and is usually carried out around 15 weeks.

Third Trimester: 28 weeks onwards

During the last 12 weeks you will become more tired as the baby – and your tummy – become much larger. You are more likely to get problems such as backache, varicose veins, constipation and piles. As the enlarging womb presses into your bladder you are also likely to need to pee much more frequently than before.

This is the time when you need to make plans for the birth itself, and also start preparing yourself for the new addition to your family. In most places antenatal classes take place during the third trimester. Remember to invite your partner along too!

If you are well, when you decide to give up work is largely one of personal choice. If you have limited maternity leave, then working right up until the birth can give the advantage of more time with your baby, but it is important not to get too tired. The first few weeks of motherhood are always the hardest, and it definitely helps to be well rested beforehand.

TESTS AND CHECK-UPS

During this time you will need to see your midwife more frequently, and in the last month it's common to be seen every week. Some hospitals also offer a routine scan to check the baby's growth during the third trimester, but in many places a scan is done only if there are concerns.

Antenatal appointments aren't just about the baby, though. They are also an opportunity for you to discuss anything to do with the pregnancy, including minor health niggles that you don't feel warrant a doctor's appointment. It also is an ideal time to discuss any questions you have about labour or the birth itself.

The birth and afterwards

The majority of women give birth in hospital, but you can, if you want, have your baby at home. However, the midwifery services for this are very stretched, so it helps if you can express your wish for a home delivery as early on in the pregnancy as possible.

If you go into hospital, and the birth is straightforward, you will almost certainly be able to go home within a day. If you have a Caesarean, expect around 4–5 days in hospital.

Once you are home, a community midwife should come and visit you until the baby is 10 days old, to check how you and your baby are progressing. During the first weeks of motherhood you are bound to feel tired, and emotional, but it's also a wonderful happy time as you start to enjoy the extraordinary pleasure of motherhood.

Spreading the news

Deciding when to tell your family, friends and work colleagues that you are pregnant can be difficult. The first few weeks can sometimes be a bit hard; my advice is usually to tell them as soon as possible, so that they will understand if you have to keep going to the loo or cancel a meal out.

What if you miscarry? Though some women may want to keep this private, others find that sympathy, understanding and sharing the experience with other women can be invaluable. And you are likely to need a little time off work, which will require some sort of explanation. Though doctors are happy to put a vague 'gynaecological problem' on a sick note, this can easily be misinterpreted.

Be well informed

You will be offered free information booklets by your midwife, and these can be very useful. However, I think it can be helpful to have at least one really good pregnancy book as well. There is a large choice available, and it's worth browsing through them before you decide which one to buy.

The rules about maternity benefits are quite complex. If you are unsure, ask your midwife for a leaflet, or contact your local social security office. Your employer will almost certainly ask for a Mat B1 form, which confirms the date your baby is due. You can get this form 26 weeks onwards from your GP or midwife.

MOTHERHOOD

COPING WITH BABIES

Look round the office – you will spot new parents because they are the ones with their eyes hanging out of their heads. If you are a single mother wandering around like a zombie through lack of sleep, tell your health visitor. There are night nanny services for those who can afford it but, if you can't, perhaps a supportive parent or friend would be willing to take on the odd night shift. This kind of help can make all the difference in the world to you and the baby, so don't soldier on alone.

Men need emotional maturity to cope with a baby too. A younger man is more likely to resent being side-lined by a demanding infant and may fail to give a woman the support she needs. What she does require is a solid emotional crutch and buckets of understanding when she has spent the day with a crying, demanding newborn who refuses to be pacified and has destroyed her confidence. A man needs to be mature enough to turn the other cheek when a tired and fraught new mother displays jealousy because he still has the freedom to escape the pressures of childcare by going to work.

Another reason to consider becoming a parent later rather than sooner is that more relationships fail among couples in their early twenties than in their thirties. Forget the old cliché about children bringing you closer. With a bit of luck they will in time, if you are grown up enough to be a parent. But a screaming, insomniac infant can drive a permanent wedge between couples who had a shaky relationship to begin with. And some men just cannot cope with attention being diverted from them to the new addition to the family. You need a committed loving bond before you can become the sort of parental partners who can cry on each other's shoulders when times are tough without pointing the finger of blame at each other. If you manage it, the rewards of being a parent are incalculable.

You may not believe this at the time, but later – and thankfully for the survival of our species – we edit out the bad bits.

YOUR RIGHTS

You will not lose your job if you become pregnant – sacking you because you are pregnant is illegal. You are entitled to 26 weeks' ordinary maternity leave, plus a further 26 weeks if you have worked for your employer for 26 weeks by the 15th week before your expected delivery date. Basically, if you are trying to get pregnant, don't change employers if you want to take advantage of this. You are also entitled to the same training and promotion opportunities as your non-pregnant colleagues and must be allowed to return to your old job after the baby arrives or, if this is not possible, be offered a suitable alternative.

THE JUGGLING ACT

Women face major lifestyle adjustments during their reproductive years. What's the best way to keep juggling all the balls of parenthood, work, home life and your relationship with your partner without dropping one of them?

Sharing your life with your partner

The first adjustment comes when you and your partner decide to live together. Even with the delicious freedom of having sex whenever you want, the initial months can be tricky because a balance of power and fair division of labour have to be established.

So start as you mean to go on. Resist the temptation to be superwoman. Irons, washing machines and cookers do not have 'women only' labels on them. His mum may have done everything for him – you don't have to do the same. Unfortunately, despite so-called liberation, most women still end up doing most of the cleaning, cooking and food shopping as well as a full week's work.

Having two jobs – one of them unpaid – is a good shortcut to becoming exhausted and resentful. If this starts to happen, nip it in the bud or it will become a life sentence. Sometimes this martyrdom is self-imposed. Women cannot resist showing off their superior skills instead of going down the far wiser path of encouraging a partner who has, for example, never ironed or cooked before to have a go.

Don't turn sex into a daily chore, either. It is not compulsory to have sex every night and if either of you does not feel like it, learn to say so. It is much more intimate and honest to admit that you would rather have a cuddle than to 'give in' when you are not in the mood and score the supreme own-goal of faking orgasm. All habits are more smoothly established at the beginning of a live-in relationship, so start as you mean to go on.

If you have the money, use it to buy leisure time. Invest in labour-saving devices such as a dishwasher or pay someone to clean your home. Although you are in the first flush of passion, don't neglect other important relationships, such as your women friends. You and your partner do not need to live in each other's pockets, and spending time apart or having separate interests is not only necessary but mentally healthy. Nor is 'me time' the height of selfishness – it will help recharge your batteries. It does not matter how you spend it – a day at the spa if you can afford it, getting stuck into a good book, shopping or browsing the internet – it is psychologically vital time when you give yourself the total freedom to do what you want instead of what other people want.

Early years with a baby

When a baby arrives there are even more demands on your time and if your partner has always shared the chores, it will make your load much lighter. Don't monopolize your infant just because you think you do things better – let your partner bathe, change and comfort her. It is his child, too, and it also will give you time for a much-needed nap. As soon as feasible, grab back some 'me time', difficult as this may be. Get your partner to babysit while you go out for the evening with friends or join an evening class. Everyone needs a break from a baby.

Some women cannot wait to get back to work, but others find it an appalling wrench to leave their child. No matter which category you fall into, a woman needs to have absolute confidence in the person entrusted with the care of her child, for peace of mind and to minimize any feelings of guilt. However, the guilt is bound to surface from time to time, even when children are older – it is something you have to learn to live with. Many women end up thinking that they are failing in their jobs and at being mothers, too, because their loyalties are so divided.

And children become sick. In an ideal world, both men and women would take it in turns to take time off to care for them, but in practice it is nearly always women who have to play Florence Nightingale. Although it is against the law to discriminate, a woman will feel her career and chances of promotion are compromised if she puts her children before her work. She will feel guilty if she stays in the office when her child needs her, or guilty for letting down her colleagues or boss if she goes home.

Being a working mother is a superhuman juggling act and it is sometimes impossible to keep all the balls in the air. You need a strong support system – your partner, friends and, with a bit of luck, your mother – as long as these people do not disapprove of your decision to combine work with motherhood. A friend is someone who makes you feel good about yourself. Anyone who takes every opportunity to undermine your choice does not fall into this category, so unless you have a strong streak of masochism in your personality, delete them from your address book.

Chatting to other working mothers and finding out how they, too, are struggling to cope can boost your confidence tremendously. You will discover that everyone finds this work/mother juggling act enormously stressful. Everyone makes mistakes and, just like you, they are not perfect.

In the same way as it is unjust to wait on your partner when you both have full-time jobs, it is unfair to run around after your children when you are a working mum. Sons and daughters should earn their pocket money by undertaking chores that make your busy life easier. Encourage them to cook, wash and iron when they are old enough and don't practise gender discrimination and collude in turning out a new generation of males who learn at an early age that mundane, low-status tasks are 'women's work'.

FOOD AND NUTRITION

These are the years when many women are forging careers and raising children at the same time, and what's needed is a diet that provides enough energy to cope physically and mentally with the many demands that life can throw at you.

Get your diet right and you will give your body all the necessary nutrients to create and repair tissue, sustain a healthy immune system and provide you with the energy to enjoy life to the full. Moreover, only minor changes will be necessary to give you the best chance of conceiving and to have healthy pregnancies.

Eating well is about moderation and balance. Our bodies need a constant supply of energy, or calories – though some calories are better than others. Latest Department of Health figures reckon a woman who leads a fairly inactive life needs around 1,940 calories a day. By 'inactive', I mean those who might drive to work, take a gentle stroll around the shops during their lunch hour, and who take no specific exercise – cycling, gym work, swimming – on a regular basis. However, age, height, activity level and body composition all affect the number of calories each individual woman needs.

The body mass index (BMI) table (see page 218) is the most accurate way of assessing your ideal weight. Accumulating fat around your middle can also be an indicator if your weight is a risk to your health, and all women should aim to have a waist measurement under 80cm (32 inches). A measurement of greater than 87.5cm (35 inches) can put you at increased risk of heart disease, no matter how much or how little you weigh.

Energy comes from four main sources:

♦ complex carbohydrates ♦ protein

♦ fat ♦ simple sugars

Women need to consume foods from these four groups every day for optimum health.

IMPORTANT INGREDIENTS FOR A HEALTHY DIET

Fibre

Complex carbohydrates, such as wholemeal flour, oats, brown rice or pasta, will provide another important dietary requirement – fibre. This stimulates the bowel and ensures nutrients are released gradually. (On food labels, fibre is sometimes listed as non-starch polysaccharides.) Refined carbohydrates, such as white flour, are not so nutritious and will not satisfy your hunger for as long as the complex ones which provide slow energy release. (See the GI index on page 224.)

Water

An average 8 glasses of water a day will help flush out waste products, keep skin, hair and organs healthy and produce digestive enzymes to enable women's bodies to get the maximum nutritional benefits from their diets. Though both tea and coffee contain water, they also have a diuretic action, which means that they stimulate the body to produce more urine. This doesn't matter if you are drinking plenty of them, but if you rely on small quantities of them, especially on a hot summer's day (when you sweat a lot), you could risk becoming dehydrated.

Fruit and vegetables

The recommended 5 daily 80g portions of fruit and vegetables will provide maximum protection from heart disease, strokes, high blood pressure and some cancers. (Fresh is best, but frozen will do.) Examples of an 80g portion of fruit would be a banana, a small glass of fruit juice or a tablespoon of dried fruit such as raisins. The equivalent for vegetables is a small bowl of salad or a couple of tablespoons of cooked vegetables.

Dairy foods

Go easy on milk and dairy foods and try to choose reduced or low-fat versions, but don't cut them out altogether – they are high in calcium, which is very important for strong bones. You need 2 or 3 portions daily. A typical portion is 40g of hard cheese, a small pot of yogurt or fromage frais or a third of a pint of milk.

Protein

Have 2 portions of daily protein (fish, poultry, offal, eggs, pulses and nuts) and pick low or reduced-fat examples. A portion is equivalent to 3 slices of cooked pork, a chicken drumstick, an egg, 2 tablespoonfuls of nuts or a medium cod fillet.

Fats and sugar

Be very sparing with foods containing fats and sugar – butter, margarine, spreads, oils, fried food, mayonnaise, crisps, cakes and puddings and fizzy drinks. And also, sad to say, chocolate!

Good and bad fats

The body cannot produce the essential fatty acids, omega 3 and omega 6, so we need to get them through our diet. However, they are a double act. They will maintain their 'good fat' status only if you get relatively balanced amounts of both. In this country we tend to consume far too many omega 6 oils at the expense of omega 3s.

Omega 3 reduces the risk of heart problems, lowers blood pressure and battles auto-immune diseases and mood disorders. It is found primarily in cold-water oily fish. Try to eat fish 2–3 times a week or take cod liver oil to redress the omega 3/omega 6 imbalance. If you don't like fish, Colombus eggs – laid by hens on an omega 3-rich diet – may be an acceptable alternative; or, for veggies, flax oil (which, like cod liver oil, is also available in capsule form). Don't cook with flax oil, though, as this destroys the beneficial omega 3s.

The most beneficial omega 6 oils contain linoleic acid which turns into hormone-like molecules that regulate inflammation and blood pressure, and improve heart, kidney and gastro-intestinal function. These oils are found in cereals, eggs, poultry, most vegetable oils, wholegrain breads and some margarine. Evening Primrose and Starflower (borage) oils are particularly rich sources, but remember, if you have too many omega 6s, you can undo some of the benefits of omega 3s.

In summary: to balance the omega 3 and omega 6 oils, you need to consume oily fish or cod liver/flax oil for omega 3, as well as cereals/eggs/poultry/vegetable oil/wholegrain bread for omega 6.

Cooking oils

Supermarkets now stock a bewildering range of cooking oils. All oil is fattening – just one tablespoon contains 13.6g of fat and 120 calories – but some options are healthier than others. Here's a run-down of the best:

◆ **Canola oil**: its mild, bland taste makes it a perfect all-purpose cooking oil. It also contains alpha-linoleic acid, an essential omega 3 fat many Western diets lack.

◆ **Extra-virgin olive oil**: the very distinctive taste does not suit everyone – a little goes a long way. However, it is rich in monounsaturated fat and contains phytochemicals that lower cholesterol and protect against cancer.

◆ **Macadamia nut oil**: its light, nutty taste makes it an ideal choice for fish, chicken, vegetables, baking and salads. Because it has a high smoking point it is also ideal for stir-frying and sautéing. Like olive oil, it is rich in monounsaturated fat.

◆ **Sesame oil**: its richness enhances many meals when used sparingly. The toasted (dark) type packs the most punch for the taste buds.

◆ **Walnut oil**: it has a distinctive flavour but works well with most baked dishes and salads. Like canola, it contains a substantial amount of omega 3 oil. Most brands are minimally processed, so refrigerate them after opening because they can turn rancid quickly.

◆ **Soybean oil**: most vegetable oils are made from this and its blandness makes it a good all-rounder for cooking. However, it does not contain as much omega 3 as canola or walnut oil.

DIET FOR PMS, CONCEPTION AND PREGNANCY

Sometimes, adjusting your diet can help alleviate pre-menstrual syndrome (PMS; see page 258) symptoms and can also help you to conceive. Try the following before you reach for the supplements (see 146):

♦ Eat less salt to reduce water retention.

♦ Reduce caffeine and alcohol intake – they can make mood swings worse, make you jittery, and there is evidence that even small amounts of alcohol can harm a developing baby.

♦ Eat less meat and dairy produce. Their saturated fat can inhibit the body's production of essential fatty acids, which could slightly affect hormone production.

♦ Try to reduce your sugar and chocolate intake, even though you crave them. They can give you an instant boost, but then your blood-sugar levels will plummet, which can result in energy highs and lows.

Many nutritionists now believe diet plays a vital role in your ability to conceive. If you want to have a baby, the very worst thing you can do is to embark on a strict weight-restricting diet. The body's reproductive system is remarkably sensitive, and will switch off if it detects a nutritional deficiency. This is self-preservation at work – why try to feed a baby when you are not feeding yourself adequately?

To give yourself the best chance of success, avoid alcohol, caffeine, refined carbs and animal fats and reduce your salt intake. Eat plenty of wholegrains, nuts, seeds, fruit and veg.

If you have built up a good supply of vitamins, proteins and minerals before conception you will need to make only modest changes to your diet during pregnancy. Pregnancy is natural – it's not an illness – but there are a few things you should *not* eat because they may be detrimental to your baby's development, and it's a good idea to start following 'pregnancy food rules' right from the moment of possible conception.

Liver

Although it's important to get enough iron, avoid liver and liver products such as pâté because, although they are rich sources of iron, they contain high levels of vitamin A, which, if taken in excess, can harm the baby. Pâté can also contain listeria, a bacteria that can infect and harm a developing baby.

Fish and shellfish

Stay clear of swordfish, shark and marlin, and limit tuna to two steaks a week, because these fish contain high levels of mercury, which can harm a baby's developing nervous system. Have no more than two portions of oily fish, such as fresh tuna, mackerel, sardines and trout. Avoid raw shellfish during this time because it can contain harmful bacteria and viruses that can cause food poisoning.

Don't take fish entirely off the menu, though. Have at least one portion a week, because it is good for your health and your baby's development.

Cheese

There are plenty of cheeses you can eat, but you should avoid soft cheeses such as Camembert, Brie and blue cheeses because they are made with mould and can contain listeria.

Eggs

Only eat eggs that are cooked long enough for the yolk and white to be solid to avoid the risk of salmonella. Salmonella won't harm the baby directly, but it can be a particularly severe illness during pregnancy.

Peanuts

Peanut allergies affect 1–2 per cent of people in Britain. If you or your close family members have allergic conditions such as asthma, hayfever or eczema, it's wise to avoid nuts and nut products while you are carrying your baby, as this can help reduce the chance of your child developing allergy problems.

Alcohol

Current guidelines say you should not have more than one or two units of alcohol a week while pregnant. However, new research has shown that even one glass of wine may be harmful, so the less you drink, the better.

Caffeine

Excess caffeine has been linked to low birth weight and miscarriage. Again, the less the better, but two cups a day is very unlikely to be harmful, and if you are used to having lots of coffee, cut down slowly to avoid caffeine withdrawal headaches.

SUPPLEMENTS

In an ideal world there would be no need for women to supplement their diets with extra vitamins and minerals. However, modern farming and refining methods have robbed much food of its full nutritional value, and at this time of life, when many women find themselves 'too busy to eat', a supplement may provide a nutritional safety net. But be warned: this is one area where, in general, you do get what you pay for. Controls on the contents of many supplements are very lax, and those huge cheap jars of supplements may contain very little in the way of active ingredients (despite what you read on the label). If you do decide to take supplements, ask your doctor or a good pharmacist to advise you about the best brands.

Multivitamins and minerals

There is little evidence that taking a mega dose of anything is likely to improve your health. The biggest support group is for vitamin C, which many claim can help to ward off coughs and colds, but good solid scientific evidence for this is lacking. If you feel you would benefit from a supplement – and especially if you know you are neglecting your diet – then my advice is to choose a balanced multivitamin and mineral, one that contains the recommended daily allowance of all the major micronutrients your body needs. That way, you are unlikely to be doing yourself any harm, and you could do yourself some good. If you are planning on getting pregnant, though, choose a formulation without any additional vitamin A, as too much of this can be harmful to the developing foetus. Look for brands specifically labelled for pregnancy.

Folic acid

All women of childbearing age – whether they plan to get pregnant or not – should consider taking a folic acid supplement. This is because foetal neural tube defects such as spina bifida occur in the first weeks of pregnancy when many women are oblivious of their condition, especially if the pregnancy is unplanned. You do get a certain amount of folic acid from fortified breakfast cereals, wholemeal and wholegrain breads and fruit and vegetables. But you need to steam vegetables or cook them in very little water to preserve the folic acid. Taking a 400mcg supplement in addition to the daily 200mcg you should get from your food is a wise precaution.

Calcium

The other important supplement for women of all ages is calcium. This is vital for both building and maintaining strong bones. Young women need a minimum of 800mcg daily and, unless you are a fan of dairy foods, you may not get this from your daily diet.

Other supplements

A huge range of specific supplements is available for different conditions. Remedies for PMSs, period problems and menopause are covered on pages 262, 249 and 299. At this age you might also benefit from:

♦ **Echinacea**: it is claimed that this can strengthen the immune system. Take 15 drops twice a day when you feel a cold coming on. Don't take it for more than 30 consecutive days because, perversely, it then starts to work against the immune system.

♦ **Zinc**: there is also some evidence that zinc can help to build up the immune system and aid speed recovery from minor viral illnesses such as colds and sore throats.

♦ **Ginseng**: it is claimed that this can increase resistance to stress and build up vitality.

♦ **St John's Wort (hypericin)**: this has been used historically to repair nerve damage, and has now been proved an effective treatment for mild depression. The recommended dose is 300mg a day of the active ingredient hypericin. It is believed to correct the balance of serotonin – the happiness chemical – in the brain, which helps to control sleeping, eating and mood. It acts in the same way as selective serotonin re-uptake inhibitors (SSRIs) like Prozac. However, do not take this if you are pregnant or breastfeeding. There is also some evidence that it can make the contraceptive pill less effective. (See also page 236.)

Supplements and natural remedies can be powerful and will sometimes interfere with conventional medical treatment. Always let your GP know what supplements you are taking.

DETOXING – EXPELLING THE MYTHS

A vast business has developed around detoxing – it seems to be the craze of the twenty-first century. But at the risk of sounding deeply old-fashioned, for most women it is completely unnecessary, and it certainly should not cost you any money.

There are two big myths about detoxing:

♦ The first is that toxic chemicals build up in the body. Actually, they don't. The body, especially the liver and kidneys, is in fact very efficient at clearing harmful substances out of the bloodstream, and waste matter is also expelled from the body in your motions.

♦ The second myth is that in order to detox you have to go on a semi-starvation diet and use expensive supplements and treatments to cleanse your body. But since there is no 'build-up' of poisons, it should come as no surprise that there is no good evidence that taking anything, be it herbs, vitamins or special foods, or applying lotions or potions, helps rid the body of anything other than perhaps some dirt. Brushing or massaging your skin may well make you feel good, but that's because it's had an effect on your mental state, not on the levels of nasty chemicals inside your body.

That said, though, there is a limit to the amount of chemicals that the body can cope with, and over-indulging in some substances can put a strain on the body's organs and lead to long-term damage. So there is something to be said for giving your body a break from potentially harmful chemicals, particularly smoke, alcohol, fatty foods and caffeine.

If you want to detox, there is no need to spend money on it – in fact, it should save you money. Here's how:

♦ Cut out alcohol and stop smoking.

♦ Eat at least 5 good portions of fresh fruit and vegetables each day.

♦ Increase the amount of fibre in your diet (to get your bowels moving).

♦ Drink at least 2 litres of pure water each day.

♦ Try to cut out caffeine, but do it slowly to avoid a thumping headache. Drink hot water with a slice of lemon or some fresh mint instead.

♦ Try to stop taking any unnecessary medications too, particularly painkillers, but don't stop any that you have been prescribed without medical advice first.

The longer you can manage to follow this regime, the better, but even if you only follow it for a few days, you should notice a difference.

HORMONE ISSUES

FERTILITY - BACK TO BASICS

It's all a question of timing. Whichever way you look at it, whether you are planning to start a family or are keen to avoid getting pregnant, knowing when you are most likely to conceive can be very useful.

To work out when you are at your most fertile, you need to know when you are most likely to ovulate, and this all depends on your menstrual cycle.

Each cycle can be divided into two sections, before and after ovulation. The second half of the monthly cycle, the time between ovulation and the start of a period, is usually pretty constant at around 14 days. However, the first half of the cycle, the lead-up to ovulation, can be quite variable – anything between 11 days and several weeks (even more in women with very erratic periods).

If you have a standard 28-day cycle, that is, 28 days between the start of one period and the start of the next, then you will ovulate halfway between the two, around day 14, counting from the first day of the last period.

If you have a slightly longer cycle, say 33 days, then you'll ovulate around day 19; if you have a slightly shorter cycle, say 25 days, then you'll ovulate around day 11.

In the days leading up to ovulation, thinner, more abundant mucus is produced from the cervix, and this can be a useful indicator that ovulation is imminent. But not all women notice this, and if you haven't a clue when you're ovulating, you are not alone!

The egg lives for a maximum of only 24 hours after it has been released, and many experts say that it can only be successfully fertilized for the first 12 hours. Sperm, by contrast, can live for up to 7 days in the female genital tract. If you want a baby, ideally fresh sperm should be ready and waiting in the fallopian tube as the egg is released.

If you have a 28-day cycle, that means having sex at least a couple of times between days 9 and 14. Because sperm live so long, you don't need to have sex every day – every 2 days or so is fine. There is evidence that ejaculating too often can reduce a man's sperm count. Though this is unlikely to be important if his sperm count is good, it could be an issue for the increasing numbers of men with sub-optimal sperm counts.

If you want to avoid getting pregnant, then you need to give yourself a margin for error, and avoid having sex for at least a week before your expected ovulation date, and at least 2 days afterwards (see page 176).

Even if you are trying to conceive and have sex at the right time, there's no guarantee you will get pregnant. Compared to other animals, humans are remarkably inefficient at reproduction, though it may not seem that way when you find yourself unexpectedly pregnant after just one misguided moment of passion. On average, it takes a young couple with perfectly good fertility 3 months to conceive a child; for a woman in her mid-thirties, it can take 6 months; and more than a year when the woman is in her forties. So don't panic if you don't get pregnant on your first attempt.

MISCARRIAGE

Unfortunately, a positive pregnancy test does not automatically mean you are on your way to having a baby. Around 1 in 4 pregnancies ends in miscarriage, and this means that miscarriage is common – around 25 per cent of women have at least one. But nature is good at getting it right next time round, and recurrent miscarriage is fortunately rare, affecting only 1 per cent of couples.

Most miscarriages occur in the first few weeks after conception, and it's only the ability to do accurate, very early pregnancy testing that has meant that what many women previously thought was just a late, heavy period is now correctly diagnosed as a miscarriage.

Sometimes the baby does start developing, but stops growing and dies approximately 6 weeks after fertilization. However, the tell-tale heavy bleeding may not occur until 2 or 3 weeks later – which is why many women used to have miscarriages at 10–12 weeks. Nowadays, early scanning, done after just slight blood loss, has meant that many of these early pregnancy losses are detected earlier, at around 8 weeks.

Why does this happen?

About half of all miscarriages are caused by abnormalities in the chromosomes of the fertilized egg. This is more common with the increasing age of the mother, but other than that, why this happens is unknown. A problem in the chromosomes of either the mother or the father can cause recurrent miscarriage, but this is rare.

Other causes of miscarriage are:

♦ Structural abnormalities in the womb, which make it difficult for the egg to implant properly.

♦ Occasionally a hormone imbalance may be to blame. Women with very erratic periods find it harder to conceive, and when they do they have a slightly increased risk of miscarriage.

♦ Anti-phospholipid antibodies can affect the blood flow to the womb and placenta, and cause miscarriage at any stage of pregnancy. They are found in up to 15 per cent of women who suffer from recurrent miscarriage, and can be detected by a blood test. Treatment with low-dose aspirin or heparin can reduce the risk of miscarriage in those affected.

♦ It is also thought that a few women may miscarry because of an immune reaction between the egg and the sperm.

Tell-tale signs

♦ Bleeding, which can vary from light to extremely heavy.

♦ Lower abdominal cramps, like period pains.

♦ But sometimes there are no signs at all. A routine ultrasound scan reveals that the foetus has not developed, or has died.

Treatment

It's important that the womb is emptied, as any remaining tissue can lead to heavy bleeding. It can also become infected, which could not only make you feel ill, but could also affect future fertility.

If a miscarriage occurs in the early stages, less than 7 weeks from the last period, then nature may do the job perfectly well. All that's needed is an ultrasound scan to check that the womb has emptied. After 8 weeks, though, a small operation is usually required. This may be done under either a local or a general anaesthetic.

Afterwards

It's usual to feel tired and drained, and the sudden drop in hormone levels adds to the inevitable depression that follows the loss of a baby. So be gentle to yourself, and give yourself some recovery time. And don't start blaming yourself – most miscarriages are just a sad quirk of nature, and nothing anyone could have done would have prevented it. There are no hard and fast rules about how long you should wait before you start trying to get pregnant again. Some doctors recommend you wait at least a month, but unless there are medical reasons for delaying, such as anaemia, you could try straight away. Check with your doctor.

Miscarriage is so common that you don't need to have any tests done if it's only happened once or twice. But if you've had three, then you and your partner should consider having investigations to check for an underlying cause.

ECTOPIC PREGNANCY

This is a pregnancy that develops outside the womb. It happens in around 1 in 100 pregnancies in the UK. The most common site is inside one of the fallopian tubes, but very occasionally ectopics occur in the ovaries or, even more rarely, in the abdominal cavity.

Tell-tale signs

These usually occur about 2 weeks after the missed period.

♦ Bleeding, which can be light for a day or so, but then usually gets heavier – but sometimes the first sign is sudden, really heavy bleeding.

♦ Pelvic pain, which, like the bleeding, can vary from slight discomfort to sudden, really severe pain.

If you have either of these, and you think you may be pregnant, then see your doctor straight away.

How is it diagnosed?

If there is even a slight suspicion that you have an ectopic, you should have a pregnancy test and a vaginal ultrasound scan.

Is it dangerous?

Yes. Very. As an ectopic pregnancy grows, it damages the fallopian tube, which may suddenly rupture, causing severe, heavy bleeding, which may be life-threatening. Ectopics still kill 7 women in the UK every year.

What can be done about it?

If an ectopic is diagnosed early, it is sometimes possible to destroy the foetus with an injection of the drug methotrexate, and no surgery is necessary. But if bleeding is heavy, then the only option is immediate surgery to remove either just the foetus or, more commonly, the damaged fallopian tube as well. Sadly, having an ectopic inevitably means losing the baby. As yet, no doctor has ever succeeded in transferring the foetus to the womb.

Alternative treatments

These aren't an option here. Ectopics need conventional medical treatment – fast.

CONTRACEPTION

But what if you don't want children – or not just yet? What's the best way to avoid pregnancy but continue to enjoy your sex life?

Contraception is an incredibly important issue for women – we're fertile for an average of 40 years, and most of us are sexually active for at least 30 of them. Which means that unless you want a huge family, or are prepared to say no, you need to find some way of stopping yourself getting pregnant.

Thankfully we've come a long way from the days when women used oiled rags or half a lemon as a barrier in the vagina to try to prevent conception, and there's now a good choice of much more user-friendly methods. Sadly, however, even in the twenty-first century, none of them is perfect. All methods have drawbacks, and can either cause side effects or be a bit unreliable. Which method you choose has to depend on your individual circumstances, especially your age, where you are in terms of having a family, and your general health. It's also important to consider protecting yourself from sexually transmitted infections, especially if you are in a new relationship (see pages 85–109).

But the good news is that it's fairly easy to switch between most methods, so if one doesn't suit, you can always try another.

WHERE TO GO FOR FAMILY PLANNING

There are several options. Nearly all GP surgeries hand out free condoms, and most family doctors or their practice nurses are happy to prescribe the pill and give contraceptive injections. Those who have had the right extra training can also insert coils and implants, and a few also offer a diaphragm-fitting service.

Alternatively, you can go to a family planning clinic run by the health authority, either near your home or near your place of work. Opening hours of these vary, but usually include some evenings, and so can be much more convenient if you don't want to have time off work just to get your supply of pills. Some clinics are aimed at a specific group of women, such as Brook Advisory Centres, which cater for young women under the age of 25.

Many hospitals also have family planning clinics, and these can be particularly good for women whose needs aren't entirely straightforward – for example, if you have other medical or gynae problems, such as diabetes, fibroids or previous cancer.

THE OPTIONS

There are two main groups of contraceptive methods – those that contain hormones and those that don't.

In general, hormonal methods are the best for doing what you want contraception to do – preventing you getting pregnant – but they are the worst for side effects. They also don't offer much in the way of protection against infections. If that's what you're concerned about (and if you've got a new partner, you should be), then you need to use a barrier method of some sort, such as a condom or diaphragm, as well.

CONTRACEPTIVES BASED ON HORMONES

THE COMBINED PILL

The pill seems to be the drug (along with HRT; see page 300) that the media love to hate – any bad news about the pill is virtually guaranteed to make the front page of at least one national newspaper. But it's not the baddy it's made out to be, and if there's one thing that really has contributed to women's lib, then it has to be the pill, for the simple reason that it works. Genuine pill failures are incredibly rare. If you take it properly, then you can enjoy sexual freedom without the risk of becoming pregnant. And whatever scary stories you may read about side effects, the bottom line is that, for every woman, being pregnant is a lot more dangerous than taking the pill. Blood clots, strokes, high blood pressure, sickness – every single bad side effect of the pill is much more common in pregnancy, even if you decide to have a termination.

How it works

Yes, it's been around for decades, but it's surprising how many women have no idea how the pill works, and the effect it has on the body. So here's a quick run-down. It contains two hormones, oestrogen and a progestogen, which is the synthetic man-made type of the natural hormone progesterone. Together these work mainly by stopping ovulation, but in the unlikely event of an egg being released, it helps to prevent implantation by altering the lining of the womb. It also thickens the mucus in the cervix, which helps to prevent sperm entering.

One big advantage of the pill is that it gives regular periods, which are usually much lighter and less painful than before. This also means it reduces the risk of anaemia occurring from heavy periods. It also usually reduces PMS (see page 258) and the breast tenderness that some women experience before a period.

Side effects

So what about those nasty side effects that somehow seem to grab all the newspaper headlines? Yes, the pill can increase the risk of deep vein thrombosis (DVT – a blood clot in the leg). It's only a slight effect, but it does mean that women with a family history of clotting need to view the pill with caution, and those who have a factor V mutation (see pages 162–3) should avoid it altogether. And any woman on the pill should take 75mg of aspirin (which has a blood-thinning effect) just before embarking on a flight of more than four hours. But overall, DVTs in young women, even those on the pill, are rare.

The pill's tendency to increase blood pressure is much more of a nuisance. It's why every woman on the pill should have her blood pressure checked at least once a year, and if it's persistently above 135/85, then the pill should be stopped.

The other common reason why women cannot take the pill is because it can make migraines worse (see page 275). Any women getting really bad migraines, with tingling or numbness in one part of the body in addition to their headache, should stop the pill straight away, as it can be an indicator of an increased risk of a stroke – another rare, but potentially very serious pill side effect.

Nausea, tender breasts and slight weight gain can be troubling in the first few months of use, but these usually settle down, though the need to wear a bra with a larger cup size usually persists until the pill is stopped.

Women who are taking the pill are at a very slightly increased risk of breast cancer. For most young women, the chances of this happening are remote, but it does mean those with a strong family history of breast cancer should consider other methods. On the other hand, it significantly reduces the risk of cancer of the ovary or womb lining.

The risk of a serious pill side effect (DVT, stroke, high blood pressure) is increased by smoking, by age and by being overweight. For this reason doctors will not prescribe the pill to women over 35 who are medically obese (BMI over 30) or who smoke. It also should be avoided by women who are breastfeeding, as the oestrogen it contains can decrease milk production.

Which one to take

There are loads of different brands of pill available. Though most contain the same amount of oestrogen, the type and amount of progestogen can vary, and it is this variation that can make one pill more suitable than another for individual women. Just because one brand suits your best friend does not mean it will suit you.

Pills that are more oestrogenic can cause bloating, weight gain and nausea, while those that are more progestogenic can cause greasy skin, acne, depression and PMS-type symptoms. Generally it's a question of 'try it and see' – but try not to give up on a brand too soon. Give it at least 3 months for your body to get used to it.

Regular periods

One advantage of taking the combined pill is that you can predict, to the day, when you are going to have a period. If it's going to be at an inconvenient time – right in the middle of your summer holiday – then simply take two packets in a row without a break. You can also do this regularly if you have awful heavy painful periods. There's really no need to have a monthly bleed if you don't want one – once every 2 or 3 months is fine.

The bottom line

The pill is a great contraceptive. It's suitable for most women, of all ages, and, as long as you take it properly, it provides really good, reliable protection against an unwanted pregnancy. It also has lots of other benefits, which often get forgotten.

Factor V leiden

Factor V leiden is an abnormal type of the protein factor V. Factor V is needed for blood clotting, and those with the leiden variant have at least an eight-times greater risk of having a thrombosis, or clot, compared to others. It's an inherited condition caused by a gene defect, which affects around 5 per cent of the population. Those who inherit an abnormal gene from both parents (around 0.1 per cent of people) have up to a 130 times increased risk.

Anyone with a family history of venous thrombosis, especially if it has happened for no good reason, should be tested for the condition. Women with factor V leiden should avoid using oestrogen-containing contraceptives, and may need anti-coagulant drugs during pregnancy. Taking precautions to avoid a blood clot in the leg (DVT) while travelling are also important.

THE PATCH

Evra, the contraceptive patch, contains two hormones, just like the combined pill, and is suitable, and not suitable, for the same women as the pill. Side effects are similar as well. The big difference is that instead of swallowing them by mouth, the hormones are absorbed through the skin.

The patch needs changing only once a week, so it's ideal for women who find it difficult to remember to take a pill. But like other patch medicines, the adhesive can irritate sensitive skins and can also leave an annoying line of glue when it's removed. It's also more expensive than the pill, which means that some doctors and clinics are reluctant to prescribe it – which is a bit of a nonsense, as it's a lot cheaper than dealing with an unwanted pregnancy.

The bottom line

A good alternative for women who can't remember to take the pill.

HORMONAL METHODS BASED ON PROGESTOGENS

Several different types of contraception are based on progestogens:

- the 'mini-pill'
- the injection
- the implant
- the intra-uterine system (IUS)

Progestogens work as contraceptives by altering the environment in the cervix and womb, making it hostile to sperm. The sperm simply die off before they can reach and fertilize the egg. However, this effect is short-lived: if the progestogen level falls, then the mucus and womb lining rapidly return to normal. So for progestogen methods to be effective, there has to be a constant supply of the hormone – this is why it is given via injections or implants.

Low doses of progestogens generally don't stop ovulation, but higher doses can. This increases contraceptive efficiency but, as always, the downside is more problems with unwanted side effects.

Progestogen methods can be used by women of all ages, including those who can't use methods containing oestrogen – for instance breastfeeding mums, or those with high blood pressure, severe migraines or a high risk of a DVT. Side effects of progestogens can include greasy skin and acne, weight gain, headaches and, occasionally, loss of libido. These are generally more troublesome with injectables than with the pill and IUS.

THE PROGESTERONE-ONLY PILL (MINI-PILL)

Often known as the POP or 'mini-pill', this can contain one of several different types of progestogen. Most brands don't stop ovulation, but the latest addition to the range, Cerazette, stands apart from the rest. The progestogen it contains, desogestrel, does appear to stop ovulation in most users, and this means it is slightly more effective as a contraceptive than other brands – which is important!

Overall, though, the POP isn't quite as good a contraceptive as the combined pill, and if 100 women use it properly for a year, one or two will accidentally become pregnant. But that's better than barrier methods. The most troublesome side effect is erratic periods, sometimes with bleeding in between – if you need to know when you're going to have a period, then this isn't the method for you. It can also very slightly increase the risk of an ectopic pregnancy (see page 155), which isn't an issue for most women, but does mean that it's not suitable for those who have already had an ectopic.

One word of warning. Unlike the combined pill (which can be taken up to 12 hours late), the POP really does have to be taken at the same time every day. If you are more than 3 hours late, then it counts as a missed pill, and you have to take pills properly for the next 2 days before you are safe again.

The bottom line

A good choice for women who either don't want to or can't use the combined pill or Mirena (see page 167). Not so good if you can't remember to take a pill at the same time every single day.

INJECTABLES AND IMPLANTS

These both slowly release a small amount of progestogen into the body each day.

The injection, usually referred to as 'depo' (a shortened version of its name, depo provera), is given into the buttock and lasts 3 months.

The implant, Implanon, is a small flexible tube, about the size of a hairgrip, that's placed just under the skin of the inside of the upper arm.

The big advantage of both these methods is that they provide long-term contraception, but side effects are common, especially erratic periods, which may last longer than before. Some women experience frequent bleeding, which, especially in the first few months of using the injection, may be quite heavy. Weight gain, bloating and a greasy skin can also be a nuisance, along with tender breasts, headaches and mood swings. If side effects are too much of a problem, then the implant can simply be removed, but there is nothing that can be done about the injection – you just have to wait until its effect wears off, which can take months.

Repeated injections of depo can 'switch off' the ovaries and there may be a delay of up to a year before they start working properly again, making it difficult for women to conceive a baby during this time.

The lack of ovarian activity also leads to low oestrogen levels. Oestrogen plays an important role in bone formation, and there are concerns that depo can reduce bone density, increasing the risk of osteoporosis in later life (see page 307). There is also some worrying evidence that using depo may reduce the build-up of bone that normally occurs in the teenage years. It's not yet known whether this can be rectified in later life, and it may be that using depo when you're young could mean a lifelong increased risk of osteoporosis.

The bottom line

Good for those who need highly effective contraception and who either can't use or reliably take other hormonal methods. But side effects can be a real problem.

THE INTRA-UTERINE SYSTEM (IUS OR MIRENA)

This looks just like an ordinary T-shaped coil (see page 172), and has to be inserted into the womb in the same way. What makes the IUS very different is that, instead of the fine copper wire that's found on a standard coil, it has a sheath of progestogen. A small amount of this is released continually, right where it's needed, inside the womb lining. This makes it highly effective: as far as contraception goes, this is top of the league. It's better than the pill – even better than being sterilized. No method can claim to be 100 per cent effective, but if you've got a Mirena fitted you are very, very unlikely to get pregnant.

Not only that, but once it's in place you don't have to worry about contraception for the next 5 years. Better still, only a tiny amount of progestogen goes into your general circulation, and this means that the unwanted side effects that can occur with other progestogen methods, such as weight gain or acne, are rarely an issue.

One good side effect of the IUS is that the high concentration of progestogen that occurs inside the womb can dramatically thin the womb lining, and this can lead to very light periods, sometimes to the extent of just a couple of tiny spots of blood. It's why the Mirena is now used as a treatment for heavy periods. However, a few women can find it alarming not to have a monthly reminder that they are not pregnant.

Like other coils, the Mirena can be painful to fit, especially in women who have never been pregnant, and cramps can occur for a day or so afterwards. Erratic bleeding can also occur in the first 3 months after insertion – so it's not a good idea to have one fitted just before you jet off on an exotic holiday. There must be no chance you are pregnant when the device is inserted, which means that if you are sexually active it's best to put it in within the first 10 days of a period.

The bottom line

A fantastic contraceptive that's not remotely like any other coil. Suitable for women of all ages, and especially good for women in their forties, as it can control the troublesome bleeding that can occur in the run-up to the menopause. Can be tricky to insert in women who have never been pregnant.

BARRIER METHODS

CONDOMS AND DIAPHRAGMS

The really important advantage of barrier methods is the protection they can give against sexually transmitted infections (see pages 85–109). They also can be a good choice for women who really don't want to put extra hormones into their body by taking the pill, having injections or implants, or using intra-uterine devices. The downside is that they are generally not quite as effective as hormone methods, and they can reduce spontaneity, but with practice they can be really easy to use.

Condoms for men are hugely popular contraceptives, and for good reason. They provide good contraception and really good protection against STIs. A huge range of different types is available, and whether you opt for those with texture, flavour or a wild colour is largely a matter of personal choice; however, make sure you opt for brands that have either the British Standard kitemark or the European CE marking. Both of these mean they have been quality tested. Different sizes and shapes are available, but because no man will ever want to buy a 'small' condom, descriptions on the packets aren't always very helpful. However, 'tight' or 'slim' fitting may feel uncomfortable on an above-average penis, which may be more suited to a 'flared' variety.

The most effective condoms for protection against both pregnancy and infection contain the spermicide nonoxynol 9, but occasionally it can trigger allergic reactions in the genital area, as can the rubber used to make most condoms.

Condoms should be rolled carefully on to an erect penis (the roll of rubber should be on the outer, not inner, surface) and any air at the end should be squeezed out. If you've got long nails, take care. After sex, the man should withdraw holding the condom in place before he loses his erection.

Never use oil-based lubricants, such as aromatherapy oils, vaseline or massage oils – they weaken the rubber and can make the condom more liable to burst.

Preventing common condom problems

'It came off.' Make sure the condom is the right size – if it only comes three quarters of the way down the shaft when he's erect it may be a disaster waiting to happen. Condoms come off most often after ejaculation if he stays inside and loses his erection. Much as you may not want him to move, make sure he withdraws while he's still erect, and that one of you – either you or him – holds the condom in place until he's clear of your genital area.

'It burst.' Condoms are actually incredibly strong – you can fill them with a litre or more of water and not a drop will leak out. They only burst if they are put on incorrectly, or if they have been weakened with an oil-based lubricant or a tiny tear from a sharp nail. Some vaginal medications can also weaken condoms, such as anti-fungal pessaries, and some oestrogen creams. Check before use.

'He says he can't feel anything.' Switching to a different brand, for example one that is thinner or ribbed, may help. 'Gel-charging' – using a non-oil-based lubricant inside the condom – can also heighten sensitivity for the man.

The bottom line

Not quite as good as hormonal methods for contraception, but if used properly condoms are still very reliable. Can play a vital role in keeping women healthy, because of the protection they give against STIs – if you are out dating you should keep one in your handbag.

The female condom, Femidom, is made of very thin polyurethane, which is lubricated lightly for easier use. It has a small ring that helps to keep it in place inside the vagina, where it acts as a protective liner. As it is loose fitting, it does move during sex, and some women liken using it to having sex with a squeaky plastic bag, but it does provide very effective protection from both pregnancy and STIs. Femidoms are available from chemists as well as family planning clinics. One size fits all.

The bottom line
Good if you feel embarrassed about asking a new partner to use a condom, but that's about it.

Caps and diaphragms are rubber devices used inside the vagina to cover the cervix, preventing sperm penetrating inside the womb. Both are made of flexible thin soft rubber, but in addition a few types of cap are made of silicone.

Diaphragms are circular domes designed to fit across the top of the vagina, while cervical caps are much smaller and are designed to fit just over the cervix itself. For extra protection, the surface in contact with the cervix should also be smeared with a layer of spermicide.

Caps and diaphragms have to be fitted to size by a nurse or doctor, and getting the hang of using them and getting the device into the right place can be quite time-consuming. But experienced cap users can slip them into place in seconds. Both devices are fairly reliable – failure rates are quoted as being between 4 and 8 per cent, and are very dependent on whether they are used properly.

Though your partner may be aware of either device, it should not reduce the pleasure of lovemaking for either of you. Caps and diaphragms can be inserted up to 2 hours before having sex, and then should be left in place for at least 6 hours afterwards. Once removed, the device should be washed with mild soap and water and dried thoroughly. Some silicone caps are disposable and should be thrown away after use.

The bottom line

Very good for women in steady relationships, or for those having occasional sex, who don't want to use hormones and who wouldn't consider a pregnancy a complete disaster. Deserve to be more popular than they are.

INTRA-UTERINE DEVICES – COILS OR IUCDS

These are small pieces of plastic, about 1.5cm long, which have a copper wire wound round the stem. They are shaped like a T or an inverted U, with either one or two very thin nylon threads attached at the base. After the device is inserted into the womb, the threads are cut so that a short length is left sticking out through the cervix and into the vagina. The thread enables you to check that the device is still in place, and also means that the device can easily be removed. They should not interfere with sex in any way – if they do, go back and see the doctor who did the insertion.

Coils work mainly by interfering with the way sperm swim up through the womb, preventing them reaching the egg. If an egg is fertilized, the device may also stop the egg implanting in the womb.

Failure rates are between 1 and 2 per cent – not quite as good as either the combined pill or the Mirena – but better than barrier methods. Their main advantage is that they provide long-term contraception, as most devices work for up to 7 years, but they are easily reversible; as soon as the device is removed, fertility returns to normal within a few days.

The main problem with copper coils is that they can make periods heavier, longer and more painful. Bleeding lasting 7 days is not uncommon, and some women also get a little spotting between periods.

Having a coil cannot cause a genital infection – you have to catch it from someone else – but it can increase the risk of STIs, especially chlamydia and gonorrhoea, spreading from the vagina up through the cervix to the fallopian tubes, causing PID (see pages 87, 88 and 105). Another downside is that if you are unlucky enough to fall pregnant with a coil in place, there's an increased risk of its being an ectopic pregnancy (see page 155), so it's not a good option for women who know they have problems with their fallopian tubes, either from a previous ectopic or from a bout of PID.

The bottom line

If you want an intra-uterine device, you're far better off having a Mirena (see page 167), unless you don't want to, or can't, use progestogens.

OTHER METHODS OF CONTRACEPTION

STERILIZATION

Both men and women can be sterilized. For women, it involves blocking the fallopian tubes, usually with small metal clips. This is done via a laparoscopy (see page 185) under a general anaesthetic, on a day-case basis. Though it is very effective, it's not foolproof – occasionally pregnancies do occur after sterilization, and if so there's an increased risk of them being ectopic (see page 155). Some women also notice that their periods are heavier afterwards – this is thought to be due to a change in the blood flow to the womb.

Male sterilization – a vasectomy – involves cutting and tying the tubes that lead from the testes to the penis. It's done under local anaesthetic, via a tiny cut on each side of the groin, beside the top of the scrotum. The operation takes only about 15 minutes, but can cause quite dramatic bruising afterwards. Unlike sterilization in women, a vasectomy doesn't work instantly – it can take between 3 and 6 months for all sperm to disappear from the ejaculate, and other contraception is required until two semen tests have confirmed no live sperm are present.

Sterilization is permanent – don't be fooled into thinking it can be reversed. Occasionally surgeons can be persuaded to attempt a reversal operation (not on the NHS though), but it's rarely successful. For this reason doctors are very reluctant to perform sterilizations on young people under 30, or on those who have never had children, unless there are medical reasons.

The bottom line

Good for those who are absolutely sure that they don't want to have any more children and have problems using other methods.

One word of warning: don't be misled by a new partner who says he's

had a vasectomy (an old ploy when he doesn't fancy using condoms).
Check for the tiny scars!

EMERGENCY CONTRACEPTION

There are two ways you can help to stop yourself becoming pregnant
after having unprotected sex.

♦ The pill method – often wrongly called the 'morning-after pill' –
involves taking just one large dose of progestogen. It's best
taken as soon as possible: if you take it within 12 hours of
having sex it's reckoned to be up to 95 per cent effective, but if
you leave it until 72 hours after sex – the latest it can be taken –
it's only 58 per cent effective. If you have unprotected sex again
after you've taken it, then you need to take another dose.

♦ The alternative is to have a copper coil fitted. This can be done
up to 5 days after your estimated date of ovulation – for most
women approximately 19 days from the first day of the last
period (14 days to ovulation plus 5 more days). Unlike the pill,
it doesn't matter when, and how often, you've had unprotected
sex. The coil can then either be left in place to provide long-
term contraception or removed after the next period has
begun.

Neither of these methods is 100 per cent effective, and neither
should be viewed as a substitute for pre-sex contraception, but they are
certainly better than nothing. Unless you're using a long-term method
(such as a coil or the injection) I think it's a good idea for all women to
keep an emergency contraceptive pill in the bathroom cupboard. You
just never know when you might need it.

NATURAL METHODS

If you can work out exactly when you ovulate, then in theory at least you can avoid having sex when you are likely to conceive. Though the egg lives for only 24 hours after it is released, sperm can live inside a woman's body for up to 7 days. This means that in order to avoid a pregnancy, you should avoid having sex for 7 days before the estimated date of ovulation, and for at least 2 days afterwards.

Ovulation usually occurs around 14 days before the next period, so if you have a regular cycle you can work out when you are likely to be safe, or (more importantly) when you are not safe. Detecting changes in the cervical mucus, and taking your temperature each morning (watch for a slight rise on ovulation), can also be helpful in identifying the time you ovulate (though they require commitment!). You can buy kits that help to detect when ovulation is likely to occur, and these can help you to time when it is safe (or not) to have unprotected sex.

The problem with natural family planning is that it takes only one blip in your cycle for it all to go horribly wrong. And it's no good at all for women with erratic cycles. But for women with regular cycles, it can be surprisingly successful, and it can be useful if you don't want to use a barrier method all the time, or are unable (for whatever reason) to use any other sort of family planning.

The bottom line

Good if you have a regular cycle, and you wouldn't mind if you accidentally became pregnant. Hopeless if you have an even slightly erratic cycle.

TERMINATION OF PREGNANCY

Accidentally becoming pregnant is very, very common, and in the UK at least two-thirds of women have one or more unintended pregnancy. They then face the decision of whether to continue with the pregnancy or have an abortion. For some this is straightforward; for others it is heartachingly difficult. I'll discuss this later; first, the facts.

At the time of writing, abortion can be performed legally in the UK until the 24th week of pregnancy. Two doctors must agree that the procedure is justified for one of five reasons; these include whether the baby is likely to be severely handicapped, whether the mother's physical or mental health is likely to be badly affected by the pregnancy, and whether the health of any of the mother's existing children is likely to be badly affected by the addition of another child to the family.

There are three types of abortion.

1. Medical abortion: this can be done until the end of the ninth week of pregnancy. First, three pills containing the hormone mifepristone are taken by mouth. This blocks the hormone that is vital for the pregnancy to continue. Two days later, a prostaglandin pessary is placed high up in the vagina. This softens the cervix, and also makes the womb contract, expelling the pregnancy – usually during the next 4–6 hours. It does cause cramps, like severe period pains, but these can be eased by strong painkillers. Most women undergo this part of the procedure in a hospital or clinic, but some private centres allow women to abort this way at home. If the procedure is done after the ninth week of pregnancy, two doses of the prostaglandin drug may be required, and it is sometimes necessary to stay in hospital overnight.

In most cases medical abortion is very straightforward, but occasionally the womb does not empty completely and needs to be scraped surgically, under anaesthetic, to prevent excess bleeding and infection.

2. Suction method: this is a surgical procedure that is carried out under either a general anaesthetic or a local anaesthetic combined with sedation. It is used from the ninth to the fifteenth week of pregnancy. It involves gently stretching the cervix, then sucking out the contents of the womb through a small tube. It usually takes between 5 and 10 minutes, and you go home the same day. It's normal to have some cramps afterwards, and to have light bleeding for a few days.

3. Surgical dilation and evacuation, C D and E: this is used from 15 weeks onwards. It is carried out under general anaesthetic, and involves stretching the cervix, then removing the contents using surgical instruments rather than suction. You may be able to return home the same day, or you may need to spend the night in hospital.

RISKS

The vast majority of abortions are quite straightforward, but occasionally complications do occur, and these can affect your future fertility. The most common are:

♦ Incomplete emptying of the womb, leading to pain and heavy bleeding. This also increases the risk of infection afterwards.

♦ Infection of the womb lining, which may spread up to the fallopian tubes, causing a severe pelvic infection, with scarring. To help prevent this, most women are screened for infections beforehand (particularly Chlamydia, (see page 87) and are given antibiotics just before the procedure.

♦ Damage to the cervix.

♦ Less commonly, damage to the womb itself by surgical instruments, leading to very heavy bleeding. Damage can usually be repaired (though this is a major operation), but there have been reports of women having to have their womb removed following a termination that has gone drastically wrong. However, I must stress that this is incredibly rare.

It's normal to bleed for a few days after a termination, like a period at first, then very lightly. Any heavy bleeding or painful cramps can be an indication of an infection, and you should see a doctor as soon as possible. Having an abortion should not affect your fertility unless there are complications, but repeated straightforward abortions can weaken the cervix and increase your risk of premature labour in a future pregnancy.

Even if you are relieved following an abortion that the whole thing is over and done with (as many women are) plummeting hormone levels mean that it's normal to feel tired, drained and upset for a week or so afterwards. Though many women do return to work the next day, this isn't ideal – try to have a couple of days off if you can. You can get pregnant within 2 weeks of an abortion, so make sure you use effective contraception before you have sex again.

PRACTICALITIES

Do not ever rush into having an abortion, even if you feel you are certain from the moment you learn that you are pregnant that you don't want the baby. Take your time – and that means several days at least. By all means go and see your doctor, but don't head straight for the clinic the same day. It's all too easy to think you know what you want to do, then regret it later.

Factors that you will need to think about include your relationship, your career, your finances and your existing family. For some, religious considerations are also important, and also your age, if you are in your late thirties or early forties. Could this be your last chance to have a baby? You don't need the agreement of the father of the child to have an abortion, and a girl under 16 can also have an abortion without telling her parents, as long as the doctors signing the form feel she fully understands the decision she is making. In practice, young teenagers especially are strongly encouraged to tell at least one of their parents, or another family member.

Remember, this is your decision. You will have to live with it afterwards, so don't feel pressurized by other people. If money seems to be an issue, check out what financial support would be available should you want to keep the baby.

Abortions are carried out by the NHS, though the availability of services varies in different parts of the country – in some areas it is much easier to get a termination than in others.

To have an NHS termination, you need to get a referral from either your GP or a doctor in your local family planning clinic. You will then get an appointment at the local hospital, though you may have to wait up to 14 days for this. At the clinic you will be scanned (to gauge how many weeks pregnant you are) and be seen by a specialist counsellor, who will talk you through your decision, and also the procedure. The abortion will then be arranged at a future date, and for surgical terminations especially this may mean waiting a further week. Many clinics are reluctant to carry out late terminations (after 16 weeks) unless you have very good reasons for the request.

Many privately run clinics (such as the British Pregnancy Advisory Service and Marie Stopes) also offer abortion services. Costs vary according to the type of termination you are having done, but start at about £400. If you are paying, you can usually have a termination done within days.

PHYSICAL HEALTH

Women in their twenties and thirties generally have excellent physical health. But there is one part of their body that can cause problems – the lower abdomen and the pelvis. Often problems in the 'gynae' system are to blame, but urinary-tract infections and irritable bowel syndrome can also contribute to pain and discomfort in the lower tummy. Sorting out the culprit isn't always easy.

ENDOMETRIOSIS

In endometriosis, tissue similar to the womb lining is found elsewhere in the body. The most common places are in the pelvis, on the ligaments that support the womb, around the fallopian tubes and in and around the ovaries. Endometriotic tissue can also occur in the wall of the womb, a condition known as adenomysosis. More rarely, endometriosis occurs in the bowel, in the bladder, even in the tummy button.

Endometriotic tissue responds to the monthly changes in hormone levels, just like the womb lining, and thickens then bleeds at the time of a period. Depending on the site, this may result in obvious bleeding, for example from the bladder or bowel, but any blood inside the pelvis is trapped. Though generally only tiny amounts are shed, it irritates the surrounding tissues, causing inflammation and pain. Eventually this can result in marked scarring. Bleeding inside the ovaries can lead to cysts developing.

Tell-tale signs

The most common symptom of endometriosis is pain, which classically builds up for a few days before each period and is then at its worst during the first days of bleeding. The pain can be really severe, and difficult to control, even with strong painkillers. But some women experience pain or a dull ache in the pelvis at other times, and find deep penetration during intercourse very uncomfortable.

Other symptoms can include low back pain and pain passing urine. Interestingly, though, endometriosis doesn't always cause symptoms – some women are found to have it quite by chance when they have pelvic surgery for an unrelated reason. Not only that, but the amount of endometriosis that a woman has doesn't always correlate with her symptoms – some have only a few tiny spots, which cause a lot of pain, while others have large areas with hardly any symptoms at all.

Endometriosis is linked with infertility, but the exact association is unclear. If the fallopian tubes are scarred, this can be an obvious reason why conceiving a baby is more difficult, but often there is no clear reason why endometriosis should affect fertility. Plenty of women who have the condition are still able to have a family without any difficulty. Overall, women with endometriosis are slightly less fertile than others – 3-year conception rates in women with endometriosis have been observed to be 36 per cent, compared to 55 per cent in women without endometriosis.

One study showed that 22 per cent of women being sterilized (after completing their families) were found to have endometriotic deposits.

Why does this happen?

Sadly, the honest answer here is that no one knows for sure. The most popular theory is that it is due, in some way, to 'retrograde menstruation'. During a period, some blood probably flows backwards up the fallopian tubes and spills into the pelvic cavity, but in most women this is mopped up by white cells from the body's immune system. A combination of a deficit in this cleaning-up process, plus maybe slight differences in hormone levels, means that the deposits of blood remain in some women.

There is evidence that there is a genetic tendency for this to happen, but it is not a condition that always runs in families.

Diagnosis and treatment

Endometriosis can be suspected from a combination of symptoms and a pelvic examination, but sadly the diagnosis is often missed, or is mistaken for something else, usually PID (see page 105). Many women suffer for years before they finally get the right diagnosis and treatment.

Endometriosis usually can't be seen or diagnosed on an ultrasound scan, and the only point in having a scan is to rule out another cause for the symptoms. The exception here is adenomyosis, which can sometimes be seen by a skilled scanner.

The only way that endometriosis around the pelvic organs can be diagnosed properly is by laparoscopy (see page 185) but it is essential that this is done by a skilled gynaecologist, as small deposits can easily be missed.

Treatment depends on the severity of symptoms, and whether or not fertility is an issue.

Drug treatment: because the tissue grows in response to hormone changes, drugs that block the hormone cycle can be very effective.

♦ This can be done by taking the combined pill for several months continuously (so there are no monthly bleeds), or giving relatively high doses of progestogens, which thin the womb lining.

♦ More effective still are drugs known as GnRH analogues, such as Zoladex, which completely stop the menstrual cycle and create a temporary menopause. These have to be given by injection, once a month. To avoid side effects, and to reduce the risk of osteoporosis, these can be given with tibolone, a special form of HRT (see page 300).

♦ Danazol, which dampens the cyclical changes in hormones, is used much less frequently now than in the past, as it has a high incidence of side effects.

To be effective, all treatments for endometriosis should be continued for at least 6 months. Many women continue for much longer than this, but unfortunately it is usually very difficult to conceive while having hormone treatment, as the drugs generally stop ovulation. So the routine is usually to have treatment for 6 months, then stop and see what happens. Some gynaecologists will perform a repeat laparoscopy to check on the response to treatment, but this is not universal practice.

Surgery: this is generally reserved for women who continue to have symptoms despite medical treatment, or to aid fertility. The aim is to remove the abnormal tissue deposits, leaving the pelvis as anatomically normal as possible. Small endometriotic deposits can be burnt away with a laser, while larger cysts can be removed. As a last resort, affected pelvic organs can be completely removed. Surgery for endometriosis should only be done by a gynaecologist with a particular expertise in the disease – it's not a job for a general gynaecologist.

Laparoscopy

This is a very common surgical procedure in women and is carried out to investigate the cause of pelvic pain, to aid in the diagnosis and treatment of infertility, and is also increasingly used as an alternative way to remove smaller pelvic organs.

It is done under general anaesthetic, on a day-case basis. First, the abdominal cavity is filled with air, then the surgeon inserts the laparoscope through a small cut, about 2.5cm (1 inch) long, on the edge of the tummy button. Two smaller cuts may also be needed further down on the tummy wall.

Afterwards it's normal to feel bloated, and some women also experience pain in the shoulder (which is due to irritation of the diaphragm, the muscle sheet between the chest and abdomen). The cuts themselves may feel slightly sore.

You'll need a couple of days off work, and you shouldn't do any vigorous tummy exercises for 2 weeks. As with any operation, you should not go swimming until the cuts have healed – again, usually 2 weeks.

POLYCYSTIC OVARIAN SYNDROME – PCOS

This is a surprisingly common condition, affecting between 10 and 15 per cent of women to varying degrees. On an ultrasound scan the ovaries can be seen to contain numerous tiny cysts – hence the name – but, despite the name of the syndrome, the cysts aren't the problem. In themselves the cysts don't cause any symptoms – they don't grow large and they don't cause pelvic pain. The real issue in PCOS is abnormal levels of hormones, particularly testosterone. No, that isn't a misprint. Although it's usually associated with men, all women have small amounts of testosterone as well, and women with PCOS tend to have more than average.

Tell-tale signs

These can include:

- erratic periods, with gaps varying between several weeks and several months
- difficulty getting pregnant
- greasy skin, with a tendency to acne
- excess body hair, especially on your face, around your lips and chin (hirsutism)
- weight problems, with a tendency to gain weight and real difficulty shedding excess pounds
- thinning hair, especially on the crown or around the temples, similar to a slightly balding man

Why does this happen?

Even experts don't really know why some women get PCOS and others don't, but as with many diseases, the current thinking is that it's a combination of an inherited genetic tendency together with lifestyle factors. It can run in families, and being overweight can also increase the risk of PCOS developing.

The symptoms of PCOS are triggered by imbalances in the levels of FSH (follicle stimulating hormone) and LH (luteinizing hormone), the hormones that control the menstrual cycle. Normally the blood level of FSH is the higher of the two, but in PCOS this ratio is reversed. As a consequence, the ovaries produce lower than average amounts of progesterone, slightly above average amounts of oestrogen and, most importantly of all, a lot more testosterone than usual.

Though testosterone is often regarded as 'the man's hormone', women have it too – it's just that men produce ten times as much. It's those high testosterone levels that lead to male-pattern baldness and make teenage boys much more susceptible to bad acne. Women certainly need a bit of testosterone – it's important for general well-being and also plays a vital role in libido. The problem in PCOS is that those abnormal ovaries produce too much testosterone, and the higher the level, the worse the symptoms.

Just to complicate matters a bit further, it seems that many women with PCOS develop resistance to the action of insulin, the hormone that controls blood-sugar levels. To try to maintain the status quo and stop blood-sugar levels rising, the pancreas pours out more insulin, and these high insulin levels affect the ovaries, triggering them to produce an even greater imbalance of hormones. This is especially likely to occur in women who are overweight.

Diagnosis and treatment

Many women are concerned that they may have PCOS when they have a pelvic scan (often for some unrelated condition, such as pelvic pain) and are told that their ovaries have a polycystic appearance. This doesn't mean you have PCOS – between 10 and 15 per cent of normal women have little cysts around the edge of the ovaries. To have PCOS you must also have a hormone imbalance, with LH levels higher than FSH, and a high testosterone level, though these may be barely outside the normal range.

Unfortunately, at the moment there is no 'cure' for the condition – there's nothing that can make the ovaries magically return to normal. But there are treatments that can help to control symptoms.

Which treatment – if any – you decide to use depends on which symptoms are bothering you most. Some GPs are great, and can offer everything that a PCOS patient needs in the way of back-up, but other women will do better seeing a specialist gynaecological endocrinologist.

♦ Skin problems can be tackled with standard acne drugs, such as retinoids and antibiotics, and this is all some women need.

♦ Excess body hair can be more difficult. Shaving and hair-removing creams are one temporary answer; electrolysis and laser treatment can provide a more permanent solution, but neither of these is available on the NHS (which is a disgrace) and both are expensive. The cream Vaniqa has recently become available for treating hirsutism. This cream, applied twice daily, can help reduce facial hair growth. Persistent use for several months is usually required for it to become effective, and hair will tend to regrow once treatment has stopped.

♦ A more effective answer can be to tackle the underlying hormone imbalance by taking the combined contraceptive pill. This overrides the natural cycle and can produce predictable monthly bleeds, but choice of brand is important. Those with a high progesterone content can make greasy skin and spots worse. Currently, the best choice of combined contraceptive pill is usually Dianette; it contains cyproterone acetate, which blocks the action of testosterone. This can lead to dramatic improvement in excess hair and acne. Unfortunately, taking cyproterone acetate on its own can lead to very erratic, sometimes heavy bleeding, so this is rarely done. For those who get side effects from Dianette (such as weight gain) a good second choice is Yasmin, which also has a weak anti-androgenic action.

♦ A useful alternative for hairiness and acne in women who can't take the contraceptive pill (for example, if you have high blood pressure, or are very overweight) is spironolactone. However, its effects are extremely variable, and it can cause very erratic menstrual bleeding.

Unfortunately, all these drugs work only for as long as they are taken. They are not a cure, and so symptoms have a horrid habit of returning once they are stopped.

Other treatments

◆ Drugs designed to treat type 2 diabetes by reducing insulin resistance can also be of benefit to women with PCOS. The most promising one is metformin, which in clinical trials has been shown to improve ovulation rates, especially when combined with clomiphene (an ovulation induction agent). It can also improve menstrual bleeding patterns, making periods more regular, and also, to a lesser degree, improve hirsutism. Side effects can include nausea and stomach upsets.

◆ Fertility drugs can also help to stimulate more regular ovulation and to improve fertility. The one most commonly used is clomiphene (Clomid), which is successful in triggering ovulation in around 80 per cent of cases, and in achieving pregnancy in 60–70 per cent.

◆ Women who don't respond to clomiphene can be given gonadotrophins by injection, though these are much more powerful, can have more dangerous side effects and so require careful monitoring. Pregnancy rates with these vary between 50 and 70 per cent, but usually several cycles are required.

Self-help

This is very important, and there is a lot you can do yourself to improve the symptoms of PCOS.

Losing excess weight is very important. Gaining weight makes the symptoms of PCOS worse, mainly because it increases insulin resistance. Studies have shown that losing between 5 and 10 per cent of body weight can make a significant difference to symptoms and may be all that some women need to do. Not only that, but losing weight can also reduce the risk of diabetes and heart disease. Trouble is, of course, that most women with PCOS find it fiendishly difficult to lose weight;

with careful dieting and lots of exercise, however, it can be done – as long as you are motivated enough.

Even if you don't manage to lose weight, good nutrition and plenty of exercise can help lower insulin resistance in their own right, and this in turn reduces excess testosterone production and so improves acne and erratic periods.

Alternative treatments

It's the same old story here – lots of alternative treatments have been tried by different women, with varying degrees of success, but there are no good large-scale clinical trials that give solid evidence of what really works and what doesn't.

Conventional medicine hasn't really got the answer yet for PCOS, particularly if you're not keen on filling yourself up with strong hormones, so it makes sense to consider alternative remedies, particularly if you're looking for a more gentle, natural approach.

- ◆ Acupuncture may be helpful for regulating periods, and may even kick-start non-existent periods.
- ◆ Medical herbalism may ease many of the symptoms due to the hormone imbalance.
- ◆ Some women have also found homeopathy helpful.

Is PCOS dangerous?

The cysts in the ovaries aren't harmful; they don't grow into whopping big cysts, and neither do they turn into cancer. However, sometimes PCOS can have damaging effects on long-term health, especially if you are one of the unlucky ones who has insulin resistance. This can increase your risk of developing type 2, non insulin-dependent diabetes (see page 355), and those who are very overweight may also develop high triglyceride levels, and high blood pressure, which can increase the risk of having both a heart attack and a stroke.

Having very erratic periods over many years can also lead to thickening of the lining of the womb, and very occasionally abnormal cells develop – a condition known as cystic hyperplasia. This can be a forerunner to endometrial cancer, and it does appear that women with bad PCOS are at increased risk of this. So if you ever get the slightest spotting or bleeding in between periods – or you're not sure if you're having a period or not – go and see your doctor and ask for an ultrasound scan. You may need to tell a GP who's not into gynaecology why this is important, but as long as you do it nicely that shouldn't be a problem!

WHEN LOVE HURTS

This may seem obvious, but having sex should be an enjoyable experience – it shouldn't hurt. However, some women do experience pain during sex. Generally, the pain can occur in two separate places: the vagina and deep inside the pelvis.

Pain in the vaginal area

A tight vagina can make entry of the penis very uncomfortable (and sometimes impossible). Occasionally this can be due to a genuine anatomical problem, such as a thick hymen, or bad suturing after childbirth, but usually tightness is psychologically based – see the section on vaginismus (page 194).

Good lubrication, which comes from glands just inside the vaginal entrance, is essential for comfortable sex. Some women lubricate very easily (especially at the beginning of a relationship), but most do require some foreplay for their vagina to feel moist. Sometimes just a little help from a lubricating jelly, such as KY, can be a good trigger to get the natural juices flowing.

Inflammation in the vaginal walls can also make the vagina feel raw and sore both during and after sex. The most common culprits are infections such as thrush and TV (see pages 98 and 94), allergies to perfumed soaps and bubble baths, and sometimes to the rubber in condoms.

Pain in the pelvis

Pain deeper inside can be positional, particularly during deep thrusting, and especially if you have a well-endowed partner. Discomfort can also occur if your partner hits your cervix during sex. Try moving to a different position, where you can control how far in he goes. If this doesn't work, and the pain continues, don't ignore it, and if it's uncomfortable ask him to stop. That pain means that something is wrong and it needs sorting out. Possible causes are:

- ◆ pelvic inflammatory disease (see page 105)
- ◆ endometriosis (see page 181)

More occasionally, other problems can be to blame, such as:

- ◆ pelvic adhesions (following surgery)
- ◆ bowel and bladder problems
- ◆ fibroids
- ◆ ovarian cysts

See your GP, who can arrange investigations and treatment for the underlying cause.

Vaginismus

This is when the vagina tightens up against your will, making sex either very uncomfortable or impossible. Many women also find the same thing happens during gynaecological examinations. Not surprisingly, vaginismus causes distress and relationship problems, and the anxiety this brings often makes the problem worse, creating a vicious circle. It's not rare – many women experience it at some time in their lives but, as with so many embarrassing problems, it's not often talked about.

It's not that you don't want to have sex – you do; and not being able to relax enough to have a smear test can make you feel very foolish. It's just that your mind is subconsciously telling your body that it's going to hurt, and so the vagina tenses up. In some women, vaginismus starts before they even begin having sex. In this case, apprehension and fear are often to blame, which then get reinforced when sex is attempted. In others, it occurs after a previously satisfactory sex life, and is often due to a traumatic sexual experience or following a difficult childbirth.

You may be able to overcome the problem yourself by using special graduated vaginal dilators, which allow you, and your vagina, to become accustomed to penetration. Many women, however, really value the support from a trained psycho-sexual therapist, which can help you to overcome inhibitions and subconscious beliefs.

While you are undergoing any sort of treatment for vaginismus, don't even try to have sex until you are really ready, or you could soon be back to square one. But you can, and should, continue to enjoy intimacy with your partner, and if possible include him in your treatment programme.

Lung cancer

What's the biggest cancer killer in women? Breast cancer, I hear you say. Actually, no, it's not. It's lung cancer. And lung cancer is *not* just a man's disease! Though breast cancer affects far more women than lung cancer (roughly 42,000 women each year are newly diagnosed with breast cancer compared to 15,500 with lung cancer), lung cancer kills around 13,500 women each year in the UK, compared to around 12,300 from breast cancer. Unfortunately, though the numbers of women dying from breast cancer are steadily decreasing (despite increasing numbers being diagnosed with the disease), the same cannot be said of lung cancer. Put simply, the treatments for breast cancer are more effective than those for lung cancer. At least 77 per cent of women diagnosed with breast cancer will be alive five years later; for lung cancer the figure is a shocking 6 per cent. Sadly, the number of women being affected by lung cancer has increased.

The biggest risk factor for lung cancer is, of course, smoking. In fact, 9 out of 10 cases are caused by smoking. Unfortunately, as smoking rates appear to be rising in young women, this means that the number of women affected by lung cancer is likely to continue rising. Living in areas with a high level of background radiation or air pollution may also increase the risk, along with exposure to high concentrations of nickel, chromium and asbestos.

Symptoms

Initial symptoms of lung cancer may include:

♦ a persistent cough

♦ coughing up blood

♦ mild chest pains

♦ shortness of breath or wheezing

Unfortunately, many cancers do not cause symptoms until they are quite advanced. Later symptoms may include:

- loss of appetite and weight loss, tiredness and feeling generally unwell
- recurrent chest infections that are slow to clear
- worsening wheezing, and severe shortness of breath
- a change in the shape of the fingernails, making them look more rounded.

The initial test for lung cancer is a chest X-ray, which may reveal a characteristic shadow. The diagnosis can then be confirmed by a biopsy of the suspicious area, which is taken via a special camera that is passed down the windpipe into the lungs. This is called a bronchoscopy.

Treatment
Treatment of lung cancer depends on the type of tumour, its size, and whether it has spread at the time of diagnosis. Small tumours that have not spread outside the lung tissue may be surgically removed, and in a small proportion of cases the operation can be curative. However, the most common type of treatment is radiotherapy, which aims to shrink the tumour cells. Unfortunately, there are no really effective drugs for the most common type of lung cancer, but chemotherapy can be used effectively for some of the rarer types. New treatments are being developed, but compared to other cancers, the progress in treating lung cancer has been very slow.

CYSTITIS AND URINARY-TRACT INFECTIONS

Never had cystitis? You're very lucky! Most women have had at least one attack, and often it's a recurrent problem.

Tell-tale signs

♦ needing to go to the loo to pass urine incredibly often, but when you go you only pass a small amount

♦ feeling as if you are passing small pieces of glass when you go

♦ lower abdominal discomfort or sometimes pain, especially after you have emptied your bladder

Why does this happen?

Cystitis literally means inflammation of the bladder, and in the vast majority of cases it's due to an infection from bacteria that have spread up into the bladder from the vulva or anus.

We women get cystitis far more than men simply because of our anatomy – the urethra, the tiny passage from the bladder to the outside, is not only very short, but it lies right next to the vagina. This means that just the simple mechanics of having sex can push bacteria up into the bladder. The friction from lovemaking can also make the delicate tissues around the whole genital area slightly inflamed, and so more prone to infection.

Though cystitis is usually only a minor problem, occasionally the infection can spread to either one or both kidneys, causing pain in the loin on the affected side and often a fever as well. Left untreated, the kidney can become scarred and permanently damaged.

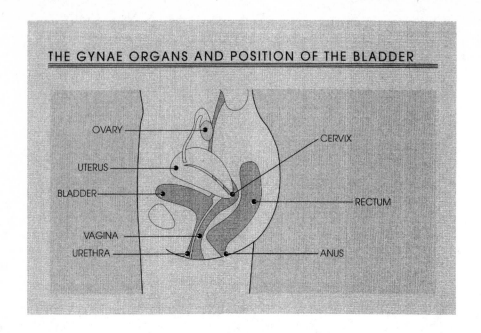

THE GYNAE ORGANS AND POSITION OF THE BLADDER

OVARY

UTERUS

BLADDER

VAGINA

URETHRA

CERVIX

RECTUM

ANUS

Treatment

At the first sign of an attack of cystitis, really step up your intake of fluid, especially water and cranberry juice. They will make you produce more urine, and sometimes this is all that is needed to flush the bugs away. Cranberry juice has an antibacterial action in the bladder and really can help to stop cystitis in its tracks.

Sachets containing sodium or potassium citrate, available from chemists, make the urine less acid and help to stop that awful 'peeing glass' sensation.

But if symptoms persist for more than 2 days, or if you have really smelly or bloody urine, see your doctor for antibiotic treatment. You should see your doctor without delay if you develop loin pain, as kidney infections rarely go away of their own accord.

To help prevent recurrent attacks

♦ Always empty your bladder either before or, better still, after you have sex, to wash away any bugs that might have entered the bladder.

♦ Wipe yourself from front to back after you've been to the loo (particularly after you've opened your bowels).

♦ Never douche or spray the shower head upwards around your vaginal area, as this can force bacteria up into the bladder. (It's not good for vaginal health either.)

♦ Avoid using bubble baths and perfumed soaps in the vulval area, especially if you've got sensitive skin, as this can cause allergic inflammation, which is then prone to an infection.

♦ Make sure your vagina is well lubricated during sex to avoid excess friction. A rubbing sensation (as opposed to gliding) is an indication that some lubricating jelly, such as KY, would be helpful.

♦ Recurrent attacks may also be linked to using a contraceptive diaphragm, because the rim can press on the base of the bladder. Try condoms for a while and see if the situation improves; if so, have a rethink about your method of contraception.

♦ It also helps to drink a glass of cranberry juice each day.

IRRITABLE BOWEL SYNDROME (IBS)

At least a third of all women have had symptoms of IBS at one time or another. Men have IBS too, but it seems to be more common in women – or at least, women visit their doctor more often to get their IBS sorted out.

Go back thirty years, and IBS was pretty much unheard of; though some say this is because people didn't complain, it does seem that IBS really is becoming more of a problem, especially in women aged between 15 and 40.

Tell-tale signs

♦ Abdominal pain, which can vary from cramps to a dull ache. It may be anywhere in the tummy, but is often low down on the left. It can occur at any time, but is often worse if you are constipated. Opening your bowels, or just passing wind, can bring relief.

♦ Feeling bloated; many women say one of the worst things about IBS is finding that trousers that were comfortably loose in the morning feel as if they are cutting you in half by the afternoon.

♦ Passing lots of gas, belching and having a noisy, rumbling tummy.

♦ Erratic bowels, with constipation on some days, diarrhoea on others. Some women find they are predominantly constipated, others find they frequently have to make a dash to the loo. A feeling that you haven't quite emptied your bowels is also quite common, along with occasional sharp pain in the back passage.

Why does this happen?

The exact cause of IBS isn't known, but it is thought that it's due to abnormal contractions of the muscle in the wall of the bowel. Overactivity of the muscle can cause cramps and diarrhoea, while if the muscle relaxes too much, the movement of waste matter in the bowel slows down, leading to constipation. In a susceptible person, cramps may be triggered by eating a meal too quickly, or just downing a large drink too fast, especially if it is full of gas. Sometimes IBS starts after a bout of gastroenteritis, when there has been an infection of some sort in the gut. But in many people there appears to be no specific trigger.

Your mental state can also have a huge influence – just think how you used to get butterflies in your tummy when you had to sit an important exam at school, or were about to go out on an important date. Stress and anxiety can certainly make IBS worse; worrying about whether there is something seriously wrong with your guts then causes more anxiety, and the whole situation gets into a vicious circle. Being over-tired often makes IBS symptoms worse.

The food you eat, and your general eating habits, can also be relevant. Too much or too little of just about anything may trigger symptoms, but common culprits seem to be:

♦ too much or too little fibre

♦ too much fat

♦ too much rich and spicy food

♦ too much alcohol, tea and coffee

♦ too much dairy produce, such as milk, cheese, yogurt or chocolate; this is because some people cannot digest lactose (the sugar in milk)

Sometimes just one food can trigger symptoms – and IBS is a common sign of food intolerance (see page 207).

Tests

There is no specific diagnostic test for IBS, but tests are important to exclude other possible causes of symptoms, such as a bowel infection, or inflammation inside the bowel. Tests normally include a blood test to check for anaemia, iron levels, general inflammation (an ESR test), and a stool test. All of these can be done by your GP.

In a few cases – if there is any doubt about the diagnosis – an endoscopy may be done to examine the digestive system internally with a fibre-optic camera. This may involve looking inside the stomach (a gastroscopy) or the large bowel (a colonoscopy).

Treatment

Irritable bowel syndrome isn't life-threatening, so in that sense it's not serious. But if it stops you sleeping, and makes your life unpredictable and uncomfortable, it can certainly cause a bit of a dent in your quality of life.

Unfortunately, there is no universal cure for IBS – it's more a question of managing your wayward innards.

Some drug treatments may be worth a try, and many of these are available directly from chemists, but before you start spending a fortune on medicines, have a chat with either your doctor or the pharmacist to work out which ones are likely to help you most.

♦ Antispasmodic tablets, such as dicyclomine, can help reduce pain.

♦ Loperamide can help to stop bouts of diarrhoea, but has to be used with care as it makes any tendency to constipation worse.

♦ Stimulant laxatives, such as bisocodyl, can help to solve constipation, but can cause cramps, and should not be used regularly.

♦ Laxatives that bulk up the stools, such as lactulose, are safe for long-term use, but can make bloating worse.

♦ Peppermint oil can also ease bloating and flatus in some, and is available in a slow-release formulation where the active ingredient is released in the large bowel.

◆ When pain is a major problem, antidepressant drugs such as amitriptylene can be beneficial, especially in those where depression or anxiety is making matters worse.

However, in my experience drug treatment is of limited use in IBS, and changing your diet and lifestyle is likely to be far more successful.

Self-help

The first thing to do is to keep a food and mood diary, which means writing down everything you ate, at what time, and your general feelings. It's a slog, and requires a lot of commitment for at least a couple of weeks, but it can pay real dividends in terms of identifying any triggers that upset your bowels.

For instance, you may find that you feel very uncomfortable after eating a large portion of leeks, but a small amount of onion is OK. Or that eating too much fibre makes you gassy and bloated, but too little makes you constipated. Lactose (found in dairy produce) and wheat are renowned for causing IBS in some women.

Sometimes it's the size of meals that is the issue – large, high-fat meals generally challenge the digestive system far more than smaller, more frequent ones.

Once you have identified a possible cause, then the next step is to remove it from your diet and see if your symptoms improve. If you find yourself cutting out a major food group, such as dairy, then make sure you get the vital nutrients it contains, in this case calcium, from another source. And try not to cut out too many foods at once – diets that leave you eating nothing but a few lettuce leaves and an occasional spoonful of rice are not a route to good health.

Some alternative remedies can be useful, especially those that help you to relax, such as hypnotherapy. Acupuncture has also been used with some success. Counselling and CBT (see page 237) can be beneficial if anxiety and depression are part of the overall IBS picture.

It has been suggested that IBS may be related to a change in the balance of the bacteria that normally live in the bowel, and some find that taking probiotics such as lactobacillus or bifidocterium can ease symptoms.

PILES

These are a classic example of a common problem that people just don't like to talk about. Piles, or, to give them their proper medical name, haemorrhoids, can occur in both sexes, but are much more common in women. At least 50 per cent of women develop one or more piles at some stage in their life.

What are they?

Piles are swollen veins at the entrance to the back passage, or anus – very similar to varicose veins in the legs (see page 340), only in a much more uncomfortable and intimate place. To begin with the swelling is usually within the back passage, but if the piles enlarge, they extend out and can be felt as knobbly lumps.

Why me?

The most common reason for piles developing is constipation, straining to go to the toilet and, when you do go, passing hard, lumpy motions. Women also often develop piles during pregnancy, due to the pressure from the baby and the effects of hormones that relax the veins and the bowel, making constipation more of a problem.

Like varicose veins, the tendency to have piles can run in families. However, you can try to avoid getting piles by eating a high-fibre diet (breakfast cereals, wholemeal bread, plenty of fruit and vegetables) and drinking plenty of water (eight glasses a day). And opt for the less dehydrating decaffeinated tea and coffee.

Tell-tale signs

The most common symptom is bleeding after you go to the toilet. The blood is bright red and the amount can vary from just a little on the tissue to spraying around the toilet pan, which can be very alarming.

Piles can cause itching, discomfort and a mucus-like discharge. They can also cause a sense of fullness in the anus, and a feeling of not fully emptying your bowels when you go to the loo.

Occasionally, a clot may form in a larger haemorrhoid. This can cause intense pain. It can also make it difficult to sit down, and agony to pass a motion.

Tests and treatment

Any bleeding from the back passage needs to be investigated – you should never assume it's 'just piles'. Occasionally, something more sinister – a polyp or cancer – is to blame.

Piles can often be easy to diagnose – the doctor can see them. To be sure of the diagnosis, it's usual to pass a small instrument, a proctoscope, into the back passage. This is a bit uncomfortable, but not as bad as many people imagine.

Constipation

It's not essential to open your bowels and pass a motion every day, but when you do go your motions should be soft and large. A healthy stool should look like a Cumberland sausage, and if you are passing little bits that are more like cocktail sausages or chipolatas, then you are likely to have constipation.

Constipation can make you feel bloated and uncomfortable, and the worse it gets, the harder it becomes to pass a motion, which puts you at risk of piles and a weak pelvic floor. Constipation is much more of a problem in women than men simply because in general we eat smaller portions of food – including those containing all important fibre, which is essential for an efficient bowel.

The best way of tackling constipation is to alter your diet to include more fibre: eat more wholewheat foods, pulses, fruit and vegetables. Best of all is to include unprocessed bran in your food every day – but don't try to eat it on its own: it's pretty unpalatable. It's also important to drink plenty of water, especially in hot weather. Regular exercise can also help to keep the bowels moving.

If you feel you need something to get your bowels moving, then agents that naturally bulk up the motions, such as lactulose or ispaghula husk (available in sachets) should be your first choice; these can be used safely long term. Laxatives that stimulate the bowel muscle, such as senna or bisacodyl, certainly can work, but can cause painful cramps. They should not be used long term as they can make the bowel muscle lazy.

If constipation suddenly occurs for no obvious reason, and does not improve with a change in diet, or if you get persistent stomach pains, then see your doctor. Occasionally, it can be a sign of a serious underlying problem, such as bowel cancer (see page 377).

ALLERGIES AND FOOD INTOLERANCE

Ever come across the situation when you try to have a few friends round and don't know what to cook? One friend can't eat wheat, another can't do dairy, and then there is another who is allergic to fish.

On the face of it we're now in the midst of a food allergy epidemic, but many people who maintain they have allergies are not actually allergic – what they have is an intolerance to certain foods. The difference is quite important. Genuine food allergy can be life-threatening, but food intolerance isn't.

Allergies are caused by an over-reaction of the body's immune system to something that is usually harmless. This can be:

♦ something you breathe in, causing hayfever, rhinitis and asthma

♦ something you eat, which can cause a reaction anywhere in the digestive tract

♦ something you touch – an offending substance, the allergen – which can trigger a severe, immediate reaction throughout the body, leading to swelling of the skin and lining of the airway, which can be enough to prevent air reaching the lungs; it's what happens occasionally when you hear of someone dying from eating a tiny piece of peanut

♦ allergic reactions in the skin, causing dermatitis and eczema

The common substances causing allergic reactions in the airway are pollen grains, house dust mite and animal fur and excretions (especially of cats and dogs).

Common foods that cause genuine allergic reactions are some types of nut, fish (especially shellfish), eggs and red fruits, especially strawberries.

Insect bites, especially wasp stings, and drugs, especially antibiotics, are also common causes of allergic reactions.

In genuine allergy, the more you come into contact with the allergen, the more the immune system is sensitized and the worse the reaction becomes. This is why the first time you have a course of penicillin you may get only slight skin itching, but the second time you have it, you may get a severe, red, itchy rash.

Intolerance is different, as the immune system is not involved – rather, a chemical in the food causes a direct effect on the body tissues. Common examples are:

♦ the amines in chocolate, cheese or red wine leading to a migraine

♦ the histamines found in salmon and tuna causing nausea and vomiting

♦ incomplete digestion of food, for example wheat, leading to wind and bloating

Diagnosis and treatment

Genuine food allergy is rare – it affects only 1 per cent of the population, though it is becoming slightly more common. But because it is such a trendy diagnosis, there's a whole burgeoning industry in 'allergy testing', which seems to be specifically targeted at women.

Testing for allergy can be done using either a blood test or a skin-prick test. For suspected skin reactions, patch tests can also be used.

However, before you have the test done, you have to have some idea of what you are reacting to – you can't be tested for allergies to everything! There is no evidence that genuine allergy can be diagnosed by passing an electrical current through the skin (a method used by a lot of alternative practitioners).

Good allergy tests measure the amount of specific IgE, a chemical in the bloodstream, which is produced by the immune system as part of the allergic response. These tests are not of any use in diagnosing food intolerance, as this part of the immune system is not involved. The usual way that intolerance can be diagnosed is by keeping a diary and noting what happens when you eat, and then don't eat, certain foods. However, new tests for food intolerance are now being developed, and will hopefully be useful in diagnosis in the near future.

Of course, with allergies prevention really is better than a cure, and the best way by far of coping with an allergy is to avoid coming into contact with the allergen. But this isn't always possible. Mild allergic reactions can be treated by taking antihistamine tablets, but more severe reactions need treatment with adrenalin. Carrying an adrenalin injection pen with you at all times, which you (or someone else) can administer, can be life saving.

Desensitization is now increasingly used for people with severe allergies, for instance to wasp stings or peanuts. The process involves giving repeated tiny amounts of the chemical involved, with the idea that the immune system gets used to it and does not over-react quite so much. However, it can be dangerous, and should only ever be done in special hospital clinics with resuscitation equipment to hand.

IN SUMMARY

The years between 20 and 39 are perhaps the most stable, physically, of a woman's life. Unless she is very unlucky, she will have settled into a regular pattern of menstruation; her skin and hair will be at their best; she will be mentally and physically energetic.

Nevertheless, there are many health problems that can arise at this time of life and need attention before they make an impact. I have emphasized the importance of beginning to take responsibility for your own medical check-ups, whether or not you are active sexually or intend to have children, now or in the future.

Luckily, many women of this age are beginning to be really interested in the subject of nutrition, both for themselves and for their partner or family. The best insurance you can give yourself against a feeble old age is to keep healthy and make sure you feed yourself properly.

The main source of frustration for many women in their twenties and thirties is lack of time. You may be a career woman with a job that takes up all your waking hours; you may be the mother of young children with all the attendant tiredness and sleeplessness; you may be looking after elderly parents and worrying about their future. Whatever your situation, remember to make time for yourself. It's not being selfish, it's being sensible. An exhausted woman who becomes ill through the sheer amount of work she has to cope with is no help to herself or anyone else.

In this positive frame of mind, the woman in her thirties can approach her forties with interest and enthusiasm as a new stage in life, something to be embraced, not feared.

CHAPTER FOUR

PERI-MENOPAUSAL YEARS: 40–49

Women in their forties can be at hugely different stages in their lives. Some will just be starting a family, with babies and small children; others will be coping with moody teenagers. Some will be living on their own, through personal choice or as circumstances dictate. Some women may even find themselves with an empty nest, if their children are old enough to leave home.

But despite all these differences, there is one thing that all women in their forties will experience, and that is the approach to the menopause.

As long as ten years before your periods stop, the ratio between the hormones oestrogen and progesterone that saw you through the reproductive years begins to alter. Welcome to the peri-menopause!

Some lucky women sail through the transition to the menopause without problems, but most women experience changes that they may find distressing and bewildering.

In this chapter you will find:

- **Staying healthy**
  - the regular check-ups you need
  - unpredictable hormones

- **Diet and nutrition**
  - controlling your weight

- dieting, diet plans and diet pills
- cellulite

- **Lifestyle and mental health**
  - stress and depression
  - anger
  - tiredness

- **Hormonal issues**
  - signs of change
  - period problems
  - hysterectomy
  - fibroids
  - pre-menstrual syndrome

- **Physical illnesses**
  - thyroid problems
  - rheumatoid arthritis and other auto-immune disorders
  - headaches, including migraine

- **Skin and hair problems**
  - alopecia and hair loss
  - flaking scalp

STAYING HEALTHY

Up to the age of 40, most women can stay reasonably healthy without bothering too much about check-ups. But once you hit your forties, regular check-ups become much more important.

Tests that every woman should have:

- ◆ **Every 3 years**: a blood pressure check.

- ◆ **Every 5 years**: a cervical smear, more often if you have ever had an abnormal smear, or evidence of wart virus infection (see page 93).

- ◆ **Every 5 years**: a blood cholesterol level check.

- ◆ **Every 2 years**: an eye test; this is the time when eyesight can begin to change.

In addition, all women in their forties should be breast aware and check their breasts regularly for anything out of the ordinary. Though benign, non-cancerous breast problems are much more common at this age, the risk of breast cancer is rising (see pages 318–25).

Regular skin checks are important too, for any odd-looking lumps, bumps or moles. This is an age when malignant melanoma is at its most common (see page 338).

Don't forget about contraception. If you are still having periods, no matter how infrequently, you are still ovulating, and unless you take precautions you can still get pregnant.

If you have, or are likely to have, a new sexual partner, then you should have a check-up for STIs (see pages 85–109). Just because you are older does not mean you are immune from them.

There are other tests you should have if your family history means you are more at risk of certain illnesses. Mostly these apply if a first-degree relative (parent or sibling) is affected, but illness in two second-degree relatives (grandparent, aunt or uncle) can also indicate an increased risk. Check with your doctor to see if you need:

- Breast screening. Those with breast cancer in the family should start having regular mammograms before the age of 50.

- Ovarian screening, with ultrasound, for those with a family history of ovarian cancer (see page 369).

- Faecal occult blood testing and/or colonoscopy, for those with a family history of bowel cancer (see page 377).

- Checks for thyroid auto-antibodies, if thyroid disease is in the family (see page 264).

- A blood glucose check once every couple of years if there is diabetes in your family, especially if you are overweight or have PCOS (see pages 355 and 186).

UNPREDICTABLE HORMONES

Hormone levels of women in this age group are beginning to change, and it's not all good news. The effects of these changes can be dramatic, worrying and annoying – sometimes all at the same time. Here's what you can expect.

The menstrual cycle before the peri-menopause

For the first 30 years after their first period, most women's hormones behave in a fairly predictable way. In response to follicle stimulating hormone (FSH), produced by the pituitary gland, the ovaries produce oestrogen and an egg starts to ripen. Oestrogen levels rise, the womb lining thickens, and then ovulation occurs, usually about 14 days after the start of a period.

After ovulation, the ovaries produce progesterone as well. Levels of both oestrogen and progesterone rise for the next 10 days, the womb lining alters slightly, then (assuming the egg isn't fertilized) the levels of both hormones fall. Once the hormone levels are below a critical level the lining is shed as a period, usually 14 days after ovulation (see chart on page 77).

Some women are not quite so lucky and don't have regular periods, but most do and know what to expect, month on month. Once you enter your forties, however, things aren't quite so predictable.

The beginnings of the peri-menopause

In the UK the average age of the menopause – which is defined as a woman's last period – is 51; this is when the ovaries finally stop working. But they don't switch off suddenly. Instead, like most of the body changes that occur with increasing age, this change occurs gradually.

The peri-menopause – the time leading up to the menopause – can be difficult to define, as the changes that occur can vary enormously from one woman to another. Some women are barely aware of any changes till the menopause is virtually upon them, and then they only notice that their periods become less frequent. Others go through years of unpredictability, not just in their periods, but in many aspects of their health, particularly their moods.

DIET AND NUTRITION

Women generally find themselves gaining a pound a year (about half a kilo) in their forties as they approach the menopause, unless they reassess their diet and lifestyle. It takes real determination and hard work to keep your weight down at this age unless you are particularly genetically blessed, because nature is working against you on several fronts.

CHANGES IN BODY SHAPE

The main reason why women gain weight at this time has nothing to do with hormones. It's all to do with a change in the body composition, especially a slow reduction in the quantity of muscle tissue. Women lose muscle from everywhere – it's why older women's buttocks are less rounded and their legs thinner.

Muscle burns calories more than any other type of tissue, and as the quantity of muscle falls, so too does the metabolic rate. Your metabolic rate falls by about 3 per cent per year, so that means if you continue eating at 45 what you did at 25, you will unavoidably gain weight.

The benefits of exercise

Of course diet is very important, but the real key to avoiding middle-age spread is exercise. Exercise burns calories in its own right but, more importantly, it helps to maintain muscles. The more muscle bulk you have, the more you will maintain your youthful metabolic rate and shape.

Try to do at least 30 minutes of moderate exercise a day. It will do wonders for your weight and body shape. Cardiovascular exercise such as swimming, running, cycling or brisk walking for 20 minutes or more will boost your metabolism and help you burn fat. Strength or weight training will maintain your muscles, raise your metabolism and strengthen your bones. Elastic resistance bands, water aerobics, walking or hiking all provide enough resistance to strengthen muscles. Pilates and yoga will enhance your suppleness, and tone and build muscle. They are also excellent at lowering stress levels.

If you find it difficult to make time for exercise (and who doesn't?), then try wearing a pedometer and make changes during your daily activities so you take 10,000 steps a day. It can be very reassuring to know that you don't always have to find that protected half an hour, and that several bursts of 5 or 10 minutes do actually add up to some meaningful activity.

Hormonal imbalance

In the years leading up to the menopause many women suffer from oestrogen dominance, which means they have too much oestrogen relative to progesterone. This imbalance can also contribute to weight gain, especially round the abdomen. So even if your weight does not alter too much, you may find you change from a pear to an apple shape, with a thickening waist.

Keeping your weight down

To some extent, all these changes are natural, and trying too hard to maintain your youthful figure can be a mistake. You really can be too thin for your own good, and as you approach fifty people are more likely to notice your gaunt face than your flat tummy. But this shouldn't be an excuse for letting yourself go. Too much fat isn't good for either your figure or your health. If you are overweight, you may develop high cholesterol and high blood pressure, plus insulin resistance, which can lead to type 2 diabetes (see page 355). All these factors can put you at risk of a heart attack.

The most reliable way to assess whether you are overweight is to calculate your body-mass index (BMI), which is a measure of weight relative to height.

BMI CHART

HEIGHT		OPTIMUM BODY WEIGHT RANGE	
METRES	FEET/INCHES	KILOGRAMS	STONES/POUNDS
1.47	4ft 10ins	40-51	6st 4lb – 8st
1.50	4ft 11ins	42-54	6st 8lb – 8st 7lb
1.52	5ft	43-55	6st 11lb – 8st 9lb
1.55	5ft 1in	45-57	7st 1lb – 8st 13lb
1.57	5ft 2ins	46-59	7st 3lb – 9st 4lb
1.60	5ft 3ins	48-61	7st 8lb – 9st 8lb
1.63	5ft 4ins	50-63	7st 12lb – 9st 13lb
1.65	5ft 5ins	51-65	8st – 10st 3lb
1.68	5ft 6ins	53-67	8st 5lb – 10st 7lb
1.70	5ft 7ins	54-69	8st 7lb – 10st 12lb
1.73	5ft 8ins	56-71	8st 11lb – 11st 2lb
1.75	5ft 9ins	57-73	8st 13lb – 11st 7lb
1.78	5ft 10ins	59-75	9st 4lb – 11st 11lb
1.80	5ft 11ins	61-77	9st 8lb – 12st 1lb
1.83	6ft	63-80	9st 13lb – 12st 8lb

You may be surprised at the weight range for each height, but remember:

● This BMI range gives you the optimum weight range for your health.

● At this level, your relative risk of dying from a weight-related disease is minimal.

● Once you are within this healthy BMI band, you can fine tune your weight depending on how you feel in yourself and on your general body build.

For this you will need metric measurements.

1. Take your height in metres and multiply it by itself. Write the answer down.
2. Weigh yourself in kilograms. Write it down.
3. Divide your weight (step 2) by the answer from step 1.

A desirable BMI for women is between 20 and 24. A BMI of 19 and under is underweight, and could mean you are at increased risk of osteoporosis (see page 307). In younger women it could also affect ovulation and fertility. A BMI of 25 or higher means you're considered overweight, and 30 and above is obese.

However, very muscular women will have a high BMI without the associated health risks, and for this reason it is also useful to measure your waist. It should be below 80cm (32 inches). Between 80cm and 87.5cm (32 and 35 inches) is overweight, and above 87.5cm (35 inches) is obese. Anyone who is obese has a 30 per cent increased risk of arthritis, heart disease, stroke and diabetes. The heavier you are, the greater the risk.

Losing weight

Sorry, but if you need to drop some pounds, there's no quick fix, despite all the hype attached to modern diet plans (see pages 221–5). You just need to employ the same old standbys – a sensible, varied diet plus 30 minutes of moderate exercise a day.

If you reduce your calories too drastically and too quickly, this will be counterproductive. When calorific intake drops below about 1,500 a day, the body believes it is starving and begins conserving fat – the exact opposite of your goal on a peri-menopausal diet. Instead, the body will use muscle tissue for fuel, thus using up the very thing that has such a voracious appetite for calorie-burning.

Not only that, but stress hormones, like cortisol, can block weight loss too. This is because the body interprets prolonged stress as famine, in the same way as it reacts to swift calorie reduction. Bingeing and yo-yo dieting can put our bodies under tremendous stress. Studies have also shown that levels of leptin, the fat hormone that helps to regulate appetite and metabolic rate, drop after a crash diet; this will increase your appetite and slow down your metabolism.

The bottom line is that if you are trying to lose weight, you have to do so slowly if you want permanent results.

Reassessing your diet

Even if you are eating well and exercising regularly, you may still gain weight at this time due to a slight fall in your metabolism, so it's time for a diet reassessment to ensure your body is not taking in more calories than it burns. Here are some tips to make this as painless as possible:

◆ Eat only when you are hungry, and only enough to satisfy your hunger. However, be careful. Many peri-menopausal women who become light-headed, get headaches or feel unduly tired are suffering from low blood sugar. The way to combat this is not by reaching for a high-sugar snack but by eating regularly.

◆ Don't skip meals – especially breakfast.

◆ There is no shame in leaving food on your plate, no matter what your mother told you.

- Be extremely sparing with high GI foods (see page 224) such as white bread, desserts and sweets, and watch your alcohol intake. Those glasses of Chardonnay are full of calories.

- Experiment, and see what works for you. Eating plenty of fruit and vegetables will keep you feeling full, so if you fancy a snack, think 'apple', not 'biscuits'. If you don't trust yourself, don't buy any.

- If you are thirsty, drink water, not a sugary or caffeine-laden drink.

- Eat plenty of lean protein, but go easy on red meat and dairy products, and don't be tempted to nibble on cheese, which is packed with calories.

- Avoid using butter to cook your food – instead use small amounts of olive oil or another healthy oil. And keep mayonnaise and cream for special occasions only.

DIET PLANS

Speak to any doctor or dietitian, and they will tell you that the best way to lose weight is to eat a well-balanced, low-calorie diet, with plenty of fruit and vegetables. Trouble is, this is boring, and it doesn't always give the instant results that many women want. It can also be quite difficult working out exactly what you can and cannot eat.

No wonder that a huge, multi-million-pound 'dieting' industry has appeared. Someone, somewhere, has made a mint out of advising women to trim their figures by eating nothing but grapefruit or watercress soup. This may help you lose a few pounds, but clearly such a restrictive diet can't be followed for more than a couple of weeks at the most. Then there are other diets that on the surface seem a little more sensible. They come beautifully packaged, promise the earth and make slimming sound so easy. But which one to choose? Here are the pros and cons of the most popular.

The Atkins Diet

This high-fat, high-protein regime involves eating unrestricted amounts of meat, cheese and eggs (protein) but severely restricting carbohydrates, including sugar, bread, pasta, milk, fruits and vegetables. The theory is that carbohydrates create insulin, which leads to weight gain and hunger. So if you cut out this food type you will reduce your appetite and use stored fat for energy instead.

According to most health professionals, the Atkins Diet is not good for your health, especially if it is followed for more than a few weeks. There is now good evidence that in many people it raises cholesterol levels, sometimes quite dramatically, and this can increase the risk of a heart attack or a stroke. Extremely high-protein diets like this and Sugar Busters (below) can also cause acidic urine. This leaches calcium from your body, which will increase the risk of osteoporosis and kidney stones. The Atkins Diet also limits high-fibre foods, which provide essential vitamins and minerals and are necessary for regular bowel movements.

Sugar Busters

This is another high-protein, high-fat, low-carbohydrate diet plan. The twist with this one is that sugar is 'toxic' so you restrict all refined sugars along with some high-sugar fruits and vegetables. On the hit-list are potatoes, corn, white rice, some breads, beets, carrots, corn syrup, molasses, honey and soda.

In my opinion, the big hole in this theory is that sugar is not actually toxic, although it's true that eating refined sugar causes a quick insulin surge. However, this diet does encourage consumption of high-fibre vegetables, whole grains and lean protein – all good, sound advice for healthy weight loss, though you can achieve the same results by watching your portions and calorie counting.

The Zone Diet

This is all about ratios. The theory is that your body reaches its peak efficiency when every meal you eat comprises 40 per cent carbohydrates, 30 per cent protein and 30 per cent fats. When you get this 40–30–30 balance right you are working within the 'zone'.

This is not as restrictive as other high-protein diets and does allow for the consumption of a broad range of foods. However, there is no long-term scientific study to support the 40–30–30 theory. There are also some concerns that those following the Zone Diet may not get all their essential daily vitamins and minerals.

The South Beach Diet

The basis of this diet, which started life in southern Florida, is to replace 'bad carbs' and 'bad fats' with 'good carbs' and 'good fats'. For the first couple of weeks many foods are banned, including fruit. However, because you are eating normal-sized meals with plenty of protein and vegetables (including nuts and olive oil dressing) you won't feel hungry.

During the next phase, when you have rebalanced your diet, you can add back some of the foods you initially cut out. Because you are now eating 'smart carbohydrates' the theory is that you will then lose weight.

You can add more of the foods you originally cut out when you reach your target weight.

The first two weeks appears to involve crash dieting, which is not a healthy way to drop weight for the reasons I've already explained. Although much of the thinking on food types is sound, you could achieve the same results just by employing a modicum of dietary common sense without banning nutritious food such as fruit.

The GI Diet

This is nothing to do with Americans who wooed women with nylon stockings and chewing gum during the Blitz. GI stands for glycaemic index, and foods are categorized depending on whether they raise blood sugar dramatically, moderately or slowly. Glucose is rated as 100, top of the GI scale.

The theory is that high GI foods, which score 70-plus, such as refined sugar and white flour, are quickly broken down by the body. They give you a swift energy high, but this is soon followed by an energy dip, which leaves you craving more of the same quick-fix foods.

Low GI foods – ones that score 55 or less on the scale – such as wholemeal bread, whole grains and porridge oats, take longer to break down, so they leave you feeling fuller for longer, which then means you are less likely to reach for an unsuitable snack. As an added bonus, many of these foods provide plenty of healthy fibre to keep your bowels in good health.

The GI diet does all the calculations for you using traffic-light colour coding. The red foods (high GI) should be avoided if you want to lose weight; the yellow-coded ones you can eat occasionally; and you can pig out as much as you like on the green (low GI) foods. The diet is simple to follow, nutritionally sound and one of the best around for women of this age.

Weight Watchers

It's no longer necessary to go to a weekly Weight Watchers meeting to be weighed these days – unless you find this a powerful motivator. You can join online and follow one of the plans at home. Different foods are awarded points – the more nutritious the food, the fewer points they carry. You try to stay within your allotted number of points each day.

The dietary thinking is basically sound and the many success stories of women who have dropped several stone to reach their goal weights are well publicized. However, as in any diet, the true goal is actually maintaining that weight once you get there. The changes have to be for life.

For me, the downside of Weight Watchers is that it often costs money to join, and these costs will accelerate steeply if you decide to buy the special Weight Watchers ready meals. Also, because you are counting points, many would argue that you can get unhealthily preoccupied with food.

DIET PILLS

Losing weight by diet and exercise is fiendishly difficult, and taking a pill that will magically make the pounds disappear would be a dream come true for many women. It's reckoned that at least a third of women have tried slimming pills at some time.

Do an internet search for 'diet pills' and you'll get a choice of more than a million websites. A lot of manufacturers make miraculous claims for their pills – but sadly they don't generally work. The only thing they trim is your bank balance.

The fact is that no pill will spontaneously melt fat away. Some can help a little with weight loss, but only if combined with diet and exercise. And any diet pill that actually works will have side effects.

Two drugs that can aid weight loss are available on prescription from doctors, and if you are desperate these are the ones I would recommend you consider first. Both can be prescribed on the NHS to aid weight loss in people who are medically overweight, which is putting their health at risk.

- Orlistat (Xenical) reduces the absorption of dietary fat. It can aid weight loss, but it's essential you stick to a really low-fat diet as well. This isn't just to help with weight loss – it's because any excess fat you eat is passed out in your motions; this means that, for instance, just adding some mayonnaise to your salad leads to oily leakage around your back passage. Other side effects can include abdominal pain, bloating and wind. It also reduces slightly the absorption of fat-soluble vitamins and for this reason should be taken for a maximum of 6 months.

- Subitramine (Reductil) works by reducing appetite. It's chemically related to some types of antidepressants, and boosts brain levels of serotonin and noradrenalin. It should not be used in people with high blood pressure or heart disease, or with a history of eating disorders. It can cause palpitations, a dry mouth, stomach upsets, insomnia, anxiety and delayed orgasm. It can be used for up to a year.

Then there are the dieting pills that you can buy. They are a different ball game altogether and need to be viewed with extreme caution, because either they don't really work or, worse still, they can be very dangerous. If you are tempted to try any type of slimming pills, always check the ingredients and their actions. If you can't find this out, then leave them well alone. It's never worth putting your health at risk for the sake of wearing a smaller pair of trousers.

They generally fall into two groups:

♦ those that claim to boost your metabolism
♦ those that claim to suppress your appetite

Metabolism boosters may include ingredients such as caffeine, or herbs that have a caffeine-like action. Any effect on your metabolism is minimal, but the side effects are not – these can make you jittery and irritable, keep you awake at night, and increase your pulse rate and blood pressure. Ephedrine, an ingredient of a lot of decongestant pills, is similar. It is chemically related to adrenalin and has even more noticeable side effects.

Appetite suppressants: the safest types of appetite suppressants are herbs or fibre products that swell up inside your stomach, making you feel full. These must be drunk with plenty of water, or they can block the intestine. Drugs that act on the brain satiety centre, such as dexfenfluramine and phentermine, which are related to amphetamines, are highly addictive and can cause damage to the heart and blood vessels in the lungs. They are no longer officially licensed in the UK, but do find their way into some rogue products, particularly on the internet. Some of these drug concoctions also contain thyroid hormone, which has nasty side effects and can be dangerous.

CELLULITE

You won't like me for saying it, but it's normal for women to have cellulite. It's that dimpled-looking skin that can occur anywhere on your body, but is most likely to make a very unwelcome appearance on your buttocks and thighs. However, 80 per cent of women have it, including really slim models. It's the very few that don't have any cellulite that you'll see in swimwear photo-shoots!

Look at cellulite under the microscope and what you'll see are fat cells, interspersed with bands of fibrous tissue that run up to the skin. It's these bands that give the dimply effect.

We all have some fat under our skin – even thin people – but whether you have cellulite or not depends on the thickness of your skin and the thickness of the fibrous bands, which are determined by your genes. In other words, you really can blame your parents if you have cellulite. Despite anything you may have read, cellulite is not caused by toxins that have built up under your skin, and neither is it due to poor circulation.

Cellulite tends to form at a time of hormonal change – at puberty and during pregnancy. Though some men do get it, it is much more common in women. It usually gets worse if you put on weight, because the fat cells enlarge and bulge more against the fibrous bands. It also gets worse with age, as the skin becomes thinner and less well supported.

Dealing with cellulite

To get rid of cellulite you need to tackle both the fat and the fibrous bands. Certainly losing excess weight can help, but getting rid of those nuisance bands is a real problem.

- Really vigorous massage may have a slightly beneficial effect, but some experts say this is only because it makes the skin slightly inflamed and oedematous (with a little retained water), which just makes the dimpling less obvious.

- Sadly, I've seen no good scientific evidence that rubbing any cream or lotion into the skin has anything other than a very temporary effect. You could spend a small fortune on cellulite products and look exactly the same.

- Similarly, diets and supplements that aim to 'cure cellulite' should be treated with a very large pinch of salt. The best way to improve the appearance of your skin is to eat a really healthy diet that keeps your weight at a healthy level, and to take plenty of exercise, which can help to keep the underlying muscles well toned.

- The only proven way to get rid of cellulite is to have liposuction, which can remove both the fat and bands. But not only is it expensive, it also comes with a health warning (see page 337). Only you can decide if that is a price worth paying.

LIFESTYLE AND MENTAL HEALTH

Emotional symptoms can affect every area of your life. These symptoms include nervousness, depression, moodiness, irritability, frustration and over-reaction, memory and concentration problems, substance abuse, phobias or feeling out of control.

Any woman can suffer from these at any age, and many do. But the time at which these mental-health problems – and yes, that's what they are – most commonly rear their head is in the peri-menopausal years. Hormone changes don't help, but often it's lifestyle factors that tip the scales, and a woman who is just about coping with the normal ups and downs of life can develop a genuine health problem.

STRESS

We can't live without stress. It is our body's fight-or-flight reaction to anything that threatens or challenges us. When the body engages the stress response, we go into overdrive and think or move faster. Heartbeat and breathing accelerate and blood pressure rises.

Positive stress can be exciting – it provides that adrenalin rush that helps us through the marathon of childbirth, enables us to think creatively, meet impossible deadlines or survive danger. We all benefit from a little stress: without it life can seem very dull, and there is evidence that, surprising though it may seem, lack of stress can be a factor in depression.

But too much stress is a different thing altogether. It makes us feel out of control, exhausts the immune system and opens the door to physical or mental illness.

Many women today experience intense stress because of the twin demands of home and work, and because they spend a disproportionate amount of time and energy caring for others at the expense of their own needs and well-being.

Physical symptoms of stress can range from headaches, hair loss and eating disorders to chest pains, cold hands and feet, high blood pressure and fatigue. Other people experience skin problems, sweaty hands, palpitations and shortness of breath.

When you are stressed out your behaviour is likely to lose you friends. You will be spoiling for a fight, whether it is with your family or with people at work. Sometimes the aggression is verbal – you will be more argumentative – but this can spill over into behaviour such as road rage or physical violence.

Apart from the major catastrophes in life, few situations are actually stressful – it is how you react to them that causes the problems. If, for instance, the train to work is delayed yet again, some people will say 'ho-hum', phone their employer to explain and then enjoy another chapter of their book. The stressed-out individual will argue with the platform staff (assuming they can find any), pace the platform like a caged lion or let out a stream of invective about the rail service to anyone within earshot.

If these negative stress symptoms sound familiar, your life needs a rethink. You need to regain control, know your enemy and identify situations that trigger feelings of powerlessness, panic and anger. If you cannot avoid these stressful situations, make a determined effort to alter how you react to them.

Stress management

Stress management takes time and practice and it starts with the recognition that you are not – nor should you want to be – superwoman. This means:

- Learn to delegate whenever possible and learn how to say 'no'.
- Make more time for yourself and spend it doing things that give you pleasure. Share it with people who make you feel good about yourself and who will listen to your problems without putting you down.

- Take exercise, listen to music, eat a healthy diet and don't try to blot out your unhappiness with drink or drugs.

- Forward planning can also minimize stress. Allow yourself plenty of time to do tasks, because chasing the clock or being late will put you under pressure. Have realistic expectations of what you can achieve in a day. Operate a strict priority system to minimize your load – some things can always wait. Tick-off lists can be helpful and are useful memory aids too.

Over half of all illnesses are now reckoned to be stress-related. If you have tried to make your life more manageable but still feel like running away, quitting your job yet again, hurting yourself, or feel that life is not worth living, see your GP and get professional help.

DEPRESSION

No one feels happy all the time – feeling sad sometimes is quite normal. It's part and parcel of leading a varied life. But you shouldn't feel sad or low most of the time. This is depression.

It can also manifest itself in feelings of emptiness, hopelessness, worthlessness and guilt. You may lose interest in things you once enjoyed, including sex, and your sleep patterns will change. Some people can't sleep, others sleep all the time. You feel perpetually tired, cannot concentrate or make decisions and you may over-eat or starve yourself. Headaches or digestive problems will not go away, despite treatment. At its worst, it can make you feel as if life just isn't worth living any more.

Depression is a genuine mental illness. It's surprisingly common amongst women, who are affected twice as often as men, though some would argue that this is because we're more prepared to admit to how awful we really feel, and that the gap isn't quite as wide as it may seem.

Causes of depression

There is no single cause of depression. Common triggers include an abusive or unhappy childhood, living in a difficult family environment, homelessness, poverty, losing your job, financial problems, divorce, bereavement or chronic illness, hormonal changes, alcohol or drug abuse, or the side effects of medication. The list is, quite literally, endless. However, sometimes there is no obvious cause at all – it just happens. People with seemingly nothing to worry about can, and do, get depressed, sometimes very severely.

Depression can run in families. Although the common assumption is that this is genetic, the sad truth is that many children of depressed parents receive early lessons in negative thinking. Chemical imbalances in the brain certainly affect how we process thoughts and how we feel, and lower levels of both serotonin and noradrenalin can lead to depression.

However, it is hotly debated whether this could be a chicken-and-egg situation. In some people it does seem that what happens in life alters the brain chemistry, but in others it seems that it is a change in brain chemistry that first altered their life. In many, though, which came first – the life pressures or the brain chemistry – is very unclear.

Whatever the cause, being depressed is nothing to be ashamed about – it is every bit as genuine an illness as thyroid problems or pelvic pain. It just happens, and being depressed does not mean you are either inadequate or mad.

Treatments

There are many different types of depression but they can all be treated, usually by a combination of methods, including antidepressants and 'talking therapies'.

Making changes to your lifestyle can help. Exercise, particularly vigorous activities that make you slightly short of breath, can lift your mood. It causes a rush of endorphins, the brain's own natural mood-lifters, and there is good evidence that it can help alleviate depression, both in the short and long term. The right diet can help too. There is evidence that eating a diet high in carbohydrates and low in protein can raise tryptophan levels in the blood, and this in turn can increase levels of serotonin in the brain. Omega 3 fatty acids (found in oily fish) are also thought to be important in helping to combat depression.

Whatever the route, the first step along the road to recovery is to admit you have a problem and to see your GP.

Antidepressants

Somehow antidepressants have become another of those groups of drugs (along with the pill) that people love to hate. But the bottom line is that when they are used appropriately (and that is very important) they really can be very effective, lifting mood, improving quality of life and giving some the will to live life to the full again.

There are two main types of antidepressants prescribed by doctors – selective serotonin uptake inhibitors (SSRIs) and tricyclics.

- **SSRIs**, such as fluoxetine (Prozac) or citalopram, generally work faster than tricyclics, and have fewer side effects, though in the first few days of use they can cause increased anxiety. There have been reports that SSRIs can (very rarely) trigger suicide; the exact reason for this remains unclear, though it may be that in someone who is severely depressed the drug brings a slight improvement in energy levels and so gives them the will to end their life. Whatever the reason, no one should start taking an SSRI without telling someone close to them that they are doing so. SSRIs generally start having an effect within a week, but can take 2 or 3 weeks to reach full effect.

- **Tricyclics**, such as dothiepin and amitriptilene, have a sedative effect, and so are particularly suitable for people who have disturbed sleep. They can also cause a dry mouth and constipation, and taking an overdose is more dangerous than with SSRIs. They also take at least 3 weeks to reach their full antidepressant effect, but some find them better at lifting mood in the long run than SSRIs.

As with so many things, the choice should depend on individual symptoms – there is no 'best' drug. Whatever the choice, the biggest mistake people make with antidepressants is to stop them too soon, the moment they feel better. Instead, they should be continued for at least 3 months after you feel back to normal. However, this doesn't mean that you will need to be on them long term; though some people do need to take antidepressant medication for years, others feel remarkably better and are able to stop treatment after 6 months or so.

Antidepressants are not addictive – there are no cravings to take another dose too soon, or to step up the dose. Neither does your mood drop the moment you stop taking them. However, suddenly stopping them can cause dizziness and 'electric shock' sensations, which tend to be worse with SSRIs. For this reason all antidepressants should be stopped gradually, over a period of a few weeks.

The herbal remedy St John's Wort has been conclusively proven, in good scientific trials, to help combat mild to moderate depression. However, it is important to take the correct dose (300mcg of the active ingredient hypericin daily) for long enough – St John's Wort usually takes at least 2–3 weeks to make a noticeable difference. It can reduce the effectiveness of the pill and can interact with other drugs, particularly other antidepressants. Always check with either your doctor or a qualified pharmacist if you are on other medication or if you have other health problems before starting St John's Wort.

Talking therapies

There is a bewildering array of talking therapists available, and it can be difficult to know which one to choose, particularly when your mind is foggy. Though you can take yourself off to a private therapist without a referral, I think it best, if possible, to get guidance from your doctor on the type of treatment that is most likely to be of benefit to you.

There are two main types – counselling and psychotherapy. Though there is a large overlap between the two, and a lot of counsellors employ some psychotherapy techniques, in very simple terms:

♦ counselling focuses on you talking and thinking your way through a problem

♦ psychotherapy works on a deeper level, helping you to understand your depression better and to alter the way you think and feel

Unfortunately, the NHS lacks the cash to provide enough counsellors to answer all the cries for mental help when people need it – and that's usually immediately. There are long waiting lists for NHS counsellors and treatment can take years. If this is your only option, antidepressants can smooth the ragged edges or see you through a crisis while you wait.

If you can pay for a 'talking cure', your GP will have a list of private, accredited counsellors. You can also contact the Association for Counselling and Psychotherapy to find someone local (see page 449 for details).

Counselling is not a magic bullet. It cannot change the external pressures of your life, but it can alter how you perceive and react to them. A skilled counsellor who employs objectivity, perception and empathy can provide insight into your behaviour and feelings and give you strategies to cope. Instead of being the powerless victim, you will be empowered by choices. Counselling can enable you to think about a problem in a way that has never occurred to you before and this can be wonderfully liberating. Equally important, it gives you the freedom to sound off about anything, slag off anyone or burst into tears in complete confidence and without fear of being judged.

Psychotherapy is often more structured than counselling, and there are lots of different types. Some are based around analysing your past life to help you to understand why you think as you do – psychoanalysis. Others, such as cognitive behaviour therapy (CBT), are based more in the 'here and now' and centre on altering abnormal, dysfunctional thought patterns. Which you choose is a matter of personal preference, but a good psychotherapist should be able to guide you to a form that is most likely to be helpful to you.

Severe depression is usually best treated under the care of a psychiatrist. Treatment usually consists of more powerful combinations of drugs along with analysis, and very rarely ECT (electroconvulsive therapy). There is a crossover between psychiatry and clinical psychology, but whereas a psychiatrist is a trained medical doctor (usually working within the NHS) and can prescribe drugs, a psychologist needs no medical qualification to practise.

ANGER

Anger can vary in intensity from mild irritation to violent rage. Everyone experiences anger sometimes. Of course it's normal to become irritated with family members from time to time, or to get cross and upset in situations that seem unfair or when you feel out of control; it's how you deal with your reactions that is important to your general well-being.

Sometimes both men's and women's moods can be subject to the effects of hormones. Though testosterone can certainly make some men very angry, they don't have the monopoly on being bad-tempered. Women's swinging hormones can certainly make them irrational and give them a short fuse.

But it's unfair on those around you to use hormones as an excuse and, if your anger is out of control and badly affecting your life, you should try to develop more insight into your behaviour by examining how you express yourself when you lose your cool.

How to control your anger

First, learn to recognize the signs that precede 'losing it', and don't let the anger build up. If you can, get away from the situation that is winding you up. Leave the room or invent a phone call or call of nature. It's the old counting-to-ten tactic. Use this 'time out' to take long, deep breaths to give your heartbeat a chance to slow down before you return to the fray.

After the row is over, talk about it with someone you trust and try to assess whether the confrontation has been caused by a misunderstanding or whether your anger is actually due to some issue unrelated to the one that ostensibly caused the row.

If you are already in the throes of a row, try to express your anger calmly and logically. Keep your delivery deliberately slow so that you have time to think before you speak. Consider the endgame: what are you trying to achieve? You may be deeply offended by the criticism being hurled at you, or feel that you are on the receiving end of some major injustice, but do not be side-tracked, and do not react in kind.

Listen to the other person carefully. What is their real motivation? Do they have a hidden agenda? Ask questions to get to the heart of the problem and see if you have some common ground that will allow room for compromise. That way, you can both save face.

If anger is taking over your life, consider making some changes to include activities that are relaxing and make you feel good.

♦ Exercise is a great way to de-stress and release endorphins, the feel-good hormones in the brain.

♦ Yoga and meditation are wonderfully calming.

♦ Painting or writing will give you the freedom of self-expression.

♦ A lot of violent behaviour has its roots in alcohol, so do not exceed your recommended 2–3 units a day.

♦ If you can, cut out the situations in your life that cause you stress or which you know will trigger some form of anxiety.

- ◆ If you feel angry about something, talk it over with a friend instead of letting it fester.

Some people need professional help. You can find this through:

- ◆ Assertiveness training, which will teach you how to express your anger more constructively.
- ◆ Counselling – perhaps through Relate, if your anger is caused by behaviour.
- ◆ Your GP will also be able to put you in touch with an anger-management programme if your temper has spilled over into physical violence.

If you are frightened or on the receiving end of violence and do not want to ring the police, you can phone the Samaritans (0345 90 90 90) for help and advice, day or night.

TIRED ALL THE TIME?

The modern disease. It's normal to feel tired sometimes – that's part and parcel of leading a busy life. But it's not normal to feel tired *all the time.*

You shouldn't feel tired when you wake in the morning, feel drained most of the day, or worn out every evening. And you should have enough energy to enjoy doing a little exercise – going for a walk shouldn't wear you out.

But this is the experience of loads of women. Chronic tiredness can happen at any age, but it seems to be most common in the peri-menopausal years. It's not so bad that it stops you functioning – you can still get to work and get things done in the house – but you just feel weary most of the time.

Why does this happen?

Swinging hormone levels certainly don't help, but they are rarely the main reason. There's usually at least one, or more often several, other contributing factors.

Poor sleeping can of course cause tiredness, but many women who are tired generally sleep quite well. The amount of sleep that people need can vary enormously, and it is true that some women can function very well on 6 hours, whilst others need at least 8. Certainly the first thing to check when you are feeling tired is just how much sleep you are actually getting, and if it averages out at less than 7 hours a night, you'll probably feel a bit better if you get some more.

But what if you are getting plenty of sleep and still feeling whacked out? Causes of tiredness are usually divided into two groups – medical and psychological – but there's a third: lifestyle.

Medical causes of tiredness

The most common medical reason is iron deficiency. Iron is essential for forming haemoglobin, the red pigment that carries oxygen around in the blood. Anaemia certainly causes tiredness, but a lot of women who aren't anaemic still have low levels of iron – their iron stores are drained – and it's now known that this can cause tiredness. It's a situation that usually develops over the years, due to slightly heavy periods and eating little red meat, which is the richest source of iron.

Other possible medical causes of tiredness include an underactive thyroid (see page 265), diabetes (see page 355), and acute infections. A lot of medicines can also cause fatigue – check the package information leaflet.

Psychological causes of tiredness

Psychological reasons for tiredness include depression, anxiety and stress (see pages 230–32). And let's face it, feeling constantly a bit unhappy is enough to make you tired.

Lifestyle

In practice, however, the main reason so many women feel tired all the time is because of their lifestyle. The average twenty-first-century woman is constantly trying to do too much, all the time, and it can just drain you. Some of the problems women can face are:

♦ running a home while doing paid work

♦ caring for young children or elderly parents

♦ getting no time to relax

♦ long-term dieting or just eating an unbalanced diet, and a little too much alcohol

♦ lack of exercise

What to do

Any woman who is feeling tired should see her doctor and get tests done to rule out an underlying medical problem. These should include:

- a full blood count, which will reveal anaemia
- an iron level
- a blood glucose level (for diabetes)
- thyroid hormone levels
- if your periods are becoming erratic it may also be helpful to have your FSH level (follicle stimulating hormone) checked as well

A good doctor will also want to discuss your mood. You may already have decided that you are feeling a bit low, or are unduly anxious, but sometimes it takes a medical professional to spot an underlying psychological problem. Treatment with counselling, antidepressants or both can be very helpful, and can gradually improve energy levels.

If you have neither a medical nor a psychological problem, then you need to take a critical look at your lifestyle, and try to make some changes.

- First, check what you eat. Don't skip breakfast, or any other meal – you may think it is the answer to preserving your waistline, but your body needs food! Aim to eat a low GI diet (see page 224), with foods that give you sustainable energy, and plenty of fresh fruit and veg. Stop for lunch – don't snack on the go.
- Check your alcohol intake. You'll feel a lot more energetic if you stick to under 14 units a week and have a couple of days when you go without alcohol altogether.
- Increase your activity levels – try to do something active every day, and do some vigorous exercise at least twice a week.
- Try to stop doing quite so much, and stop feeling you have to be at everyone else's beck and call. Learn to delegate, so the family helps you out, don't always feel obliged to answer the telephone the moment it rings, and prioritize tasks.

- ◆ Get to bed at a reasonable time, and avoid building up a sleep deficit. If you have a late night, try to go to bed a bit earlier the next night.

- ◆ Make sure you have at least half an hour of relaxation time every day. Far too many women feel guilty when they stop, but honest, it is OK to sit and just read a book or watch your favourite TV programme and do nothing else, just for a while.

HORMONAL HAVOC – PERIODS AND PERIOD PROBLEMS

This is where the peri-menopause becomes a bit of a nuisance. Don't women have enough to cope with, without constantly wondering when the next period will occur, how long it will last, and how annoying the associated symptoms will be?

SIGNS OF CHANGE

The first sign that something is changing is that the menstrual cycle shortens, with periods occurring every 26 days, instead of 28. This commonly occurs in a woman's early forties, but it does not mean the menopause is imminent. This pattern often continues for many years. Neither is it a sign of infertility – many women with these shorter cycles in their forties can, and do, conceive. So unless you want an addition to the family, you've still got to be careful about using contraception. All that's happening is that ovulation is occurring earlier, after 12 days instead of 14. No one knows why this happens, only that it is often an indicator that the menopause is on its way.

Another reason for changing menstrual cycles is that, with passing time, the ovaries gradually become less responsive to FSH (follicle stimulating hormone), and as a result it can take longer for the egg to ripen. It may take 3 weeks, maybe 4 weeks, maybe 3 months. Overall, though, this results in a longer gap between periods. Sometimes the egg is released at the normal time, but the post-ovulatory phase shortens and a period occurs 10 or so days later, instead of 14, resulting in a shorter gap between periods.

Then there is a third possibility. Sometimes no egg is released at all – an 'anovulatory cycle'. When this happens, the oestrogen produced by the ovaries continues to stimulate the womb lining, but there is no balance from progesterone. Instead, the womb lining builds up until it becomes destabilized, and then it breaks down. Timing? Sometimes 2 weeks after the last period, sometimes 3, sometimes a bit longer. The result though is usually a very heavy period, at an unpredictable time, and often with large clots. Not fun.

In ovulatory cycles (when an egg is released) a woman may have some idea of when she is going to have a period because she still gets symptoms of PMS – just at a different time. And the changing levels of oestrogen and progesterone may mean the PMS is worse than usual (see page 258). But with anovulatory cycles, the lack of progesterone can have slightly different effects on the rest of the body.

Progesterone acts as a balance to oestrogen and, in its absence, oestrogen can lead to bloating and tender breasts. It may also contribute to the mood swings, sleep disturbances, tiredness, forgetfulness and increased anxiety that many women experience at this time.

But it's not just the lack of progesterone that can cause problems. The ovaries 'wind down' in a very erratic fashion. Some days they produce a lot of oestrogen, some days they produce hardly any at all. No wonder you can feel on top of the world one day and want to murder the cat (and your partner, and your boss) the next.

How long all this goes on can vary enormously between different women. Some women feel that they are peri-menopausal for years, others for just a few months. The average age of onset of the peri-menopause in the UK is 47½, but it can be much sooner or later than this.

Tests and treatment

The best way to tell what is going on is to check the level of FSH (follicle stimulating hormone). As the ovaries become less responsive, FSH levels rise. It's the body's way of trying to maintain the status quo. Unfortunately though, during the peri-menopause the levels of FSH can vary quite a lot from day to day, as sometimes the ovaries respond to it (so the levels go down) and sometimes they don't (so the levels go up). So one measurement alone isn't terribly helpful – 2 or 3 are needed on separate days really to establish what is going on.

Levels of under 12 suggest that the ovaries are still working well – you are not peri-menopausal. Levels above 50 suggest the ovaries have run out of steam – you're menopausal, and hardly producing any oestrogen at all. In between these two – you're peri-menopausal. The higher the level, the closer you are to the menopause.

Measuring oestrogen levels (which might seem the obvious thing to do) isn't helpful because they vary even more than FSH. What you need to do – if anything – depends on your symptoms.

ERRATIC PERIODS

Erratic periods can be a real nuisance, but they aren't dangerous – 'toxins' don't build up in the womb lining, and there is no biological need to have a period once a month. Having less frequent periods can have the advantage that you are less likely to become iron deficient, but of course the opposite is true if you have periods every 2–3 weeks, and you should watch your iron levels.

Why is this happening?

Erratic periods are a sign of hormone disarray – the cyclical rise and fall of oestrogen and progesterone on a monthly basis just isn't happening. There are times when this is quite normal, and can be expected – for instance, when the ovaries are just getting going in the early teens, and when you are weaning a baby (when varying levels of the hormone prolactin interfere with ovarian function). Erratic periods are to be expected in the years approaching the menopause, and are also very common in women using progesterone-based contraceptives (except the Mirena device; see pages 164 and 167).

Erratic periods at other times can be a sign of PCOS (see page 186) and, less commonly, of other hormone disorders, such as thyroid problems (see page 264) or high prolactin levels. They can occur in women who are underweight or very overweight, or who take a lot of exercise. Stress can also upset your hormone balance and send your cycle completely out of kilter.

Treatment

Any underlying cause should be treated, but if it turns out that the ovaries simply aren't working quite as they should be, one option is to do nothing – remember there is no biological necessity to have a period once a month. However, if you want some predictability in your menstrual life, there are several options that you can discuss with your doctor:

♦ **Drug treatment**: though one obvious answer is to take drugs that can get the cycle going and stimulate ovulation, such as clomiphene, because of potential side effects these are used only in women who are trying to conceive. In others, there is no need to ovulate. You can control the cycle more safely in other ways.

♦ **Contraceptive pill**: the combined pill produces a very regular cycle, and is especially good if you want contraception as well. It's not only suitable for younger women – in most women it can be taken right up to the menopause, and it can be a great way to iron out the other problems that widely fluctuating hormone levels can cause in the mid to late forties.

♦ **Progesterone**: for peri-menopausal women, boosting up progesterone levels for 2 weeks each month can be helpful in regulating an erratic cycle. Natural progesterone can't be taken by mouth (it is broken down in the stomach) but it can be administered via suppositories placed in either the vagina or the rectum. Alternatively, synthetic progestogen tablets can be taken by mouth. A natural progesterone cream is available on private prescription, but it is very expensive and the amount that is absorbed can be variable.

♦ **HRT**: the right combination of HRT (see page 300) can also help to regulate periods in peri-menopausal women. However, the dose of hormones it contains is quite low and 'breakthrough bleeding' – having periods at the wrong time – can be quite common. So it's not often used purely for cycle control.

Natural remedies

Several natural remedies are available from chemists or health-food shops.

♦ **Phyto-oestrogens**: these are chemicals from plants that have a weak oestrogen-like action, and are often marketed for peri-menopausal women. So are black cohosh and dong quai, which again are thought to be weakly oestrogenic. Most period problems in peri-menopausal women are caused by unopposed oestrogen – oestrogen not being balanced by progesterone. That means that taking these products, if anything, will make a tendency to heavy or erratic periods worse. If you are still making oestrogen, then you don't need any more.

♦ **Wild yam**: this is a bit different. A lot of synthetic hormones are made from wild yam root, including progesterone. But you can't take natural progesterone by mouth because it is broken down by the stomach, so I'm not sure how much of the hormones in wild yam (if any) are actually absorbed into the bloodstream.

Sorry to sound sceptical here. Natural remedies can sometimes take the edge off menopausal symptoms, and can be useful for PMS, but I honestly don't think they can do much for the menstrual chaos that can occur in the peri-menopause.

BLEEDING BETWEEN PERIODS

The only time that vaginal bleeding should occur is during a period. Bleeding at other times is not normal, though it is quite common when first starting the combined pill, especially with low-dose brands. It can also be due to a cervical erosion (see page 104), particularly after sex – not dangerous, but a nuisance. But it can be due to a polyp in the womb lining or PID (see page 105). And much more rarely, it can be due to cancer of the cervix or womb. So don't ignore it. See your doctor and get it checked out.

HEAVY PERIODS

It can be difficult to know if you are really having heavy periods – what seems heavy for one woman may be normal for another. But as a general rule, if you need to change a super tampon or towel at least once every two hours, if you have to wear two pads at once, or if you pass several clots larger than a 50p piece, then your periods are heavier than normal. This also applies if your periods last more than a week, with heavy flow for more than 4 days.

Although they may seem nothing more than a nuisance, heavy periods shouldn't be ignored. Apart from the cost of buying all that sanitary protection, repeated heavy periods can drain a woman's iron stores and are a very common cause of anaemia. They can also be an indicator of an underlying gynaecological problem.

Why is this happening?

The womb does tend to get slightly larger with increasing age, particularly after having a baby, and this means that periods do tend to become a bit heavier, especially during the thirties and forties. Fibroids that distort the womb lining (see page 257) can also increase menstrual blood flow.

Heavy periods can be a sign of a pelvic infection, though in this case there are usually other symptoms, such as bleeding between periods or after sex. Less commonly they can be due to a polyp. These are small benign outgrowths, usually around the size of a small grape, which grow out from the womb lining.

However, in many women there is no clearly identifiable cause for heavy periods. Gynaecologists call it 'dysfunctional uterine bleeding', and it is probably due to changes in the balance between the levels of oestrogen and progesterone. Though cancer of the womb can cause heavy periods, there are usually other symptoms as well, especially spotting in between periods.

Tests

All women with heavy periods should have a pelvic examination to check for a possible underlying cause, and usually a pelvic ultrasound scan. Blood tests should also be done to check for iron levels and anaemia.

Treatment

This depends to a large extent on the underlying cause. Here are some of the options you may wish to discuss with your doctor.

For straightforward heavy bleeding, taking anti-prostaglandin tablets, such as ibuprofen or mefenamic acid, can help a little. For best effect they should be started 2 days before the period is due and taken regularly while the heavy bleeding persists.

Tranexamic acid (available on prescription) can also be helpful – it works by closing down tiny bleeding blood vessels in the womb lining. This only needs to be taken for the duration of heavy bleeding.

Taking the combined contraceptive pill can dramatically reduce menstrual blood flow, or alternatively a Mirena IUS can be inserted (see page 167). The progesterone this releases thins the womb lining and leads to dramatic reduction in monthly bleeding.

Frequent, heavy periods can be due to anovulatory cycles (see page 245), where oestrogen is acting alone on the womb lining. Taking a synthetic progesterone for 2 weeks each month can help to regulate periods (so that they occur only once a month), but unfortunately does little to reduce the blood flow.

Surgery is only ever an option for those women who continue to have heavy periods despite trying all possible medical treatments. In the past, a D and C (dilation and curettage) or 'scrape' was often performed, where the upper layer of the lining was removed. It's now obsolete, for the simple reason that it just doesn't work for more than a month or two. However, the newer version of D and C, a hysteroscopy, is sometimes performed. Under anaesthetic, a tiny camera is passed up inside the womb, allowing the gynaecologist to view the womb cavity directly. It's more accurate than a D and C, and means that tiny polyps, which otherwise might have been missed, can be removed.

If heavy periods are due to fibroids, then it is sometimes possible to remove these – a myomectomy operation.

In cases where there is no obvious cause for heavy periods, one possible treatment is to burn away most of the womb lining, using either microwaves or a fluid-filled thermal balloon. The operation, known as endometrial ablation, is performed under either local or general anaesthetic on a day-case basis. It's effective in 80 per cent of women, most of whom report that their periods return to normal – in other words, they are not heavy any more. But it doesn't work on everyone – in some, periods stay the same, and others find their heavy periods return within a few months. Around 10 per cent of women who have an endometrial ablation end up having a hysterectomy (see below). It's also unsuitable for women who may want a family at a later date, as the thinner womb lining will not be able to support and nourish a growing baby. However, the operation itself doesn't stop you conceiving, so you still need to use some sort of contraceptive afterwards.

The final treatment option for heavy periods is to have a hysterectomy. Though this may sound drastic, if you have found yourself organizing your diary around when you are likely to be bleeding, it can give you a completely new lease of life.

HYSTERECTOMY

It's understandable that many women balk at the idea of losing their womb. It is, after all, the place where an unborn baby grows, and for many it represents the very core of their femininity. Even if your family is complete, or you are not keen on the idea of having a child, there is a world of difference between not wanting children and being physically unable to have a child. That said, though, a woman's uterus can cause her a lot of problems – heavy bleeding, pelvic discomfort or pain and urinary disorders, especially stress incontinence (see page 381). There are thousands of women who will testify that having a troublesome womb removed is the best thing they ever did.

Despite women's emotional attachment to their wombs, the womb actually has only one biological function, and that's to incubate babies. It doesn't produce any hormones, and though the lining is shed once a month, that's only a response to the lack of a pregnancy. So removing the womb alone has only two consequences – you don't have periods any more, and you can't bear a child. There is no change to your hormone levels, so you don't suddenly become menopausal, and there is no reason suddenly to pile on weight.

However, the continued cyclical secretion of hormones from the ovaries can mean that you still get PMS, even though you don't have any periods. Your sex life should not be affected, as the vagina stays the same – in fact, many women find their sex life improves, because they no longer suffer from heavy periods, or pelvic pain, which previously interfered with lovemaking.

Things are a little different if the ovaries are removed as well, which is sometimes necessary. This can result in a sudden fall in hormone levels, and plunge a woman into an abrupt menopause (but only if the ovaries were working beforehand; if you are post-menopausal your ovaries have stopped working, so removing them doesn't make much difference).

There are three main types of hysterectomy:

Abdominal hysterectomy. This involves removing the womb through a cut in the lower tummy wall, usually across the top of the pubic hairline, but occasionally a vertical cut may be required straight down the middle of the lower tummy, below the tummy button. The stay in hospital is usually about 5–7 days.

Vaginal hysterectomy. This involves removing the womb through a cut in the top of the vagina. It involves carefully cutting and tying the ligaments to the womb – it's not done by suction. A vaginal hysterectomy has the advantage of not leaving any visible scars, and recovery afterwards is often much quicker. However, it's not suitable for all women: wombs enlarged by fibroids can't usually be removed this way. A 3–4-day stay in hospital is normally required.

Laparoscopic hysterectomy. Increasing numbers of hysterectomies are now being performed via keyhole surgery. This is done via three small incisions in the tummy wall. It usually only involves a 2-day hospital stay, and there is less pain afterwards, so the overall recovery time is much shorter. However, as with any keyhole surgery, it is important that it is performed by a surgeon skilled in the method to avoid possible complications, such as accidental damage to the bowel or bladder.

Why me?

Having a hysterectomy does mean saying a final goodbye to your chance of having children, so, unless you are well past wanting babies, this is a major decision that should be considered very carefully, without rushing. It's not something that can be put to rights later.

A hysterectomy is usually offered by gynaecologists only when all other treatments have failed, or when there really is no other option. It is done for:

- ◆ heavy or painful periods
- ◆ chronic PID, which is causing severe pain (see page 105)
- ◆ severe endometriosis (see page 181)
- ◆ large fibroids (see page 257)
- ◆ lax womb ligaments leading to prolapse
- ◆ and, less commonly, for cancers of the pelvic organs – the cervix, womb, fallopian tube or ovaries

Afterwards

You do need time to rest after a hysterectomy, and most women need at least a month off work. You should not drive until you can do an emergency stop without pain or discomfort, which usually takes a couple of weeks. You should not have sex until the top of the vagina has healed, which usually takes about a month. Younger women, under 45, who also have their ovaries removed should be offered HRT (see page 300), not only to stop sudden menopausal symptoms, but also to help prevent osteoporosis (see page 307). Whether to take it or not should be a personal decision based on personal circumstances – you don't have to if you don't want to.

The cervix is nearly always removed along with the rest of the womb, so there is no need to have smear tests any more after the operation. The exception to this is women who have had a hysterectomy for cervical cancer, or who had an abnormal smear in the 3 years before the operation. These women should continue to have smears taken from the top of the vagina – a 'vault smear' – at time intervals recommended by their doctor.

FIBROIDS

These are balls of muscle and fibrous tissue that develop in the wall of the womb. They are usually quite small, often only the size of a pea, but they can grow very large, to the size of a grapefruit. There may be just one, or several.

Fibroids are common – at least 20 per cent of women over 30 have at least one, but many are unaware of them. They are much more common in Afro-Caribbean women. No one knows why some women get them and others don't, but they do grow in response to oestrogen. This means that they often develop during pregnancy, when oestrogen levels are high, and they shrink after the menopause, when oestrogen levels fall.

Fibroids are not dangerous – they never turn cancerous – but they can cause problems. If they distort the lining of the womb they can cause heavy and more painful periods, and occasionally recurrent miscarriages. However, fibroids do not affect your cycle – how often you have periods – and neither should they cause a vaginal discharge or severe pelvic pain. They can cause pelvic discomfort though, or cause a bulge in your lower tummy, making you look as if you are in the early stages of pregnancy. Large fibroids can also press on the bladder, making you feel you need to pee more frequently.

Diagnosis and treatment

Depending on their size, fibroids can be felt during either an abdominal or a pelvic examination. The diagnosis can be confirmed by an ultrasound scan. Treatment of fibroids isn't easy. Those that aren't causing any troublesome symptoms can be safely left alone.

If they are causing heavy periods, then treatment for this may be helpful (see page 251).

The best way to shrink fibroids is with drugs known as GnRH analogues, such as Zoladex. These work by switching off production of FSH by the pituitary gland. This in turn means that the ovaries no longer produce oestrogen, and so the fibroids shrink.

Unfortunately, the lack of oestrogen can also lead to menopausal symptoms, particularly hot flushes and sweats, and can also increase the risk of osteoporosis, so treatment for more than 6 months is usually not recommended. GnRH analogues can't be given by mouth – they have to be given by injection, usually once a month.

It is possible to remove large fibroids surgically, shelling them out of the wall of the uterus. This is often the best option for women who want to retain their fertility, but the operation can be technically difficult. The most common operation is to remove the whole womb – a hysterectomy (see page 253).

Uterine artery embolization is a relatively new treatment for large fibroids. It involves blocking the blood supply to the fibroid with a chemical that's injected into the uterine arteries. As a result the fibroids shrink. The long-term safety and effectiveness of this technique are still being evaluated, and as yet it's not widely available on the NHS.

PRE-MENSTRUAL SYNDROME

It's rare to find a woman who says she has never suffered from PMS. Sometimes it starts in the teenage years; other women find it becomes noticeable after the birth of their first child. But the time it can become really severe is when the hormones are fluctuating in the peri-menopausal years.

Symptoms

There are more than 150 identified symptoms of PMS. The most common are:

- mood swings
- aggression
- tearfulness
- pelvic pain
- fluid retention
- muscle cramps
- food craving

- going off sex
- bloating
- weight gain
- painful breasts
- headaches
- sleep disruption

Symptoms may vary from month to month and can be aggravated by stress or illness.

Severe emotional changes such as depression, irritability or anxiety have been labelled by some as pre-menstrual dysphoric disorder, but my view is that this is just a more severe form of PMS – it's not a separate illness.

Why me?

You can blame many of these physical and mental symptoms on your changing hormone levels. After ovulation, during the last 2 weeks of your cycle, progesterone levels should be twenty times higher than oestrogen. But commonly, at this time in the cycle the gap between the two hormones either narrows or widens, throwing your body out of kilter.

Progesterone stimulates normal sex drive, relaxes the muscles of the uterus and is a natural antidepressant. It also acts as a brake on another hormone called aldosterone, which causes water retention. In PMS, though, an imbalance between oestrogen and progesterone means that either you don't get enough progesterone, or its actions are wiped out by too much oestrogen.

If you are still having periods but experiencing new or changing PMS symptoms, keep a 'mood diary' to see if there is a correlation between your emotions and the time of the month. This is very important. PMS occurs only in the 2 weeks leading up to a period, and in some women for a couple of days around ovulation (when hormone levels are changing rapidly). If you have symptoms at other times as well, then the chances are PMS alone isn't to blame for how you feel.

It is apparent that many women with mild depression or chronic anxiety feel worse before their period, and somehow blaming everything on PMS is more socially acceptable than admitting there is something else going on. But if you want to feel better, you must be honest with yourself and with those trying to help you, and PMS remedies alone are unlikely to be the answer.

Diet

In managing PMS, first of all, check your diet. Tiredness, tension and mood swings can all be eased by stabilizing your blood-sugar level. That means eating regularly, every 3 hours, and concentrating on carbohydrates that will give you sustained energy, such as wholemeal bread, pasta and cereals. Much as you may crave chocolate or something sweet, it will only give you a high, then a plunging low sugar level – not good. Don't skip meals.

If you are prone to bloating, cut down on salt, especially in the 2 weeks before your period.

Caffeine, particularly in large amounts, can make you irritable and can make tension and anxiety worse – and it can stop you sleeping. Cut it down, but do so slowly to avoid thumping caffeine-withdrawal headaches.

Exercise

Exercise has now been proven scientifically to reduce PMS, and to be more effective than hormone remedies. Even if you feel tired, do something active, every day if possible, in the run-up to your period. If you can manage to do half an hour's exercise that makes you short of breath, chances are you really will feel less moody.

Avoiding stress and tiredness

If possible, avoid getting over-tired – it can give you a short fuse on its own. Adding in unfriendly hormones is a recipe for rows at home or at work.

Alternative remedies

There are several supplements that may alleviate PMS symptoms. Though good scientific evidence to support their medicinal claims is scant, many women have found them helpful; as long as you can afford them, they may be worth a try.

Don't give up on one of these because it doesn't work instantly – give it a 3-month trial. It's very much horses for courses. Something may work wonders for one person and do nothing for another.

Here are some of the most common pre-menstrual allies:

♦ **Evening primrose oil** contains gamma linoleic acid (GLA) and is often recommended for abdominal swelling and breast discomfort. The suggested dose is 1,000mg a day throughout your cycle. However, its official licence for treating tender breasts was withdrawn because of lack of evidence. Some women do find it helpful, but if anything, starflower oil is likely to be more effective, as it contains twice the level of GLA as evening primrose oil.

♦ **Agnus castus** has been used for centuries to balance female hormones, and there is some good research showing that in some women it can alleviate breast tenderness, bloating, anxiety and fatigue.

♦ **Wild yam** contains both natural plant oestrogens and phytoprogesterone, a natural form of the hormone progesterone. Taking it during the second half of the menstrual cycle may be helpful. (See also page 249.)

♦ **Dong quai** (Chinese angelica root) also has natural oestrogen properties and so may help to balance hormone levels. But beware if your periods are heavy – it could make them worse.

♦ **Vitamin B complex** (particularly with added magnesium and chromium) has been claimed to relieve sugar cravings, irritability and bloating. Vitamin B6 is particularly popular, but don't exceed the dose because it could damage the nervous system. Try taking 100–400mg of vitamin B6 daily, beginning 10 days before your period is due. Don't take it all the time.

♦ **Magnesium and calcium** supplements have also been found by some women to relieve severe pre-menstrual symptoms, and you may benefit from a small supplement of these.

♦ **Herbal teas** – camomile, as well as slightly stronger natural diuretics such as dandelion and juniper – can work gently to reduce pre-menstrual water retention. Drink these teas 2–3 times a day in the week or fortnight before your period.

Help from your doctor

There are various drugs that can be prescribed by your GP and that may help to alleviate the symptoms of PMS.

♦ **Hormone supplements.** On the basis that PMS is due to a hormone imbalance, progesterone supplements used to be a very popular remedy, and on the same basis some doctors prescribed oestrogen. Sadly, there is no good evidence that either of these work and they are no longer recommended.

♦ **The combined contraceptive pill.** What can help is switching off the menstrual cycle and so stopping the fluctuating hormone levels that cause PMS. The easiest way of doing this is the combined contraceptive pill – lower-dose formulations are particularly suitable for women in their forties.

♦ **GnRH analogues** (see page 258). These stop the ovaries working and create a temporary menopause, but this is so drastic that they are used only for women with very severe symptoms.

♦ **Danazol and bromocriptine.** Other ways of reducing fluctuating hormones include low doses of these two drugs, which are both particularly good for cyclical breast tenderness.

♦ **Diuretics.** These increase urine production and can help to ease bloating. They should only be used, however, for a few days each month, not all the time, as they can cause an imbalance in salt and potassium levels and can cause thirst, especially in the summer months.

♦ **SSRI antidepressants** (see page 235). These have also been shown to be effective in PMS. This may mean that many PMS sufferers actually have depression, but the fact is, they work. Many women are reluctant to take them, but if your life (and that of your family) is wretched half the time, then I think they are worth a try. They are not addictive, and only low doses are required, so there should be no problem stopping them when you feel better.

PHYSICAL ILLNESSES

Auto-immune disorders. This is the time of life when a rather strange group of illnesses becomes more common. We all have an immune system that is designed to attack invading bugs and prevent infection. But sometimes the immune system starts attacking the body's own healthy organs, leading to illnesses known as 'auto-immune disorders'.

Though they can occur in both sexes, these disorders are more common in women. Quite why the female immune system should behave in this way is a mystery, but genes are certainly involved as many of these illnesses have a strong tendency to run in families. They include thyroid disorders, rheumatoid arthritis and less common disorders such as lupus. For more about these, see below.

Headaches. Increased stress, combined with hormonal havoc, can also make headaches a particular problem in the peri-menopausal years.

Breast disease. Breast problems can also occur, and though at this age benign breast disease is more common, the risk of breast cancer is beginning to increase.

THYROID PROBLEMS

The thyroid is a small gland that sits in front of the windpipe in the neck. Its function is to produce two hormones, thyroxine (T4) and tri-iodothyronine (T3), both of which have a powerful effect on the body's metabolism. They also have effects on growth and mental development.

Activity of the thyroid gland is strongly influenced by the thyroid stimulating hormone (TSH), which is produced by the pituitary gland in the base of the brain.

Why is this happening?

Thyroid problems are ten times more common in women than men, and have a tendency to run in families. While they can start in young women, the most common time for them to appear is in middle age.

Many thyroid problems are auto-immune – which means they are due to a defect in the body's immune system which normally develops antibodies against thyroid tissue. Those with other forms of auto-immune disease in the family, such as some types of diabetes or arthritis, are more at risk of auto-immune thyroid disorders.

HYPOTHYROIDISM (MYXOEDEMA): UNDERACTIVE THYROID

When the thyroid gland is underactive, it produces less thyroid hormone than normal. This can slow the metabolism. It is an often-quoted cause of weight gain, but in practice this is only a minor symptom – many women with an underactive thyroid don't notice much change in their weight, and most women with weight problems don't have an underactive thyroid.

But those who do have an underactive thyroid may notice the following symptoms:

- ◆ they feel tired and really sluggish, and often depressed as well
- ◆ their skin and hair feel dry and out of condition
- ◆ constipation
- ◆ feeling cold all the time
- ◆ periods may become heavy and erratic

Left untreated, hypothyroidism can cause an increase in LDL cholesterol (see page 351) and so increase the risk of heart disease and stroke. In severe cases, it can also cause quite marked changes in personality – so-called myxoedema madness. This is thankfully quite rare.

Why is this happening?

Hypothyroidism may be due to the thyroid gland simply running out of steam (which is more common in older women) or to thyroid antibodies. More rarely, it may be due to a lack of iodine in the diet, as iodine is required for thyroid hormone production.

Diagnosis and treatment

Hypothyroidism is diagnosed by a blood test that checks the levels of thyroid hormone. In those under the age of 60, most doctors also check for thyroid auto-antibodies (which can mean the problem is more likely to run in the family).

Treatment is with replacement thyroid hormone, thyroxine tablets, usually for life. The usual practice is to start with a fairly low dose and then monitor it with blood tests until an ideal level in the blood is reached. This should be checked on an annual basis.

HYPERTHYROIDISM: OVERACTIVE THYROID

This is when the thyroid produces too much thyroxine. The symptoms most women notice are:

- ◆ they are a little trembly, restless and find it difficult to keep still
- ◆ palpitations on slight exertion are also quite common
- ◆ the increased metabolic rate the hormone causes leads to excess sweating, feeling hot (even when the ambient temperature is cool)
- ◆ it also leads to slight weight loss despite a good appetite – though as with an underactive thyroid, many women don't notice a dramatic change in their weight

Why is this happening?

Most cases are caused by auto-antibodies, which stimulate the gland to produce excess amounts of hormone. In some cases, the antibodies eventually damage the glandular tissue, leading to hypothyroidism (see above).

The auto-antibodies associated with hyperthyroidism may also cause swelling of the tissues behind the eyes, making them protrude, with an unusual amount of white visible – a classic sign of thyroid disease.

Occasionally, hyperthyroidism is due to a small localized area of the thyroid gland that just goes out of control.

Diagnosis and treatment

Diagnosis is by blood tests, which can reveal not only excessive amounts of thyroid hormone, but often very high levels of thyroid auto-antibodies as well. Special scanning, using radioactive isotopes, can help to reveal whether there is a localized overactive area.

The drug carbimazole can block the production of thyroid hormone, and this may be the only treatment that's required, along with regular blood tests to monitor thyroid hormone levels. Beta-blocking drugs, such as propranol, can help to stop unpleasant tremors and palpitations. Occasionally it may be necessary surgically to remove a small overactive part of the gland or, less commonly, to remove the whole gland. If this is done, then replacement thyroxine should be given to prevent hypothyroidism.

RHEUMATOID ARTHRITIS AND OTHER AUTO-IMMUNE DISORDERS

I suspect that most women consider arthritis to be a problem of the elderly, and to a large extent it is. Osteoarthritis, the 'wear and tear' arthritis, becomes much more common with increasing age (see page 421).

Rheumatoid arthritis (RA), though, is a very different type of arthritis. It can strike at any age, and symptoms often start in the early forties. It can occur in both sexes, but it is three times more common in women.

Why is this happening?

Rheumatoid arthritis is an auto-immune disease – it's caused by the body's own immune system attacking the lining of joints. This makes them inflamed, swollen, stiff and painful.

As with so many diseases, the exact cause is not known. It can run in families, though most relatives of people with RA do not get it themselves and genes are only part of the story.

There is some evidence that lifestyle factors may be relevant – RA is more common in people who smoke and eat a lot of red meat, and slightly less common in people who have a high intake of vitamin C or who drink alcohol in moderation. But in the majority of people, there is no identifiable cause.

Tell-tale signs

Rheumatoid arthritis can affect any joint in the body, but often targets the shoulders, wrists, fingers and neck joints. It may start slowly, with just a bit of aching and stiffness, and some women have symptoms for months before they seek medical help. Often it's the other symptoms – tiredness, depression and irritability – that prompt a visit to the surgery. In a few people, though, the disease develops rapidly, with sudden onset of severe pain and swelling of affected joints.

As inflammation continues, joints become more stiff and swollen, and increasingly painful. The course of the disease can vary enormously in different people – in some it stays mild, whilst in others it becomes progressively worse, and severe inflammation leads to destruction of the joint tissues, with the result that joints become deformed.

RA doesn't just affect joints, though. The auto-immune process can affect the eyes, causing dryness, the lungs and, rarely, the tissues around the heart.

Tests and treatment

A diagnosis of rheumatoid arthritis is usually made by a combination of assessing the symptoms and blood tests for inflammatory markers –

ESR (erythrocyte sedimentation rate) and C reactive protein.

Rheumatoid factor is a protein produced by the abnormal immune reaction, and a test for this is positive in 80 per cent of people with RA. In the early stages X-rays look normal, but later on they can reveal characteristic changes in joint structure.

Early treatment is very important, as it can help stop permanent damage to joints. Anti-inflammatory drugs are used for very mild cases, but increasingly doctors use stronger agents that help to dampen down the abnormal immune reaction, including gold injections, steroids and methotrexate. More recently, newer drugs that act more specifically on the inflammatory process, known as anti-TNF agents, have been introduced.

Staying as active as possible is also important, both to prevent stiffness and to keep the muscles strong that help to support and strengthen joints. However, it's vital to get the balance right, as doing too much and putting affected joints under strain can make the inflammation worse.

See also 'Diet and arthritis', page 354.

Alternative therapies

♦ Cod liver oil, evening primrose oil and vitamin C supplements have been reported to help some patients with RA.

♦ Acupuncture may also be beneficial (and is available on the NHS in some areas).

♦ Homeopathy has also been used by some, but there is no good evidence that it works for RA.

♦ Some supplements, herbs or Chinese medicines promoted for RA may interfere with conventional drugs, so check with your doctor before taking them.

LUPUS

Very few people have heard of lupus, yet it's more common than leukaemia. It affects over 30,000 people in the UK, 80 per cent of them women. It is more common in Afro-Caribbean and Asian women, and in those from the Far East.

Otherwise known as systemic lupus erythematosis (SLE), this is another auto-immune disorder where the immune system attacks the body's own tissues, including the joints, causing pain and stiffness, and the skin, causing a rash on the cheeks. It can also cause kidney problems, flu-like symptoms and inflammation of the tissues covering internal organs, including the heart. It is also associated with an increased risk of miscarriage.

The symptoms can vary enormously between different people. It may be triggered by changes in hormone levels, or by a viral infection, but often there is no obvious cause.

The diagnosis is usually made by a combination of characteristic symptoms and blood tests which show raised levels of particular auto-antibodies, specifically anti-nuclear antibodies and those against double-stranded DNA.

There is no cure for lupus, but symptoms can usually be controlled by steroids and immunosuppressant drugs, which are best prescribed by a specialist (usually a rheumatologist) with expertise in the disease.

HEADACHES

Headaches have to be one of the most common health problems in women. Like many other ailments, they can occur at any age, but they often become more noticeable in the reproductive and peri-menopausal years.

Again, like so many other female ailments, our hormones can be partly to blame. The brain has receptors for both oestrogen and progesterone, and changing hormone levels can contribute to headache directly this way. Hormones can also have a powerful influence on the other factors that can cause headaches, especially stress and tension.

Tension headache

Tension headache – and yes, that is actually what medics call it – is caused by slight tightening of the muscles of the scalp, but the pain is often felt across or behind the eyes, across the forehead or right inside the skull. These headaches are commonly caused by stress, anxiety or tiredness, and are often linked with a slightly stiff, tender neck, which on its own can be a sign of anxiety and stress. Tension headaches may last only a few hours, and in some women occur only when there is an obvious cause. But in other women they become a chronic problem that starts on waking and lasts right through the day with increasing severity.

Analgesic abuse headache

Tension headache can lead to another common cause of headache – analgesic abuse headache. 'Abuse' here doesn't mean addiction; it just means taking too many ordinary painkillers, often paracetamol or ibuprofen, on a regular basis. The brain gets used to them and doesn't like it when it has to do without.

Other causes of headache

Headaches can also be due to any of the following:

♦ hunger and dehydration (particularly when it's caused by an excess of alcohol)

♦ any acute illness – most people with flu have a thumping headache

♦ a sudden drop in caffeine intake

♦ food intolerance

♦ sinusitis can cause a throbbing pain in the front of the head that gets worse when you bend down

♦ a headache that starts behind the eyes, then extends over the head, can be a sign of eye strain, and a need for glasses

♦ occasionally, headaches can be due to high blood pressure

♦ more commonly, they can be due to a reaction to medicines. If you are taking any tablets and start getting headaches, check the information leaflet inside the packet, or see your doctor or pharmacist.

Is it dangerous?

A headache on its own is rarely the sign of anything serious. It is true that occasionally a headache is a symptom of meningitis, or a brain haemorrhage or tumour, but in these cases either the headache is very severe or there are other symptoms, such as vomiting, dizziness or feeling disoriented. That means, though, that if you suddenly develop a really severe headache, or start getting frequent headaches for no apparent cause, or if you are concerned, you should see your doctor for a check-up.

Self-help

Though it may be tempting automatically to reach for a painkiller when you have a headache, it's always worth having a large glass of water and something to eat first. Then try to relax, and, even if you are at work, take your eyes away from any form of screen for at least 15 minutes. If you are at home, a relaxing bath with some lavender oil, or a shoulder and neck massage, can be more effective than taking pills. For a headache caused by a cold or blocked sinuses try a steam inhalation with a few drops of menthol and eucalyptus oil added to the water.

Prevention is the key to tackling frequent headaches. This means trying to deal with underlying stress and making a real effort to avoid getting over-tired. Eating regular meals, drinking at least 2 litres of water each day and cutting down on alcohol are also important.

Too much caffeine can cause headaches, but so can cutting it out too fast, so switch over to de-caff very gradually.

Keeping a food diary can help to identify food intolerances – a headache caused by food usually starts within a couple of hours of eating it. Excessive amounts of monosodium glutamate and synthetic colourings and flavourings are often to blame.

Keep a note of how many painkillers you are taking. If it's more than 30 a month, then they are likely to be contributing to your headaches. Cutting down can be difficult, as the headaches often get worse, and you may need the help of alternative types of pain-modifying drugs, such as amitriptilene. These are available on prescription from your doctor.

MIGRAINE

This is no ordinary headache. It's a severe, thumping headache, usually (but not always) on one side of the head, which is often preceded by flashing lights in the eyes, nausea or vomiting.

It's thought migraine is caused by changes in the blood vessels inside the brain, triggered by a small change in serotonin activity. There may also be symptoms elsewhere in the body, such as pins and needles, numbness or, more rarely, slight weakness in one part of the body, usually a hand. This may then spread up the arm to involve the face.

A migraine can last anything from a few hours to a couple of days. It can make it impossible to carry on with your normal daily activities – instead you just have to lie down in a quiet dark room until the awful pain goes away.

Why is this happening?

Migraines are much more common in women – yes, it's those hormones again, particularly oestrogen. They tend to occur when hormone levels are changing rapidly, which means they often start just before a period. They can also be triggered by the combined contraceptive pill (much less so by progestogen-only contraceptives) and also to a lesser degree by HRT (see page 300). Thankfully, migraines become much less common after the menopause.

Migraines can also be triggered by eating certain foods – chocolate, cheese, citrus fruits and red wine are the famous ones – and by tiredness, stress, a change of routine or even a change of climate.

Managing migraine

Ordinary painkillers, such as paracetamol, usually barely take the edge off migraine, but they can help a little. The best treatment are triptan drugs – such as sumatriptan (Imigran). For best effect they need to be taken at the start of an attack, and in most people they can stop full-blown migraine developing. Most types are available only on prescription, but low-dose Imigran is available directly from chemists.

Other medicines that can help include anti-sickness medicines, high-dose anti-inflammatory painkillers, and ergotamine.

If you get frequent attacks – say once a month or more – then taking preventative action is worthwhile. The herbal remedy feverfew works for some. Check you take a brand that contains at least 0.2 per cent of the active ingredient parthenolide for every 125mg feverfew leaf powder. Otherwise, beta-blockers or pizotifen (available on prescription) can be helpful. All of these need to be taken all the time, for several months, to have an effect.

SKIN AND HAIR

Our skin and hair are perhaps our most noticeable features, and many women spend a lot of time and money looking after them. So it's a bit of a shock to a woman to discover that there are some unavoidable changes in her skin and hair. The question is, how to deal with them?

During her forties a woman's complexion does change – loss of collagen means that lines and wrinkles inevitably appear, the skin visibly loses some of its youthful bloom and generally becomes drier.

But despite all this, at an age when they are buying their daughters acne products, some women get spots. Doesn't it seem unfair?

Stress is often to blame – it drives the production of testosterone from the adrenal glands at a time when the balancing act of oestrogen is less reliable. The result: an extreme combination skin, with oiliness across the forehead and chin, and dryness around the eyes and on the cheeks.

Tackling the underlying cause – usually a frantic lifestyle – is the best cure, but in the meantime two sets of skin care (for the different areas of oiliness and dryness) are vital. Avoid using very strong anti-acne products. They are designed for teenagers, and can be too harsh for more mature skins, quickly causing flaking and dryness.

Rosacea is a slightly different form of acne that occurs in women in their late thirties and forties. Pustules appear on the cheeks, along with redness and flushing, which is particularly noticeable after having hot drinks, alcohol or spicy food. Occasionally it can be due to using strong steroid creams on the face, but in the majority of cases the cause is unknown. An overgrowth of the normal skin bacteria appears to be partly to blame.

Rosacea can be treated with antibiotics (usually tetracyclines or erythromycin) taken by mouth, or by applying metronidazole gel. Unfortunately, it's a condition that can persist for years, but in many, luckily it does improve after the menopause.

ALOPECIA – HAIR LOSS

Women can lose their hair at any age, from childhood onwards. Throughout life, hair goes through a cycle where it grows, rests and then is shed, and it is normal to shed up to 100 hairs a day. The longer your hair, the more dramatic this can look in your hairbrush or the bath plug. Losing more hair than this may not be immediately obvious, particularly if you usually have a thick head of hair, but the appearance of thin, and especially bald, patches can be very distressing and worth investigating.

Like all other organs in the body, the hair follicles, where hair grows, require the right nutrients for optimum function. Some causes of hair loss are:

◆ Crash dieting, or long-term portion restriction, which can make you lose hair as well as fat.

◆ The wrong diet. In particular, healthy hair growth requires a reasonable amount of protein.

◆ It also requires a good supply of micronutrients, especially iron and zinc. Many women have sub-optimal iron levels, and though the blood lower limit of 'normal' in general is around 20mmol/litre, experts reckon that a level of at least 50 is required for optimum hair growth. Zinc deficiency is more rare, but, like iron deficiency, it's worth having it checked.

◆ Stress is also a common cause for hair loss, and many women find their hair suffers along with their mental state when a relationship breaks down, after a bereavement or after a severe illness.

◆ Hair thinning can also be due to an underactive thyroid gland (see page 265).

◆ Hair changes with age, and it is normal to lose some fullness during the peri-menopausal years – it's rare to find a woman who has the same full head of hair at 45 that she did at 25. This natural age-related thinning tends to be much more noticeable in those with finer, thinner hair.

♦ Thinning on the temples and around the sides – the way men tend to lose their hair – is more likely to be due to an excess of testosterone and is often a sign of PCOS (see page 186).

Treatment

Any underlying cause should be tackled first, but hair growth can often be boosted by using minoxidil lotion. This was originally marketed for male-pattern baldness, but it works in women too. However, its effects are shortlived – hair growth will revert back to how nature intended once its use is stopped. It's not available on the NHS, and is not cheap, but it can be a useful way of getting yourself over a hair crisis.

ALOPECIA AREATA

This is an altogether different condition. In alopecia areata, completely bald patches suddenly appear – the scalp is smooth, with no hair growth at all. It may affect just a small area or, at its worst, the whole scalp. Very occasionally, the eyebrows and eyelashes fall out too.

It is thought to be an auto-immune problem, with the body's own immune system reacting against the hair follicles. In many, this is thankfully a temporary state of affairs; in others it may last for years.

Treatment is difficult and is best supervised by a specialist. Local application of strong steroid cream may help, and some experts prescribe steroids or stronger immune-modulator drugs by mouth with the aim of dampening down the abnormal immune reaction. Sometimes the only answer is to buy a wig until, hopefully, the hair regrows.

FLAKING SCALP

This is often due to contact dermatitis and can be triggered by chemicals in styling or colouring products. If you are having any sort of colouring, even if it is just a few highlights, always do a patch test first.

Occasionally psoriasis can be to blame as well – this tends to cause larger scales, with a well-demarcated edge, and redness of the underlying skin.

Shampoos containing coconut oil and salicylic acid can be helpful, but generally both dermatitis and psoriasis are better treated with prescription-only medicines – mild steroid scalp applications, and Dovonex scalp lotion for psoriasis.

However, the most common cause of scaling is dandruff. It's caused by an overgrowth of the yeasts that normally live on the scalp and is best treated with special anti-fungal shampoos containing either selenium sulphide or ketoconazole.

IN SUMMARY

The peri-menopause is all about the unpredictability of hormones. Many women will begin to feel physical changes at the beginning of their forties; others will not notice anything until they are over 50. A healthy woman in her forties will probably be as busy as a 20- or 30-year-old, if not more so, and she may well have more responsibilities than she did twenty years before, but her energy levels may be decreasing for the first time in her life.

Many women suddenly find they are putting on weight in their forties, despite never having had a weight problem before. Those of us who have always had to keep an eye on our weight may gloat that our skinny friends have to face the same problem at last! It's a phenomenon that cannot be avoided, and a statistical fact that most women will – if they are not careful – gain a pound a year after the age of 40. But we already know from earlier chapters that we all need to watch our diet and do the best we can to feed ourselves and our families with care.

This is an age when depression, stress and tiredness are very often factors in a woman's life. Don't push these problems away as not worth considering, or as something you just have to cope with on your own. Deal with them by tackling them head-on and getting help.

This is the time to consolidate all the good practice I have stressed in earlier chapters: in other words, to keep an eye on your diet; have regular check-ups; make time to relax; and be as well-informed as you can about what is happening to your body. With good mental and physical health, you will be able to deal happily with the changes involved in the menopause, as described in the next chapter.

CHAPTER FIVE

THE MENOPAUSE YEARS: 50–59

A re you one of the lucky women who revels in being in her fifties? You have got your life back. You can cross pregnancy off your worry list. You are at the peak of your earning power in a career you enjoy. Your children are virtually independent and you have a stable, loving relationship with your partner. You have fantastic health and sail through the menopause with no problems.

Or – more likely – are you a 50-year-old facing a whole new crop of problems? Either your children are firmly entrenched in the family nest and demand room service along with their subsidized accommodation or, if they have left home, you and your partner are finding it hard to adjust to life without them. Or maybe your partner has left too, and you are coping alone, and the nest seems very empty indeed. And just when you manage to carve out a little time for yourself, your parents (who probably live far away from you) hit their eighties and cannot manage to live independently without your help.

On top of it all, you lose your oestrogen. It's been with you for the last 40 years and has been like your best friend – irritating and annoying at times, but essential for your well-being and always there to support you. It's hard not to notice that it's gone.

In this chapter you will find:

- **Staying healthy**
  - essential tests for women in their fifties
- **Food and nutrition**
  - preventing heart disease and osteoporosis
  - exercise
- **Lifestyle and mental health:**
  - caring for elderly relatives
  - family rows
- **The menopause**
  - symptoms and diet
  - HRT
  - bleeding after the menopause
  - osteoporosis
- **Breast problems**
  - breast awareness
  - tender breasts and lumps
  - breast cancer
- **Skin care and cosmeceuticals**
  - ageing skin
  - tanning and smoking
  - face creams
  - cosmetic surgery
  - varicose veins

STAYING HEALTHY

Your body is like a car – as it grows older it's more liable to develop faults; so, just like a car, it's essential that every woman of 50-plus has a regular health MOT. This should include:

♦ **At least every 3 years**: a mammogram; more often if you can afford it. At this age you can't ignore your increased chance of getting breast cancer.

♦ **Every 5 years**: a cervical smear test; more often if you have previously had an abnormal smear. Ask if you can have a pelvic check at the same time, for swelling of the womb or ovaries.

♦ **Every 2 years**: a blood pressure check.

♦ **At least every 3 years**: a blood cholesterol check; more often if the level is slightly raised (which it is in at least 50 per cent of women).

♦ **Every 2 years**: an eye test. By now your eyesight is likely to be changing and you'll probably need glasses.

Breast disease: in addition, you should practise breast awareness (see page 314) and check your skin for abnormal moles or lumps.

Other screening: those who know they are at increased risk of specific illnesses, such as bowel or ovarian cancer, either because of family history or for other reasons, should continue to have regular screening.

Osteoporosis: all women should also become more 'bone aware' after the menopause, and those at increased risk of osteoporosis should have a bone density scan (see page 309). Early diagnosis and treatment of bone loss can help to prevent osteoporosis in later life.

Any unusual symptoms: most importantly, this is an age when any abnormal symptoms, of any sort, should never be ignored. A persistent cough, a change in bowel habit, pain or discomfort anywhere, abnormal bleeding from the back passage or the vagina, or unexplained weight loss should trigger a trip to your doctor.

FOOD AND NUTRITION

Just because you have gone through the menopause should not mean that you automatically put on weight. However, as you age your metabolism does slow down, so I'm afraid you do need to adjust your calorie intake downwards. For example, a 50-year-old woman weighing 57kg (9 stone) will typically require around 1,900 calories a day, while the same woman in her early twenties would need closer to 2,100. The trouble is, what you need and what your appetite wants are two different things. Until your stomach gets used to smaller portions it takes willpower to adjust.

Oestrogen helps to protect women from many serious illnesses, such as heart disease and osteoporosis, during their reproductive years; but the sharp drop now means it's important to adjust your diet and lifestyle to compensate.

PREVENTING HEART DISEASE

Coronary heart disease (CHD) is the biggest killer of women in this country and accounts for 17 per cent of female deaths. Oestrogen is protective, but after the menopause a woman's risk of heart disease rises rapidly to match that of men. Eating a low-fat, low-salt, high-fibre diet, rich in fresh fruit and vegetables and wholegrain cereals, is the best nutritional defence against heart disease.

At least 50 per cent of women have a cholesterol level that is higher than it should be, and this is a major contributing factor to heart disease. To keep your cholesterol level low, cut down on saturated fats found in dairy and animal products (see page 351).

Trans-fatty acids, found in fried food, cakes and biscuits, can also contribute to atherosclerosis (thickening and hardening of the arteries; see page 372). Watch your salt intake – too much can raise blood pressure, which can lead to heart disease and stroke. You need fewer than 5g of salt a day – about a teaspoonful (see page 353).

PREVENTING OSTEOPOROSIS

To protect your bones you need at least 800mg a day of calcium. The best sources are:

♦ dairy foods – milk, cheese, yogurt
♦ non-dairy sources such as tofu and soya
♦ pulses such as chickpeas
♦ green vegetables

- ◆ dried fruit
- ◆ nuts
- ◆ seeds
- ◆ tinned sardines (especially if you eat the soft bones, too)

The body can absorb only about 500mg of calcium at a time, so spread your intake over the day. Calcium carbonate, the most common type of calcium supplement, should be taken with a meal.

Calcium works in tandem with vitamin D. This is found in:

- ◆ tuna or salmon
- ◆ eggs
- ◆ milk products
- ◆ we also absorb it through our skin when it is exposed to sunlight. Dark-skinned women, or those who always cover up outdoors, should consider taking a supplement

VITAMIN E – THE MENOPAUSAL VITAMIN

Vitamin E has sometimes been called the 'menopausal vitamin' because it behaves in a similar way to oestrogen and in the United States is sometimes used as an oestrogen substitute. Some claim it helps to relieve hot flushes as well as the psychological symptoms of menopause.

Vitamin E is also a powerful antioxidant that helps keep cells healthy and protects against heart attacks. Research indicates that it may have an action in helping to prevent bad, artery-clogging cholesterol from hardening into arterial plaque, which in turn causes heart disease. It also raises levels of HDL, the good cholesterol (see page 373). Rich sources are found in:

- ◆ wheatgerm oil
- ◆ eggs
- ◆ green leafy vegetables
- ◆ cereals
- ◆ dried beans

EXERCISE IN YOUR FIFTIES

By now you may well have noticed how everything in your body suddenly seems to have shifted south. Fifty years of gravity have taken their toll and your breasts, your inner arms, your butt – frankly, they're all a bit droopy. Not fair!

But although it doesn't have to be this way, it is a fact that if you want to stay trim and toned, you really do have to work at it and make a place for regular exercise in your weekly routine. Exercise isn't just good for your figure – it's also essential for your general health, particularly your heart, lungs and bones.

There's very little that women of 50 can't do – I recently met a wonderful 58-year-old who had taken up climbing at the menopause ('I had to prove to myself I wasn't getting old') and had just scaled Everest! Just because you are 50 does not mean you can't take up a new sport, or take one you are already doing to a new, more challenging level.

However, you do need to be a little prudent, particularly if you've had a fairly sedentary lifestyle up to now. Don't suddenly launch yourself into a strenuous fitness regime – start gently, and slowly build up the amount you do. Warming up beforehand is also very important:

the older you are, the more easy it is to injure yourself. So always do some stretches the moment you put your trainers on.

Sadly, by the age of 50 the cartilage cushions on the ends of bones are a little worn, and this means that prolonged, hard, weight-bearing exercise, though excellent for maintaining bone strength, can trigger joint problems. Several orthopaedic surgeons I know strongly advise against women over 50 doing a marathon – they say the training involved really can do long-term damage to the knees. Be prudent – at this age you need to treat your body with some respect!

Exercise programmes

An ideal exercise programme for the 50-something woman should include some activity, every day, that makes you slightly puffed for at least 20 minutes – but this doesn't have to be a dedicated session at a sports club. Hoovering, digging the garden, a brisk walk with the dog all count.

On top of this you should do exercises, at least three times a week, that specifically strengthen and tone muscles, especially those that support the trunk, which are the back and abdominal muscles. Pelvic-floor exercises are important too at this age. You can learn to do all these at home, but the challenge often is finding the time! (For more information on pelvic-floor exercises, and how to do them, see page 383.)

If you have any concerns about your health, and what exercise you should or should not do, see your doctor.

LIFESTYLE AND MENTAL HEALTH

CARING FOR ELDERLY RELATIVES

One of the big tasks for women at this time of their lives can be coping with elderly relatives.

There are known to be 6.6 million carers in the UK – most of them women – and 3.5 million of these have jobs too. The true figure is probably a great deal higher, because many people do not acknowledge the role they play in supporting someone who cannot cope on their own.

If you work outside the home and also care for an elderly person, these twin roles will make great inroads into your spare time. You are likely to become short-tempered and stressed, especially if you neglect your diet or do not get enough sleep or 'hours off' to do what you want. The fact that you no longer have the time or energy for other people and for activities you once enjoyed – you may even feel too tired to make love – can knock your self-esteem and compromise relationships on which you depend.

Most elderly people needing help are widows who live alone. Many mums today do not live round the corner but many miles away, so popping in to do the odd job they can no longer manage, or shopping for them, is not an option. Your elderly mum will want to retain her independence as long as she can, and there is plenty you can do to help.

If friends or neighbours living near her offer to take on the odd chore – shopping or giving her lifts – take them up on it. Swap phone numbers so they can be benevolent 'spies' who will alert you to problems your mother might be minimizing.

If your parent has limited mobility, ask social services to assess her home for safety and to suggest the siting of handgrips for support. If she has trouble getting in and out of the bath, ask them if she qualifies for cash help to install a shower or walk-in bath. You can also ask social services or your local Citizens Advice Bureau for information about other community care services, such as meals on wheels and home helps.

Combining work and caring

Three out of 5 people will become carers at some stage in their lives – and it can happen suddenly, usually precipitated by a medical crisis. If you are working, an understanding employer can make all the difference if this happens to you.

Your first move is to find out from your human resources department, union representatives or colleagues if your company has an established scheme to support carers. If it hasn't, and other people who work with you are in the same situation, you may be able to find ways to juggle your job with your caring responsibilities – flexi-time, part-time, job-sharing or working from home – if your boss is sympathetic.

You have the right to take a 'reasonable amount' of time off work to deal with a crisis involving a dependant, which gives you limited protection against victimization or dismissal. However, whether you get paid while you are away is at your employer's discretion. Find out whether your firm offers compassionate leave for emergencies and whether you will get paid if you take it.

If there is a sudden crisis and there is no way you can work and cope with caring, see if you can take a career break so that you can return to your job when the emergency is over. One in 10 people in their eighties lives with one of their children – usually a middle-aged, married daughter. This can be a source of friction, especially if you have never got on well with your mother, or if your partner begrudges sharing a home with her. If this is the case, be honest about it and look at residential-care options.

Support for carers

Unless you are a saint, there will be times when you feel guilty, angry, frustrated and resentful. The person you care for may be feeling much the same, so try to be honest with each other. If communication is impossible, obtain emotional support from your friends or family, or consider counselling. The Carers' National Association runs carer groups which will give you a chance to meet other people in the same situation. Many offer social activities and carer training, as well as campaigning for better services and providing information on available help.

Make sure your GP knows you are a carer and that it is written in your notes so that she has a better picture of your home life. This will make it easier for her to treat you if you become stressed or depressed. Also establish a good relationship with your parent's district nurse and social worker.

FAMILY ROWS

Like it or not, a happy family life, like marriage, is all about compromise and accommodation of other people's needs. Let's face it, that's a tall order for years on end, and rows are an inevitable part of relationships. But it is far better to have it out with someone than to sulk or find some other, more devious way to undermine them.

If your children are still at home you may be in a volatile mother-and-adolescent-daughter situation, or dealing with the sulky and aggressive behaviour of a teenage boy. Relationships with this age group can be even more highly charged when stepchildren are involved. Your only chance of maintaining the upper hand is for you and your partner to present a united front on behaviour and house rules. Children exploit the divide-and-conquer tactic before they are old enough to speak – by their late teens they have the technique honed to perfection. If the two of you disagree over an issue involving your children, do it privately and not in front of them.

The worst arguments are often about something trivial and tend to blow up when people are feeling tired, grumpy or have too much to drink. Christmas and holidays provide fertile ground for conflict because they are times when high expectations are often followed by disappointment. No one can wind you up as expertly as the people who know you best.

To minimize escalation of a family row, follow the golden rule: control your tongue. If you get carried away on a wave of anger, your heart rate will go up, you will find it difficult to concentrate on the logic of your argument and you are likely to raise the temperature even further if you resort to character assassination. Even an apology afterwards is unlikely to wipe out the memory of name-calling, ridicule or scorning of achievements.

However, be grown-up enough to say sorry if you are to blame; and if someone apologizes to you, don't throw it back in their face or it might start another row. Agreeing to differ on some issues and deciding to tolerate things that irritate you is sometimes the wisest course of action.

Arguments fall into three main categories:

♦ Avoidance – you blow up about one issue when the real source of irritation is something much deeper that you dare not mention.

♦ Volatile – the so-called Italian marriage, where rows are explosive and furious and insults are traded mercilessly.

♦ Resolution – a fair exchange of views, the cause of the conflict pinpointed and a solution agreed upon by both parties.

Needless to say, this last example is the type of row you should aim for and the one that is most likely to make a lasting contribution to domestic harmony.

THE MENOPAUSE

The medical profession defines the menopause as the date of your last period. If only it were as simple as that.

The reality is that 'the menopause' (like puberty) isn't a single event – it's something that happens gradually over a period of many months. For some women, the events surrounding the menopause can go on for years.

The menopause usually occurs between 47 and 53; overall the average is between the fiftieth and fifty-first birthday. The age it happens is to some extent determined genetically – if your mother had an early or late menopause, chances are you will follow in the same pattern, though smoking can bring the age forward by a couple of years. Occasionally the menopause occurs at a much earlier age, sometimes as young as the twenties, though this is rare.

What actually happens at the menopause is that the ovaries finally stop working. It marks a very definite end to a woman's natural fertility, as ovulation no longer occurs and, more importantly for most women, oestrogen production ceases.

SYMPTOMS OF THE MENOPAUSE

In some, the only sign of the approach to the menopause is a change in the pattern of periods. They may suddenly stop, but more usually the cycle becomes increasingly erratic, with unpredictably longer gaps between periods. In some lucky women, that's all that happens. There really are some women who go through the menopause without ever having a hot flush or a sweat.

However, more usually, plummeting oestrogen levels cause a range of symptoms, from an occasional feeling of warmth, with slight perspiration, through to drenching sweats and an uncomfortable hot sensation that starts in the chest and works up to the face. These can last anything from a few minutes to up to half an hour, then your body returns to normal. If it happens at night, and it often does, then it wakes you up. Many women say one of the worst things about the menopause is the disturbed sleep pattern it can cause.

Other common symptoms caused by plummeting oestrogen include headaches, mood swings, depression, tiredness, a loss of libido, and attacks of both anxiety and dizziness. Many also notice that their skin and hair suddenly become drier.

How long all this goes on for can vary enormously from woman to woman. Some have just a couple of months of discomfort, while in others it can go on for a year. A few unlucky women have flushes for 5 years or more, though this is unusual. But however long it lasts, it can make life pretty unpleasant, and it's not unusual to have times when you feel you are 'losing the plot' and going slightly insane.

The loss of oestrogen at the menopause also has a significant effect on a woman's future health. Oestrogen plays an important role in maintaining bones, and bone density can fall rapidly after the menopause, increasing the risk of osteoporosis (see page 307). It also has a protective effect on arteries, and the risk of heart attacks and strokes rises rapidly once periods stop.

Oestrogen also helps to maintain suppleness and lubrication in the tissues of the genital area, so during a woman's fifties these gradually become drier, which can cause irritation and itching, and can make having sex very uncomfortable. It can also increase the risk of getting urinary infections.

Other problems related to lack of oestrogen include less supple, more aching joints, and a general lack of energy.

Diagnosis

Often, the symptoms alone are enough to tell a woman she is menopausal – no tests are necessary. However, if you want to be certain, an FSH (follicle stimulating hormone) can be helpful – the higher the level, the less oestrogen is being produced. Levels of 25 or more indicate an imminent menopause, while a level greater than 50 suggests the ovaries have stopped working.

However, the ovaries can be a little unpredictable, and for this reason, regardless of any tests, a woman should continue to use contraception for a year after her last period.

What to do

There are several different ways that the effects of the menopause can be tackled. What you do must depend on your individual circumstances – no woman is the same.

Simple self-help measures:

♦ Wear several layers of light clothing, rather than one thick layer; this can make it easier to cope with hot flushes. That way you can shed, and then add, layers as required.

♦ Choose clothing, especially underwear, made of natural fibres, such as cotton, linen or silk, which allow sweat to evaporate. At the menopause, polyester and especially tight lycra are best avoided.

♦ Cut down on caffeine and alcohol, which can widen blood vessels, making flushes and sweats worse. Smoking can have the same effect – yet another reason to stop.

Diet and supplements

You can boost oestrogen levels through both diet and supplements, and in some women these really can make a difference. As always, though, there's huge individual variation, but they are worth a try.

Phyto-oestrogens

Phyto-oestrogens are naturally occurring plant chemicals that have a very weak oestrogen-like action. They work by stimulating oestrogen receptors throughout the body, but are only 1/1000 times as strong as the body's own oestrogen. They are part of a group of chemicals known as isoflavones (a term you may see on labels), but of the thousand or so isoflavones found in plants, only four with oestrogen activity are found in the human diet – diadzen, genistein, formononetin and biochanin. Rich sources of these include red clover leaves, soya beans, chickpeas and lentils.

Interest in phyto-oestrogens started when it became apparent that Japanese women have a much lower incidence of menopausal symptoms (and also some hormonally related cancers) than Western women, and this was linked with the fact that the average Japanese diet contains thirty times more isoflavones. It's not the whole story – genes and other environmental factors are also involved – but the difference in diet can't be ignored.

You can boost your phyto-oestrogen intake by eating more pulses, such as chickpeas and lentils, beansprouts, linseeds, green leafy vegetables, and especially soya products, such as soya milk or tofu. It's reckoned that just 60gm (2oz) of natural soya product is enough to give a phyto-oestrogen effect.

Soya has little flavour of its own but it takes on the taste of the ingredients it is cooked with, so if you replace half the minced meat in a recipe (for example, bolognese sauce or shepherd's pie) with soya mince, it is highly unlikely anyone will notice. It's cheaper and lower in fat too. You can add linseeds to a lot of dishes, and special breads containing them are also available.

A wide variety of supplements containing phyto-oestrogens are now available, such as Aria and red clover leaf extract, and in some women they can help take the edge off menopausal symptoms. Flaxseed (linseed) supplements also contain phyto-oestrogens (as well as a lot of omega 3 fatty acids).

Other health claims have also been made for phyto-oestrogen products, again based mainly on the difference in disease incidence in the Japanese and their higher phyto-oestrogen intake. These include helping to protect against osteoporosis and reducing the risk of breast cancer. However, there is no long-term safety data for the use of phyto-oestrogen supplements, and any effect they have is likely to be very small. Some experts feel that because phyto-oestrogens stimulate oestrogen receptors, large doses, taken over a long time, may actually increase the risk of breast cancer.

The bottom line is we just don't know how safe these supplements are, and taking a mega dose in a pill is not the same as eating healthy food for most of your life. Take them for flushes by all means, but don't kid yourself that they will help you live a longer life.

Other supplements

There are several other supplements that can be used to alleviate menopausal symptoms:

♦ **Black cohosh** (black snakeroot) is thought to have oestrogenic properties, and it can reduce the incidence of menopausal flushes. It also has a mild diuretic effect. However, black cohosh has been linked with liver damage, and most experts recommend that it is used for a maximum of six months.

♦ **Wild yam** root certainly has oestrogenic properties, along with progesterone and testosterone-like actions – many synthetic hormones prescribed by doctors are derived from wild yam root. So it's worth a try.

- ♦ **Liquorice root** is reported to have both oestrogen and progesterone-like actions but, unlike the other supplements mentioned above, it may cause fluid retention. It can also lower blood potassium levels and so should be avoided by anyone taking diuretics or other medication for high blood pressure.

- ♦ **Grapeseed** is thought to act on the pituitary gland, ovaries and oestrogen-dependent cells. In clinical trials it has been shown to reduce menopausal symptoms.

- ♦ **Ginseng** (again in the natural form) has oestrogenic properties and is also a stimulant, so it can be useful if you are feeling tired and jaded. Don't take it in the evening though.

You need to take all these supplements for a few weeks before you notice any difference. Keeping a diary detailing your menopause symptoms may help you to assess what effect they are having.

HRT

Hormone replacement therapy (HRT) used to be called 'the elixir of youth', but concerns over long-term safety, particularly the risk of breast cancer, have meant that it is now much less popular than it was a few years ago.

That said, though, it really is the best remedy available for relieving hot flushes and sweats, and all the other troublesome symptoms of the menopause. That's because HRT is just what its name says – hormone replacement therapy. Its main ingredient is oestrogen, the hormone that the body is saying it so desperately needs. The overall dose is much less than that in the combined pill, as the idea is just to replace what nature is lacking, rather than to override the natural cycle.

The majority of HRT formulations contain oestrogen derived from soya, but those of the Premarin range, which includes Prempak, contain oestrogens derived from the urine of pregnant mares. They contain a mix of ten different oestrogens, and this means they can suit some women better than other soya-based brands, which contain only one.

Using oestrogen alone can cause thickening of the lining of the womb, which in the long term can cause erratic bleeding and may lead to the development of abnormal cells, increasing the risk of cancer of the womb. Adding in progesterone counteracts this, and ensures that the lining remains thin and safe. The progesterone component can be given either cyclically or all the time. In peri-menopausal women, and those within a year of their last period (who still may have some ovarian activity) it is given for 2 weeks each month, after which there is a withdrawal bleed. For other women, a 'continuous combined' preparation is usually used: it contains a constant amount of both hormones, which are taken all the time.

One formulation, tibolone, has oestrogenic and progestogenic properties, plus some additional androgen-like activity. It is particularly useful for women who want HRT but who complain of a low libido.

HRT is available as pills, or patches and a gel which are applied to the skin. They all come in a range of doses. Pills are probably the easiest to use, but fine dose control is easier with gel; it's quite possible to rub just a tiny amount on each day – just enough to relieve symptoms, but giving the minimal risk of side effects. With this, however, the progesterone component must be taken separately. Patches supply a more constant dose, and again this may help to stop side effects, especially nausea.

Implants, which are inserted under the skin, are now used much less frequently than in the past; this is because initially they can give very high levels of oestrogen in the body and, as these fall, flushes and sweats may re-occur, even if the absolute level is still above normal. It's a condition known as tachyphylaxis – in effect, the body's thermostat for oestrogen is re-set to a higher level. This wouldn't matter so much if high levels of oestrogen weren't so potentially dangerous to the breasts.

There's no one formulation that's best – as with so many medicines, it's a matter of personal choice.

It's normal to start with a low dose, and to increase this only if necessary, as the few advantages of larger doses are generally more than outweighed by the disadvantages, particularly the increased risk of breast cancer.

HRT – the advantages . . .

It could be said that in many ways HRT puts your body back to where it was before the menopause. It gives you oestrogen back again, and you can say an instant goodbye to flushes and sweats. Not only that, but many women say it improves their energy and vitality levels and helps to stop their creaking joints. It has also been scientifically proven to improve skin and hair thickness.

Many women say it just makes them feel normal again. Better still, it can help to stop the decline in bone density that normally occurs after the menopause, and so helps to prevent osteoporosis (see page 307).

There is conflicting evidence about Alzheimer's disease (see page 429). Some research has claimed HRT has a protective effect, whilst others say it may increase the risk – in other words, the jury is still out on that one.

. . . and the disadvantages

There is one very important reason why HRT has fallen out of favour, and that is because there is no doubt that it can increase the risk of breast cancer (see page 318). The risk is greater if you take both oestrogen and progesterone, and the longer you take it.

If you take 1,000 women aged 65, who have never taken HRT, 50 can be expected to get breast cancer.

If the same group of 1,000 women had taken oestrogen-only HRT for 5 years, there would be one additional case of breast cancer. After 5 years of both oestrogen and progesterone HRT, there would be 6 extra cases.

After 10 years of oestrogen-only HRT, there would be 5 additional cases of breast cancer; and after 10 years of oestrogen and progesterone HRT use, there would be 19 additional cases.

These risk levels are for standard-dose HRT; there is some evidence that the risk is lower for smaller doses (1mg oestradiol). The risk seems to be confined to those actually taking HRT. Once you stop it, the risk soon falls back to the background level for your age.

However, the risk of endometrial cancer from oestrogen alone is greater, so most doctors still advise women with a womb to take a preparation containing both hormones, even though this is more risky breast-wise.

The other important side effect is the slight increased risk of a DVT (deep vein thrombosis – a blood clot in the leg), and for this reason any woman on HRT should take a low-dose aspirin before embarking on a flight of 4 hours or more. It also means that HRT should be discontinued before any major surgery.

Other possible side effects include nausea, flatulence and slightly tender breasts. There is no evidence that HRT leads to weight gain, though many doctors do report that women taking high-dose preparations can have trouble with weight control – but that may be because they feel more hungry.

The bottom line

HRT remains the best way to relieve unpleasant menopausal symptoms, but because of the risk of breast cancer it's always a good idea to try other options first. But if flushes, sweats and sleepless nights are still making your life a misery, then it is worth a try. However, it's not suitable for all women, and certainly it should be used with caution in those with breast cancer in the family.

Stopping HRT

It's now recommended that HRT should only be taken for a couple of years, to see you through the worst phase of menopausal symptoms. Anyone who chooses to take it for longer than this should be aware of the increasing risk of breast cancer. For many, however, this is a price that is worth paying for an improved quality of life.

HRT should not be stopped suddenly, as the abrupt fall in oestrogen levels often triggers flushes and sweats all over again. Instead, it should be tailed off slowly, over at least a couple of months. Switching to gel can make this easier.

Vaginal dryness and discomfort can be eased by oestrogen cream specifically designed for use in the genital area. Very little of this is absorbed into the bloodstream, so it does not help relieve general menopausal symptoms, but neither does it increase the risk of breast cancer. Long-term use can, however, cause some thickening of the womb lining, although this can be prevented by taking occasional courses of progesterone tablets (see page 365).

Testosterone – the forgotten hormone

Oestrogen is not the only hormone produced by the ovaries. They also produce testosterone, and though men overall produce significantly more, ovarian testosterone can play an important role in a woman's well-being. It has a particular influence on her libido.

Testosterone is also produced by the adrenal glands, but overall at the menopause levels do fall, and this can be enough to cause quite a noticeable lowering of a woman's sex drive. HRT can help with this, particularly tibolone, which has some testosterone activity, but not all women want to go down this route. Opting to improve your sex life at the risk of increasing your chance of breast cancer is not every woman's choice.

An alternative is to boost just the level of testosterone. Testosterone implants specifically for women are available, but, as with other implants, they can give quite a high dose to begin with. This may cause side effects, such as greasy skin and acne, and a tendency to make any hair loss worse. A testosterone gel is also available, and though it is only currently licensed for use in men, women can use it too, though in much smaller amounts. It is available on prescription from some specialists and from a few GPs with a special interest in women's health.

GYNAECOLOGICAL PROBLEMS AFTER THE MENOPAUSE

Just because your womb and ovaries have stopped doing anything useful does not mean that they can be ignored. Sadly, this is the time when the really serious diseases – cancers – can rear their heads. This means that any symptoms – discomfort, pain, swelling and especially bleeding – should never be ignored.

BLEEDING AFTER THE MENOPAUSE

It can be difficult to know whether your periods have stopped or not, and gaps of 3 months between periods are quite common. But once you have turned 50, any bleeding – and that includes just slight spotting – that occurs after a gap of more than a year needs to be investigated, as occasionally it is due to cancer of the womb.

The most common cause of bleeding is vaginal dryness; this is the type of bleeding that occurs after sex (which probably felt uncomfortable). Slight bleeding can also be due to inflammation of the vagina caused by infections or allergy. More importantly, though, bleeding can be due to a polyp or abnormal thickening of the womb lining. Though polyps are rarely malignant, general thickening of the lining – a condition known as cystic hyperplasia – can turn cancerous if left untreated.

Tests and treatment

A vaginal examination is mandatory. If the bleeding has only been light, and there is very obvious dryness, then no further tests may be needed. However, it is prudent for every woman to have an ultrasound scan of the pelvic organs, to check especially on the thickness of the womb lining. If there is any suspicion that something might be wrong, then a hysteroscopy should be done. This involves looking directly inside the womb, under anaesthetic, using a tiny flexible camera. Any abnormal areas should be biopsied and then sent for analysis.

Treatment depends on the underlying cause. Polyps just need to be removed, but cystic hyperplasia usually requires curettage – or a scraping – to remove the whole womb lining, and occasionally hormone treatment afterwards. (For cancer of the womb and ovaries, see pages 366–71.)

OSTEOPOROSIS

It may not show any symptoms until you are in your seventies, but the time you really need to be aware of osteoporosis is at the menopause. It's a condition that is likely to affect 1 in 3 women – and it's not something you can ignore.

When you have osteoporosis your bones are thin and fragile, and liable to fracture. Often the first sign of osteoporosis is a broken wrist or, worse, a hip, after a relatively trivial fall.

As with so many diseases, this isn't a state of affairs that happens overnight – it's a gradual process. Bones are living tissues that are continually being built up and broken down. In childhood, and especially in the teenage years, the building-up process is more dominant.

Our bones reach their maximum density in our mid twenties, and then the two processes should be fairly balanced till the thirties, when the breaking-down process becomes slightly more dominant and the bones slowly become thinner.

The hormone oestrogen helps to keep them strong, but at the menopause, when oestrogen levels fall, this protective action is lost, the breaking-down process becomes much more dominant and bone density starts falling more dramatically.

It's a silent process: you don't get any aches and pains from thinning bones. In the later stages, though, osteoporosis can cause loss of height due to a change of shape in the bones of the back, which gradually become crushed and wedge-shaped, leading to a curved spine and the classic 'dowager's hump'.

The effects of osteoporosis

Osteoporosis can have devastating effects on your health. Though it's rare to die of a broken bone, lying immobile in bed with a broken hip can put you at increased risk of pneumonia or a DVT, which can be fatal.

It can also cost you your independence, and crushed bones in the spine can be excruciatingly painful. The statistics are horrific – every day forty people in the UK die as a result of an osteoporotic fracture.

Unfortunately, even with modern drugs, there is no cure for osteoporosis – once bones have become thin there is little that can be done to build them up again. So prevention is all-important, and though women of all ages should take care of their bones, you need to be pro-active about this once you reach the menopause.

Why me?

Osteoporosis can affect any woman, but some are more at risk than others. They include:

- those with a family history of the condition. However, chances are your mother and grandmother were never diagnosed with it – they just got shorter, or acquired a curved spine. Have a careful look at family photos

- thin women, and those with a small frame

- those who have had anorexia (see page 56), particularly if their periods stopped for more than 6 months; those with poor nutrition; and those who have avoided dairy products and not taken calcium supplements

- smokers

- those who have had an early menopause or had their ovaries removed before the age of 45, and have not taken HRT

- those who have had prolonged periods of inactivity, or taken steroid tablets for several months

- heavy drinkers

Rather surprisingly, the list also includes women who have taken a lot of exercise, especially if they are thin and their periods have stopped as a result.

Diagnosis

The only accurate way to diagnose osteoporosis is with a bone density, or DEXA, scan. Unfortunately, availability of these is patchy – some GPs can arrange it directly, others can't and have to refer women to a specialist first (which just costs the NHS even more money). An ultrasound scan of the heel can also be helpful, but is not as accurate; however, it is better than nothing.

Ordinary X-rays cannot be used to diagnose osteoporosis. There may be a comment that the bones appear to be thin, but that only tends to occur when the disease is advanced.

The real value of a DEXA scan is that it can tell you exactly how thin your bones are, so it can be used not only to diagnose established osteoporosis, but also the earlier stages of the disease, when the bones are thinner than average (osteopenia). The results are usually expressed as a T score, which is a comparison with young healthy bones. The Z score is a comparison of women in the same age group.

- a T score of 1 or above is normal
- −1 to −1.5 is a bit lower than average
- less than −1.5 is osteopenia
- −2.5 or less confirms osteoporosis

Taking action as soon as possible can help to stop the bones becoming any thinner.

Treatment

There are three types of drugs that can be used to treat established osteoporosis.

- Biphosphonates, such as Fosamax, are generally the most popular, and there is evidence that they can not only halt bone loss, but also help to build up a little new bone. They can cause irritation of the oesophagus and are not easy to take (they can't be taken when you go to bed, or near a mealtime), but most only have to be taken once a week. A once-a-month Bonviva preparation is also available.
- One alternative to these is a strontium-based powder (Protelos).

◆ Another alternative is raloxifene, a selective oestrogen receptor modulator. This stimulates oestrogen receptors in bone, but not in the breast. Hot flushes can be a troublesome side effect.

All these drugs can prevent further bone loss, and there is also evidence that they can promote some new bone formation; in some people, bone density may improve by 2–3 per cent over a 2-year period. That's not a cure – your bones are still thin, but there is a gradual reduction in your risk of having a fracture.

Any treatment has to be long term – indefinitely really – as bone turnover is such a slow process. None of these treatments works fast, and the moment they are stopped nature will revert back to its usual pattern and bone loss will begin again. Osteoporosis treatment is for the rest of your life.

Up until recently, the main way of treating those with osteopenia – those with thinner than average bones – was with HRT, but this is no longer recommended because of the increased risk of breast cancer (see page 300).

There have been no large-scale trials with the drugs used to treat established osteoporosis, so no one is sure whether they work or indeed whether they have any harmful effects on bone if given in the early stages of the disease. My feeling is that they are almost certainly beneficial and worth prescribing to women with osteopenia. However, this is a controversial area, and their cost means that many doctors will only prescribe them to women with established thin bones. Of course, treating a fracture is far more expensive, but if it happens twenty years down the line that's someone else's budget problem.

Drugs aside, there are other ways you can help to keep your bones strong – see below.

Prevention

Prevention is better than cure. Though it's those who already have thin bones who should take most action, osteoporosis is so horribly common that all women should take steps to preserve their bones. Ideally these steps should start in the teenage years – the stronger the bones are to begin with, the better they will last. But it's at the menopause when 'bone care' should be part of your regular health routine.

This means you should:

♦ Eat at least 800mg of calcium every day, 1000mg or more if you have established disease. Calcium is vital for building bone, along with vitamin D and small amounts of magnesium. The best source of calcium is dairy food and, frankly, unless you are keen on milk, cheese and yogurt, you're unlikely to be getting enough. Take a supplement. We get most of our vitamin D from the action of sunlight in the skin. Many elderly women who stay indoors don't get enough of that either. Again, a supplement is the answer.

♦ Take regular weight-bearing exercise, for instance walking, running, tennis. Sadly, swimming, which is often recommended for those with arthritis, isn't weight-bearing – the water is doing that job.

♦ Keep your alcohol consumption under 14 units a week.

♦ And don't smoke.

BREAST PROBLEMS

Look at any survey about the health issues that really worry women, and one thing comes out a clear winner – breast cancer.

In fact, the biggest killer of women, by some margin, is heart disease (see page 372), but that doesn't mean that breast cancer isn't a huge problem – 1 in 9 women in the UK will develop it at some stage in her life. It's a frightening statistic.

Not all lumps are cancerous: the majority are benign – that is, non-cancerous. But breast cancer can, and does, occur in women of all ages. However, the chances of a lump being cancerous varies hugely with age.

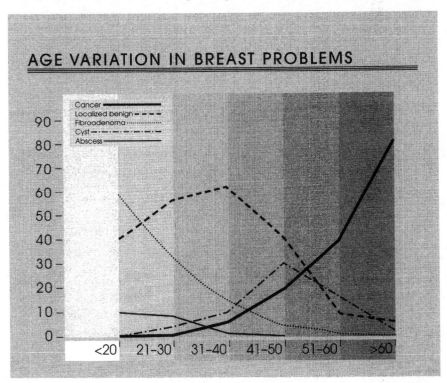

AGE VARIATION IN BREAST PROBLEMS

Cancer ——————
Localized benign – – – –
Fibroadenoma ················
Cyst –·–·–·–·–·–·
Abscess ——————

90
80
70
60
50
40
30
20
10
0

<20   21–30   31–40   41–50   51–60   >60

Lumps in young women are much more likely to be benign, but the chance of a diagnosis of cancer increases with age, especially after the menopause.

What is normal?

The breasts consist of glandular tissue and fat; most women have a remarkably similar amount of glandular tissue, and it's generally a difference in the amount of fat that is more important in determining your breast size. Naturally large breasts are quite rare in thin women.

The breasts change not only at different times of the menstrual cycle, but also at different times of a woman's life. Changing hormone levels in the week before a period can lead to fluid retention, making the breasts more lumpy and tender. This usually resolves itself in the first day or two of a period.

The breasts enlarge during pregnancy, even more so during breastfeeding, and then shrink again afterwards, usually (and unfortunately!) with a little less support.

Then after the menopause, when the influence of oestrogen is lost, the glandular tissue shrinks and is usually replaced by fat. The breasts become softer, generally less lumpy, and are often a little more droopy.

BREAST AWARENESS

By examining your breasts regularly you can get to know what is normal for you and swiftly be able to detect something unusual.

The best time for breast self-examination is just after a period. After the menopause, choose a time that you are likely to remember, such as the beginning of each month. Many women find that during or after bathing or showering is a good time.

First of all, examine the shape of your breasts in a mirror, checking for the position of the nipples and any dimpling of the skin. Ideally you should do this with your arms by your sides, then on your waist, and then finally raised above your head. This means you don't ignore the tail of breast tissue that extends into the armpits. Check the skin of your nipples too for scaling, cracking or discharge.

Next check for lumps. Press in gently, using the flats of the fingers. Don't squeeze bits of breast tissue between your fingertips. Do this methodically, starting at the nipples, and working outwards. Check right up into the armpit on each side.

If you find something unusual, don't panic – the vast majority of breast lumps are not due to cancer. If you find a lump in the week before your period, check again as your period is ending. Otherwise, see your doctor as soon as you can.

TENDER BREASTS

Fluctuating hormone levels can lead to quite marked breast tenderness, especially in the few days before a period. This can occur at any age, but is often at its worst in the peri-menopausal years, especially during anovulatory cycles, when there is oestrogen dominance (see page 245).

To ease this discomfort, make sure you wear a comfortable, supportive bra, including at night if need be. Make sure it is big enough and doesn't squash your breasts – some women need a larger cup size for just a few days each month.

Some women find a gammolenolenic acid supplement helpful – either evening primrose oil or starflower oil. It doesn't work for everyone, but it's worth a try. Bromocriptine or low-dose danazol (available on prescription) can also be helpful.

Breast pain is rarely a sign of breast cancer; however, any woman with persistent pain should see her doctor for a check-up.

BREAST LUMPS

Lumps in the breast aren't just caused by breast cancer – they can also be due to benign fibrous tissue, cysts, and localized areas of inflammation or mastitis. The two most common types of lump are fluid-filled cysts and fibroadenomas. Cysts feel firm, but not hard, while fibroadenomas, which are made up of a mixture of glandular and fibrous tissue, are usually smooth and quite mobile within the breast. However, though experienced doctors can make a good guess about the nature of a breast lump, research has shown that even they can get it wrong. That means every woman with a persistent breast lump should have thorough investigations at a specialist hospital breast unit.

Tests done will include an examination by a breast specialist, followed by either a mammogram or a breast ultrasound, or both.

♦ Mammograms (see below) have their limitations in younger women, as the breast tissue appears too dense for areas of calcification to be distinguished clearly.

♦ Breast ultrasound is mainly used to examine a small area of breast. If a cyst is found, it can often be drained under ultrasound guidance. If a lump is identified, tiny biopsies are usually taken, using a special needle, again under ultrasound guidance. These are then sent to the laboratory for analysis.

Most hospitals now offer all these tests in a single appointment, but results of any biopsies may take several days.

Treatment of lumps that have been proved to be non-cancerous mainly depends on their size and on individual circumstances.

Small lumps, less than 4cm (1¾ inches) across, are generally left alone; not only do they often disappear of their own accord, but some women are prone to forming benign lumps repeatedly, and to keep removing them could leave the breasts scarred like a battlefield. However, many women do prefer to have larger lumps removed. This is usually done on a day-case basis, under either a local or a general anaesthetic, depending on the position and size of the lump.

Mammograms

A mammogram is an X-ray picture of the breast. Each breast in turn is placed on a special small flat plate, then another flat plate is pressed down on to the breast, which helps to give a clear X-ray picture. Usually two pictures are taken – one from above and one from the side. There's no doubt that having a mammogram is uncomfortable, and some do find it painful, but this is only for the few minutes it takes for the films to be taken.

Though well-developed breast cancers nearly always show up clearly on mammograms, there will always be the odd one that is missed, or doesn't show up – it's reckoned that at least 10 per cent of breast cancers are missed by mammography, and that means that even if you have a normal mammogram it is important to continue checking your breasts for lumps or other abnormalities.

But it certainly is better than nothing – mammograms can reveal abnormalities that suggest breast cancer even when there is nothing abnormal to be felt. And at the other end of the spectrum, abnormalities can be detected that are not due to cancer.

About 1 in 20 women (5 per cent) undergoing routine screening mammograms in the UK are called back for more tests. However, only 1 in 8 of these will turn out to have breast cancer – that's about 7 out of every 1,000 women screened. The others will have abnormalities caused by non-cancerous changes in the breast.

It's reckoned that the UK breast-screening programme, where women over 50 are offered a free mammogram once every 3 years, has saved at least 300 lives each year, simply by detecting breast cancers at a stage when they can be successfully treated.

Like all X-rays, mammograms expose the breast to radiation, which can very slightly increase the risk of breast cancer. However, it's been estimated that there is less than a 1 in 25,000 risk of a mammogram causing breast cancer. But it is a reason not to have them too often – every few months would give you too much exposure to radiation.

However, the 3-year screening interval set by the NHS in the UK is a compromise between best practice and what is affordable, and, frankly, it's too long – a lot of cancers develop, and are detected, after 2 years. Ideally, women over the age of 50 should have mammograms more often – say every 12–18 months, and, if you can afford it, I suggest you pay to have one done halfway between your free NHS ones.

BREAST CANCER

Every year, over 41,000 women are diagnosed with breast cancer in the UK, and breast cancer accounts for almost 1 in 3 of all cancers in women. No wonder we are all so worried about it. And to be fair, it doesn't just affect women – 300 men a year get it too.

But the good news is that, thanks to earlier detection and better treatment, more women than ever before are beating breast cancer. Death rates from the disease are falling every year and, overall, 80 per cent of women with the disease are alive and healthy 5 years after diagnosis.

Breast cancer becomes more common the older you get. It's rare in women under 30, but becomes more common after the menopause, and is even more common in women in their sixties and seventies. Unfortunately, however, in younger women the disease can be much more aggressive than in older women.

But whatever your age, it is devastating for any woman, and for her family, to be told that she has breast cancer.

Why me?

Your family history can mean you are at increased risk of breast cancer. The genetics of breast cancer are complex, and not yet fully understood, and in most women the genetic influence is not that strong – rather it is a mix of lifestyle factors interacting with genes that triggers the disease.

Breast cancer is so common that a lot of women have somebody in their family – a grandmother, an aunt – who has had it. Generally this does not put you at any significantly increased risk unless it is a first-degree relative (mother, sister) who was diagnosed with breast cancer before the menopause. The greater the number of close relatives affected, and the younger their age, the greater the risk.

The breast cancer gene

Estimates suggest that between 5 and 10 per cent of breast cancer is caused by a genetic predisposition due to a mutated, or abnormal, gene. So far, three genes, BRCA1, BRCA2 and p53 have been identified as significantly increasing the chance of breast cancer. There are probably many others as well – they just haven't been found yet.

BRCA genes normally help to prevent cancerous cells developing, but when mutated they lose this protective effect. They can be inherited from either parent, and also appear to increase the risk of cancer of the bowel and ovary, and, to a lesser extent, cancer of the womb. A check of a family carrying one of these genes reveals several members with these cancers, usually at an early age.

These genes can now be identified by genetic testing, but this is only available on the NHS for those obviously at risk. Because of the hugely increased risk of breast cancer, many women who are carriers of these genes opt to have a bilateral mastectomy as a preventative measure, but this is obviously a very personal and difficult decision.

Other factors in breast cancer

The vast majority of women who get breast cancer, however, do not have a strong family history of it, and just because no one in your family has had it does not mean you are immune. Any woman can get breast cancer.

Other factors can also put you at slightly increased risk, including:

♦ you have never had children, or had your first child after the age of 30

♦ your periods started early (10 or younger) or you had a late menopause (after 53)

♦ being overweight, and eating a high-fat diet

♦ regularly drinking more than 2 units of alcohol a day

- taking HRT

- women on the combined pill are also at slightly increased risk, but only while they are taking it, not afterwards

- having certain types of benign breast disease (lobular carcinoma in situ and atypical lobular hyperplasia) can also slightly increase the risk of breast cancer

Diagnosis and treatment

Treatment of breast cancer is now a very specialized affair, which should always be done under the care of a team with expertise in the disease.

Treatment should be tailored not only to the patient and her wishes, but also to the type of tumour that she has. Factors that should be considered include:

- the size of the tumour

- the grade of tumour – 1, 2 or 3. This is an indication of how aggressive, or fast growing, the tumour is. Grade 3 is the most aggressive

- whether the tumour has spread to the lymph nodes in the armpit

- whether the tumour has receptors for oestrogen and progesterone

- whether the tumour has receptors for the protein HER2

Surgery: treatment usually involves removing the tumour, but whether this means removing just the lump and a small area of surrounding tissue, or the whole breast (a mastectomy, see page 323), depends on the size of the lump and whether there is a likelihood of diffuse spread of abnormal cells within the breast, which does occur in some women.

Most women are offered a choice of treatment. Research has shown that lumpectomy followed by radiotherapy can be as effective at curing cancer as mastectomy, and this is all many women require.

Breast cancer spreads mainly via the lymphatic system, and the main drainage node in the armpit (the sentinel node) is usually removed to help give an indication of whether the tumour has spread, and therefore to aid future treatment plans.

If the chance of the cancer spreading or coming back is low, then no further treatment may be necessary. However, most women are offered treatment with chemotherapy or hormonal therapy, or both, to reduce the chance of the cancer returning.

Radiotherapy is also usually given to the remaining breast tissue, or the breast wall, to prevent local recurrence of the cancer.

Chemotherapy is usually given via a course of intravenous injections over a period of 4–6 months. Side effects are very common, and can include tiredness, lowered resistance to infection, anaemia, a poor appetite and nausea and vomiting, though these can usually be reduced by special anti-sickness drugs. Hair loss is also common, though wearing a 'cold cap' during treatment can help to reduce this. Even so, most women undergoing chemotherapy for breast cancer choose to wear a wig temporarily, till their hair regrows. Chemotherapy may also induce an early menopause in some women.

Hormonal therapies, which include drugs such as tamoxifen and aromatase inhibitors, can slow or stop the growth of breast cancer cells. They do this either by altering levels of oestrogen and progesterone or by preventing these hormones being taken up by breast cancer cells. They are most effective for women whose cancer cells have receptors for oestrogen and/or progesterone on their surface. Hormonal therapy is usually given for 5 years after the initial treatment.

Herceptin is a type of treatment known as a monoclonal antibody that attaches to HER2 receptors on breast cancer cells. This stops a factor required for tumour growth from stimulating the cells. Herceptin can reduce the chance of breast cancer coming back after initial treatment, but it is only effective in women whose cancers have a large number of HER2 receptors on their surface (about 1 in 4 breast cancer patients).

Mastectomy

Having a breast removed can obviously be very distressing for any woman and is something that surgeons try to avoid if at all possible. However, it may be necessary if the lump is large, or just behind the nipple, or if there are several areas of cancer in different parts of the breast – and nearly all women opt for the best chance of a cure, even if it does mean having such major surgery.

A new breast shape – reconstructive surgery – can usually be created either at the same time as the original surgery, or months or years later. Having a mastectomy usually requires a hospital stay of between 3 and 5 days, and inevitably the wound is painful and sore for a few weeks afterwards.

If any lymph glands are removed as well, there may be swelling of the arm on that side – lymphoedema. This can be eased by physiotherapy and exercises, together with a supportive bandage.

Secondary breast cancer

In many women, initial treatment is very successful, and they remain free of cancer – some for the rest of their life. Others are not so lucky, and at some stage in the future – usually years later – the cancer returns. If this is in the same area as the original tumour, in the breast, or in the chest wall, it is known as a local recurrence.

Secondary breast cancer occurs when breast cancer cells spread, usually via the lymphatic system, to other parts of the body. This is often referred to as metastases, or secondaries. Breast cancer most commonly spreads to the bones, liver and lungs. Less commonly, it can also spread to the brain.

Secondary breast cancer cannot be cured, but it can usually be controlled for many years with further chemotherapy and radiotherapy. Being told you have secondary breast cancer can be devastating, and many women say dealing with the mental distress is worse than the physical effects of treatment. There are several excellent support organizations for women with breast cancer, and many women find their help invaluable.

Though complementary therapies cannot treat the disease itself, they can be very helpful in promoting physical, psychological and emotional well-being.

♦ massage and aromatherapy can promote relaxation

♦ some herbal remedies can relieve any hot flushes triggered by hormonal treatments

♦ acupuncture can help relieve pain and inflammation, or nausea caused by chemotherapy

♦ psychological therapies such as CBT (see page 237) can help reduce stress and anxiety

SKIN CARE AND COSMECEUTICALS

WHAT HAPPENS TO YOUR SKIN AS YOU GET OLDER?

The ageing of the skin on our faces, hands and necks is all too obvious, especially from our forties onwards. Fine lines appear and multiply, wrinkles develop and deepen and, inexorably, women's faces appear to droop. From the age of about 50, our skins also get slightly thinner. What is going on?

Some of the changes simply reflect the fact that the skin, just like the heart, kidneys and other organs, is getting older. The movement of our faces also contributes to wrinkles, which is why the deepest ones are often in the places that crease up when we smile or frown – for instance between the bottom corners of the nose and the corners of the mouth. Ageing also leads to the downward redistribution of fat in women's faces, making the cheeks look less plump, the nose and ears larger and the lips thinner.

SUNSHINE AND CIGARETTES

But age itself has less of an impact on our skin than outside factors –
most notably ultraviolet light from the sun, and smoking. Some
dermatologists estimate that around 80 per cent of all skin ageing is
due to the effects of sunlight. To get an idea of how true this is,
compare the soft, smooth skin on the insides of your upper arms with
that on your hands and face, which will have been exposed to far more
sun.

The sun's ultraviolet light damages skin because some of it
penetrates through the outer layers of skin to the collagen underneath.
It's the collagen, which is a protein, that gives skin its elasticity. The sun
damages the collagen, making the skin more saggy and wrinkled.

Some people's faces are naturally better protected from the sun
because their skin contains more dark (melanin) pigment, which
prevents some of the sun's rays penetrating to the collagen below. At
one end of the spectrum is black African skin, which is least vulnerable
to the sun's rays (although it can still burn if exposed for too long).
People with Asian and southern Mediterranean skins, who tend to go
brown rather than red in the sun, are in the middle; and skin that is
typical of people from northern European countries, such as Scotland,
are at the palest, most vulnerable end. This is why black-skinned
women generally look younger than white-skinned women of the same
age – they are naturally better protected from the sun.

The more you can hide your skin from sunshine (and this means
keeping clear of sunbeds, which also produce ultraviolet light), the more
slowly your skin will age. That means:

- wearing wide-brimmed hats

- wearing sunglasses and clothes that cover you

- staying out of the sun when it is at its hottest (between about 11a.m. and 3p.m.)

- wearing sunscreen with a sun protection factor (SPF) of at least 15

- make sure, too, that your sunscreen is 'broad spectrum', which means that it will protect you against both UVA and UVB rays. Confusingly, the SPF factor shows how well the product protects you from UVB rays, while the star rating shows how much UVA protection you'll get. Look for a product that carries four or five stars, which is the highest level of protection. Too few face creams currently carry this level of information, but it is worth asking manufacturers about their products because they should be able to tell you and your questions will encourage them to be more forthcoming on packaging

- avoid burning at all costs, because it will age you more dramatically than anything else and it could also give you skin cancer. And remember that even a tan is a sign that your skin has been damaged

But don't hide from the sun completely. You need a short time (the exact amount depending on your skin type, lifestyle and where you live) with some of your skin exposed to the sun, two to three times a week, for your body to manufacture enough vitamin D. There is some evidence that vitamin D helps to protect against some cancers and it is also vital for strong bones. About 90 per cent of it is made naturally in the body when the skin is exposed to the sun. You do not need to get a tan to have enough vitamin D.

After sunshine, the next most important influence on your skin is cigarettes. You have only to look at a picture of a woman who has smoked all her life to see how the habit has left her with fine lines (especially around the mouth) and lifeless skin. Smoking causes tiny blood vessels called capillaries to narrow, and that in turn means less oxygen and other nutrients for your skin. Giving up smoking will give your skin a major boost and it will also have huge benefits for your health overall.

DO FACE CREAMS MAKE A DIFFERENCE?

The short answer is that protecting yourself from the sun and not smoking are far more beneficial than any ingredient in a face cream, no matter how expensive it is.

The only ingredient that is proven to make a major difference is sunscreen, because it helps to protect your skin from the ageing effects of ultraviolet light. So when you're shopping for a face cream to wear during the day, the most important thing to look out for is whether it contains a broad-spectrum sunscreen with an SPF of 15 or above. This is because the sun is by far the biggest single ageing influence on your skin and the sunscreen will help to protect your skin from it. Don't, however, let even a sunscreen give you a false sense of security – you still need to cover up and stay out of the sun in other ways (see above).

Some dermatologists now favour 'physical' sunscreens such as titanium dioxide and zinc oxide, because they are less likely to cause an allergic reaction than widely used 'chemical' sunscreens with unpronounceable names. Physical sunscreens sit on the surface of the skin and prevent some of the sun's rays from getting through to the collagen below, whereas chemical sunscreens actually penetrate the skin.

At night there is, of course, no need to cover your face with sun-shielding chemicals, but you may want to apply a moisturizer if your skin feels dry.

What about other magic ingredients?

The cosmetic companies' claims. The term 'cosmeceuticals' has been conjured up to imply something between a cosmetic and a pharmaceutical drug, and to justify a hefty price tag. It sounds better than a mere moisturizer, after all. Face-cream companies are endlessly coming up with new ingredients which, they hint, will make us look young again. Vitamins A, C and E, green tea and scientific-sounding chemicals such as CoQ10, neuropeptides and phosphatidylcholine are now turning up in their products.

However, cosmetics are not legally allowed to alter the structure or function of the skin. If they did make such a major difference, then they would be classed as drugs and their manufacturers would be forced to carry out expensive tests to prove their products were safe and effective.

Furthermore, while the law requires companies to have proof (for instance from scientific testing) that the claims they make for their products are true, companies appear to be reluctant to let the public see this evidence and the law is not well enforced. If you want to test this for yourself, ask your local trading standards office to examine whether claims made by your favourite skin cream are backed up by hard, scientific evidence.

Exfoliating creams. Dermatologists have some faith in creams that exfoliate your skin – that is, they remove some of the very top layer of cells to reveal the younger ones below, making your skin look and feel smoother and softer. This won't actually remove wrinkles, but it will help moisturizing cream to penetrate the surface of the skin, which can make it look plumper. Beware, though, that too enthusiastic or frequent exfoliation can leave your skin red and flaky.

Skin peels. There is also some evidence that gently peeling off the outer layer of your skin, once a week, with a cream containing a chemical such as salicylic acid, can help with the appearance of your skin because it increases the rate at which the skin renews itself. However, again there is a risk that it will make your face sore and, ironically, this is most likely to happen to fairer-skinned people whose skin naturally ages most quickly.

Retinoids. Another ingredient in skin creams for which there is some positive evidence. It is derived from vitamin A. A product called Retinova has actually been given a licence as a drug that can help in the treatment of sun-damaged skin, as well as some other skin conditions. However, again it can actually make the skin irritated and more vulnerable to being damaged by the sun, so special care must be taken to shield the skin. It is only available in this country on prescription.

Researchers are examining the effects of other face cream ingredients, but so far the only ones known to have long-term benefits are: sunscreens.

I'll say it again: by far the most important two things you can do to keep yourself looking younger are:

- protect your skin from the sun
- stop smoking

Nothing else comes close.

COSMETIC SURGERY

We've all seen pictures of celebrities who seem to become magically younger with every passing year. We do know that clever computers have airbrushed away all their lines and wrinkles; yet we still believe the evidence of our eyes when we look at the glamorous women on the front pages of glossy magazines. Then, of course, we apply this reasoning to ourselves: 'If she can look that good, so can I.'

We live in a youth-orientated age, where it's deeply unfashionable to grow old gracefully. This means that increasing numbers of women are prepared to go to extreme lengths to take away the evidence of the passing years.

Cosmetic procedures – be it fillers, peels, botox or going under the knife – are now big business. Cosmetic treatments that seem quick and easy are now readily available on the high street, and you can pop out in your lunch break and come back a changed woman. Forget just having a new hairstyle – you can have a new smile.

But of course, cosmetic procedures can, and often do, go wrong. Having a bad 'face job' is much worse, and harder to rectify, than a disaster at the hair salon.

Why?

Cosmetic surgery should never be done on the spur of the moment. You should think very long and very hard about why you want to have it done. Questions to ask yourself should include:

♦ Are you expecting it to change your life? If so, is this realistic? Is it really going to make a huge difference if you have a different nose shape or plumper lips?

♦ Are your expectations of the procedure realistic? Ugly duckling into swan?

♦ Are you having it done to please yourself or someone else?

Changing your appearance may not be the best answer to improving your relationship, or your self-esteem, and it's always worthwhile considering other routes first, such as counselling (see page 237).

If you do decide to go ahead with a cosmetic procedure, then it's vital to do as much homework as possible. You need to know all about both the procedure itself and about the place, and especially the person, who is going to be doing it. Then go and discuss the whole thing with your GP. She can help you decipher any qualifications you don't understand, and can also advise you if there are any medical reasons why you may need to reconsider your plans. It is always better to forewarn your GP of what you are about to do anyway, in case things go wrong afterwards.

Which procedure and where to go?

First, you need to work out exactly what you are trying to achieve, and how much you can afford.

There are two main groups of treatment:

♦ **Cosmetic procedures**, such as fillers, botox, laser treatments and chemical peels. These are readily available and can be done by someone with a worrying lack of experience or qualifications.

♦ **Surgical procedures**, when someone (hopefully a well-qualified surgeon) takes a scalpel to your skin. Liposuction also comes into this category.

Cosmetic procedures

There is a disturbing lack of regulation in this industry. Many clinics offering dermal fillers and botox go unchecked, with no inspections of either care standards or staff qualifications. Always check out several clinics, and ask:

♦ Who exactly will be carrying out the procedure? 'One of the staff' is not good enough. Check their qualifications and experience, and whether they have professional indemnity insurance.

♦ The cost, including any 'extras'. Who pays for any complications?

♦ About the treatment itself. This can be revealing – you should not feel pressurized into making a decision, and you should have both the procedure and the risks involved fully explained.

♦ To see 'before and after' photographs, and ask if it is possible to speak to someone who has had the same treatment at that clinic.

Any clinic where the staff fight shy of giving you this information and cannot supply personal recommendations is to be avoided.

Surgical procedures

All clinics offering cosmetic surgery must, by law, be registered with the Healthcare Commission and have regular inspections. Check on their website (healthcarecommission.org.uk) for the latest report on any clinic you are considering.

You also need to be sure of the qualifications and experience of the doctor (and yes, it should be a doctor) who is going to be doing your operation, and make sure you have a full consultation with him or her beforehand.

Any doctor doing cosmetic surgery should have, in addition to basic medical qualifications:

♦ a surgical qualification: FRCS

♦ this may be in a particular field – FRCS (Plast) means the surgeon has a specialist qualification in plastic surgery

♦ ideally the surgeon will also be a member of the British Association of Aesthetic and Plastic Surgeons

Common procedures

There isn't space in this book to go through all the procedures available – there are just too many of them. But here are the most common:

♦ botox

♦ dermal fillers

♦ laser skin resurfacing

♦ chemical peels

♦ liposuction

♦ face lifts

♦ breast implants

♦ breast reduction

Botox. This is a prescription-only medicine. It's a toxin which blocks nerve impulses, which in turn paralyses and relaxes muscles. It can be injected into the face with the aim of smoothing out fine lines and wrinkles. It takes effect after 3–7 days, and lasts 3–6 months. With repeat treatments, the effect lasts longer.

Botox can result in facial muscles that don't move at all, giving your face a mask-like appearance. Other possible side effects include double vision and drooping of an eyebrow or lid.

Botox should only ever be injected by a doctor experienced in using it, or a well-trained nurse working under a doctor's supervision.

Dermal fillers. These aim to fill out lines and wrinkles, and make lips or sunken scars appear fuller. There are many different types, including:

- ◆ hyaluronic acid
- ◆ Gore-Tex
- ◆ collagen
- ◆ fibril

Injections are usually done into several points near the edge of the area being treated. It can hurt, particularly in sensitive areas like the lips. Effects usually last between 4 and 9 months. The more dermal filler you have put in, the greater the effect and the longer it will last (which is bad news if you end up looking like a trout).

Other possible side effects are allergic reactions, infection at the injection site, lumpiness and scarring. Dermal fillers may also re-activate cold sores.

Fillers should only be injected by experienced doctors and nurses.

Laser skin resurfacing. Lasers heat and destroy tissue, which then repairs itself with new cells. There are several different types of laser, which can penetrate the skin to different depths. Laser resurfacing can be used to remove acne scars, birthmarks, sun damage and wrinkles. Be warned that it can hurt.

The skin takes 7–10 days to heal, and may be red for weeks afterwards. Aftercare – regular careful cleansing and moisturizing – is very important.

If not done very carefully, laser treatment can cause burns and scarring. It can also damage the eyes, so it's important to wear protective goggles during the treatment.

All clinics offering laser treatment have to be registered and, though treatment is best done by an experienced doctor or nurse, some trained beauty therapists can use low-powered laser machines.

Chemical peels. These aim to accelerate the removal of old dead cells on the surface of the skin, and to promote new skin growth. Different solutions may be used to give a varying depth of peel:

♦ superficial (usually using alpha-hydroxy-acids)
♦ medium (using tri-chloracetic acids)
♦ deep (using phenol)

A similar effect can be obtained using dermabrasion or skin resurfacing, where the top layer is sanded off using either a wire brush or fine particles.

The effect, and how long it lasts, depends on the depth of peel, from around 6 weeks for a superficial peel to many years for a deep peel.

Side effects too vary according to the depth of peel, but it's normal to have redness and stinging afterwards. The skin can also become infected and is prone to sunburn.

Superficial peels can be done by beauty therapists; deeper peels should only be done by qualified doctors or nurses.

Liposuction. This removes fat under the skin by suction. It is done under either a local or general anaesthetic and, depending on how much is being done, can take up to 2 hours. A small cut is made in the skin, then the surgeon passes in a small hollow tube and massages the fat layer to break up the fat cells, which are then sucked out. Sometimes fluid is injected, or ultrasound is used to help break up the fat beforehand.

It's common to have bruising afterwards, and to feel sore. To reduce swelling, you have to wear a special compression garment after treatment. Possible side effects include:

♦ nerve damage

♦ unevenness in the area treated

♦ scarring where the tube has been inserted

♦ those having ultrasound-assisted liposuction also risk internal and external bruising

♦ liposuction can also occasionally cause heavy bleeding, and there have been reports of patients needing blood transfusions afterwards, though this is rare

The results are permanent, but only as long as you are careful with your diet. If you over-eat, you can put all the fat back on again.

Liposuction should only be done by a qualified surgeon in a registered clinic.

Face lifts. There are many different types of face lift, but the aim is usually to tighten the skin on the face, removing sagging, lines and wrinkles.

The surgery is carried out under a general anaesthetic and can take up to 6 hours. An incision is usually made in the hairline from the temples, round behind the ears and into the hairline. The skin is freed from the underlying tissues, lifted up and backwards, the excess skin removed, and then it is sutured back into its new position. Face lifts can also be done using keyhole methods, which leaves smaller scars. An overnight stay in hospital is usually required, and at least 2 weeks off work afterwards.

Results can be impressive – many women report that a face lift has made them look ten years younger. However, risks can include infection, numbness and loss of movement in the face, giving you an obvious mask-like appearance, with a loss of character. You may also end up looking a bit asymmetrical.

Breast implants. Implants can enlarge your breasts to a size you want – from just one cup to several cup sizes bigger.

Most implants are made from a silicone shell filled with more silicone or a salt solution. They are inserted under a general anaesthetic, via a tiny cut in the armpit on each side, or just under the nipple. Occasionally a cut is made under the breast itself.

It's important to support the breast afterwards with a good bra, and to rest – you'll need at least a week off work.

Common problems are:

- ◆ 'Capsular contracture', the most common risk, when a layer of scar tissue grows around the implant, making it lose both its shape and softness.
- ◆ Occasionally the tissue around the implant can crease, causing discomfort and an odd appearance.
- ◆ You can also lose some sensation in the breast.
- ◆ Implants can also affect your ability to breastfeed (though most women can, at least a little).

If you don't like the implants, or if they give problems, they can usually be removed, but this isn't always a straightforward procedure. Some implants do need to be replaced after about 15 years.

Breast implants should always be inserted by a surgeon with the relevant experience and qualifications, in a registered clinic or hospital.

Breast reduction. This reshapes the breasts by removing fat, glandular tissue and skin. It is done under a general anaesthetic and the operation usually takes 2–4 hours. It's a much more major procedure than having implants. A cut is made around the nipple area, then vertically down the lower half of the breast, and along the crease under the breast. Excess tissue and skin is removed, and then the nipple is repositioned before the skin is sewn up again. You need to stay in hospital overnight and have at least 2 weeks off work afterwards, with no heavy lifting or physical exercise for 6 weeks.

The surgery leaves visible scars, which may become lumpy, and there may be some loss of sensation in the nipple. It is common not to be able to breastfeed afterwards.

As with all breast surgery, reduction procedures should only be done by well-qualified surgeons in registered clinics or hospitals.

VARICOSE VEINS

Whatever your age, varicose veins can ruin the appearance of your legs. In many women, they are purely a cosmetic problem, but larger veins can cause leg ache and discomfort. They can also lead to varicose eczema and to leg ulcers.

At least a quarter of all women will get varicose veins – that's twice the rate in men. They can vary from tiny thread veins in just a small area of the leg to much larger, knobbly ones that run from the ankle to the thigh.

They are caused by damage to the tiny valves inside the affected vein. These usually act as dams to prevent blood flowing backwards down the leg with gravity. Any weakening of these valves leads to pooling of blood in the vein below, which then eventually becomes stretched and distorted – a varicose vein.

Varicose veins usually only occur in the veins of the legs just beneath the skin; this means they generally do not increase the risk of having a leg thrombosis, or clot, as these usually occur in the deep veins.

Why has this happened?

♦ Varicose veins become more common with increasing age. There also seems to be a genetic component to them – if your mother had them, then you are more at risk.

♦ Varicose veins often develop during pregnancy, partly because the extra weight of the baby puts pressure on the veins, and also because the pregnancy hormones relax the walls of veins. Though the veins may be much less obvious once the baby has been born, there is usually some permanent damage, especially after several pregnancies.

♦ Being overweight increases the risk in women, but strangely not so much in men!

♦ Spending hours on your feet, particularly if you are standing still, can increase the risk.

Self-help

Some women unfortunately get varicose veins no matter what they do, but you can help to prevent them:

♦ Keep your weight down and stay active. Anything that exercises the calf muscles, such as walking or swimming, is especially good, as contraction then relaxation of the muscles helps to promote blood flow inside the deep veins.

♦ Graduated support socks or tights can help to keep blood flowing in the superficial veins, but avoid wearing hosiery that has a tight band on the thigh or below the knee (such as pop socks) as this can have the opposite effect.

♦ Wearing high-heeled shoes alters the shape of the calf muscles and does not help blood flow – so avoid wearing them for long periods, especially if you are likely to be standing still.

♦ When you are sitting down, it can help to raise your legs so that they are above the level of your chest. This too helps to promote blood flow back up the legs.

Treatment

Small veins, especially thread veins, generally don't need to be treated for medical reasons, but if you want to improve the appearance of your legs, they can be obliterated with either laser or high-intensity light treatment, or by injecting with a sclerosant chemical, which glues the walls of the vein together. This can cause some staining of the surrounding skin. As these procedures are done for cosmetic reasons they are not generally available on the NHS.

Veins that itch, or ache, or are obviously very large and tortuous are a different matter. These types of vein are at risk from becoming inflamed (phlebitis) and the very slow flow of blood within them can lead to dry skin and eczema around the ankles, and can also increase the risk of leg ulcers, though these usually take many years to develop.

Traditionally, treatment involves removing, or stripping out, the whole of the affected vein. This should only ever be done after a special ultrasound or Doppler examination has been carried out to determine how many veins are damaged, and to what extent. It can also be used to check blood flow in the deep veins. This is important, as stripping out a superficial vein inevitably diverts some blood to the deeper veins, and therefore these must be healthy beforehand.

The operation is usually done as a day-case procedure, and involves an incision in the groin and one further down the leg. Several additional small cuts may also be made to remove smaller veins.

After the operation you'll need to wear special strong support stockings for at least a couple of weeks, and also to take daily walks. It's normally possible to resume your usual activities in a week or two.

A new technique for treating larger veins is now available, and involves inserting a tiny catheter into the affected vein, which delivers radiofrequency energy to the vein wall, causing it to heat, collapse and seal shut. This does not require any cuts and recovery times are quicker – though it's still necessary to wear strong support stockings afterwards. Long-term results of this procedure are still not known, and as yet it is not generally available on the NHS.

IN SUMMARY

This chapter has been all about coping with the second huge physical upheaval of a woman's life. At least this time round you will know what is happening and why, and hopefully be sure enough of yourself to cope with the nuisance and indignities of the menopause. Teenagers often seem assured on the surface, but are hiding their ignorance with bravado. Women in their fifties have so much more experience and knowledge, having managed to deal with whatever life has thrown at them. Now the years of menopause and post-menopause become just another challenge to be understood and welcomed.

This is the age when check-ups become really vital. If you have neglected them before, start thinking about them now and act on your thoughts. So many serious diseases can be caught at an early stage through regular medical check-ups, from cancer to heart disease to osteoporosis. Catching the first symptoms will give you the best chance of overcoming these problems and giving yourself a healthy later life.

And again, nutrition plays its part. Don't give up and accept that older women must pile on weight. Keep an eye on your intake of the most nutritious foods and, most of all, stay active. It's a time of life when the physical pressure of having small children has often gone away and we can put our feet up. Enjoy it, but don't slide into laziness!

Once you are past your fifties, you can look forward to another period of stability in your physical state. Many women in their 'third age' experience a positive rejuvenation in mind and body, and the next chapter will help you to cope with any difficulties which arise.

CHAPTER 6

ACTIVE RETIREMENT YEARS: 60–75

The retirement years bring new challenges. At some point between the ages of 60 and 75 you are likely to stop work. At last you have freedom from the daily grind, but this usually brings a huge drop in income. You may also experience other unwelcome side effects from retirement, such as a loss of focus in everyday life and a drop in your self-esteem. Our lives are so bound up with work – if I'm not a worker, who am I?

Not only that, but adjusting to being in your home much more than before, either on your own or with your newly retired partner for company, can be difficult.

This is also a time when your body may start to let you down, and 'high maintenance' can take on a whole new meaning. Feeling and looking good now takes time and effort, and, chances are, you won't just have to pay more attention to yourself – you'll probably have to keep an eye on your partner as well. But it can pay dividends. At this time of your life, you can have excellent health, and at long last you have the time to do those things you always wanted to do.

Like all other things in life, though, it's all about perspective and attitude. If you try to see your situation from a positive angle – time for yourself, time to get to grips with those hobbies that you've only dabbled in before, less stress – you will see how wonderful this period in your life can be.

In this chapter you will find:

- **Staying healthy**
  - checks you should be having now
- **Food and nutrition**
  - controlling your weight
  - eating for a healthy heart
  - special diets for arthritis and diabetes
  - supplements for the over-sixties
- **Lifestyle and mental health**
  - planning your retirement
  - looking after your partner
- **Hormone problems**
  - vaginal dryness
  - cancer of the womb
  - ovarian cysts and ovarian cancer
- **Physical illnesses**
  - heart disease
  - bowel cancer
  - bladder infections
  - incontinence
- **Skin and hair**
  - ageing skin
  - skin cancer
  - thinning hair

STAYING HEALTHY

Many women do enjoy wonderful health right through to their eighties and beyond. However, the human body is, in many ways, just like a car – as it gets older it does have a habit of not functioning quite as well as it once did. This is an age when many potentially serious diseases start to occur, such as high blood pressure, diabetes, arthritis and many cancers. But, just as with a car, regular maintenance can really make a difference, and detecting a problem in the early stages can help to stop it developing into a major issue.

Regular health checks are important. These should include:

♦ **Every 2 years**: a blood pressure check.

♦ **Every 2 years**: a blood cholesterol check – more often if the level is raised.

♦ **Every 2 years**: a thorough eye test.

♦ **Every 3 years**: a blood glucose check.

♦ **Every 3 years**: a mammogram – more often if you can afford it (see page 317). Automatic invitations for NHS screening stop at 65, but you are still entitled to screening after this age – you just have to ask for it. Your GP or practice nurse can arrange this for you.

♦ A final smear test in your early sixties.

Routine 'self checks' should include:

♦ being breast aware, and checking your breasts approximately once a month

♦ checking your skin, all over, for lumps, bumps or marks that are itchy, enlarging or changing colour

- taking note of the appearance of your stools

- checking your weight once a month: losing a couple of pounds is always easier than losing an extra couple of stones, but unexpected weight loss should not be ignored

Any unusual symptoms should always be checked out. This applies particularly to:

- bleeding from anywhere, but especially from the back passage, from the vagina or in your urine

- any change in bowel habit

- shortness of breath

- a persistent cough

- night sweats

- pain or discomfort in the chest or abdomen

FOOD AND NUTRITION

Even if age-related medical problems have begun to emerge, a great deal can be done to minimize their impact by eating wisely and well. Choosing the right foods really is an important part of maintaining good health into later life.

CONTROLLING YOUR WEIGHT

One of the biggest challenges for many older women is controlling their waistline, and some do find that the pounds creep on, even though they are eating pretty much the same as they always did. The main reason is a low metabolism, and though the best way to tackle this is with regular exercise, that's not always so easy if your joints are beginning to get a bit creaky. So if you want to keep your weight down, you probably will have to make some adjustments to your diet. It doesn't have to be drastic – just small changes, in the long term, can make a difference.

Let's look at, for instance, how cutting back a little on fat and sugar can have a big impact on your overall health.

Fat contains twice as many calories as starch or protein, and most people eat far too much of it. Eating 30 grams (1oz) less each day, which is actually fairly easy, saves 252 calories and can really make a difference if you are trying to lose weight. Not only that, but it will reduce your risk of heart disease as well.

The most important fat to cut down is the saturated fat (which is so bad for arteries) found in biscuits, cheese, cooking fats, hard margarine, pastry, pies, meat fat, full-fat milk, dairy products and chips. Some vegetable fats are also mainly saturates.

Cutting down your fat consumption does not have to entail a major diet overhaul. Here are some easy ways to do it:

♦ choose lean cuts of meat and trim off all fat

♦ eat more fish and poultry

♦ grill instead of frying

♦ if you do fry, use a tiny amount of oil, preferably olive oil

♦ choose semi-skimmed or skimmed milk and use low-fat spreads

♦ always read the labels on foods such as cakes, biscuits and savoury snacks to check the fat content

Sugar: eating 30 grams (1oz) less sugar each day cuts out 112 calories. Try not to add sugar to drinks and cereals and use dried fruit such as raisins to sweeten puddings and cereals instead. Even after a lifetime of use, you will be surprised at just how fast your tastebuds will adapt to a sugar-free cup of tea or bowl of cereal.

A HEALTHY DIET

Here are some pointers to healthy eating for the over-sixties:

♦ Wholegrain versions of bread, pasta, rice and cereals will provide you with important fibre and keep your hunger at bay for much longer than refined white types.

♦ Fresh fruit and vegetables are low in calories, packed with fibre and really can help to fill you up, and it's surprising how few women manage to munch their way through the recommended 5 portions a day. So try to get used to raiding the fruit bowl instead of the biscuit barrel when you're hit with a hunger pang.

♦ High-carbohydrate foods, such as pasta, rice and potatoes, are lower in calories than foods high in fat and provide valuable vitamins and minerals, so don't ban them from your diet. What makes them fattening and high in cholesterol is the butter and rich sauces you add to them.

♦ One of the biggest problems for women over 60 is eating enough calcium – you need at least 1000mg a day to help to keep your bones strong. The best sources are dairy products, such as milk, cheese and yogurt – and the good news is that semi-skimmed and skimmed milk contain more calcium per pint than full cream. Calcium is also found in wholemeal bread, baked beans, boiled cabbage and fish such as sardines. Soya milk is often calcium-fortified too.

EATING FOR A HEALTHY HEART

You can help to keep your heart healthy by eating a low-cholesterol and low-salt diet, and also making sure you eat at least 5 portions of fruit and vegetables each day. These changes will also help to reduce your blood pressure and your risk of a stroke.

Cholesterol makes its way round the body by hitching a ride on two fat proteins (lipoproteins). About 70 per cent of cholesterol attaches itself to low-density lipoproteins (LDL). These are the baddies that contribute to fatty deposits in artery walls and increase the risk of heart disease. The rest attaches itself to high-density lipoproteins (HDL) which prevent cholesterol build-up in arteries. Women tend to have higher levels of this 'good cholesterol' than men.

Only about 25 per cent of cholesterol comes from diet; the rest is produced by the liver. However, a diet high in saturated fat can cause the liver to produce more LDL – the bad cholesterol – and, overall, it's possible to reduce your cholesterol by up to 10 per cent just by eating healthily. That, in turn, reduces the risk of a heart attack by 20 per cent.

Reducing saturated fat

Your first dietary move should be to reduce your fat consumption, especially saturated fats, as these have the biggest influence on raising blood cholesterol levels. Instead, use small quantities of unsaturated or monosaturated fats, which can help to lower cholesterol levels.

Foods high in saturated fat: biscuits, cakes, red meat, hard cheese, butter, cream and foods that contain coconut and palm oil are all high in saturated fat.

A few vegetable fats and a great deal of processed food contain saturated fat too, so read the labels carefully. If you see the word 'hydrogenated' it means some of the polyunsaturated fat has been converted to saturated, which is seriously bad news!

Egg yolks, offal and meat all contain some saturated fat too, so try to limit these – and certainly don't eat them every day.

Good sources of unsaturated fat: most vegetable oils, such as sunflower, olive, corn and rapeseed, nuts and seeds, and avocados. A particularly good source of unsaturated fat is oily fish, such as salmon, herring, mackerel and fresh (not canned) tuna. Try to eat these twice a week.

Fish generally has less cholesterol than meat, but the content in shellfish varies – prawns are quite high in saturated fat.

Cholesterol-free foods: fruit, vegetables, grains, cereal, nuts and seeds contain no cholesterol. Another good reason for eating your recommended daily allowance of fruit and veg is that, along with pulses and oats, they contain soluble fibre which helps to lower cholesterol. There is also evidence that foods containing plant sterols do the same – they are found in specially developed products, such as butter-substitute spreads and yogurts. However, be warned – they cost considerably more than their 'normal' versions, and can make a dent in your purse as well as your cholesterol levels.

Salt

Eating too much salt can contribute to high blood pressure, which in turn can increase the risk of heart disease. The maximum recommended daily amount is 6g.

Processed foods, such as ready meals, are full of salt and account for 75 per cent of the salt we eat. Labels can be misleading. On the whole, they merely state the sodium content, despite salt containing both sodium and chloride. You need to multiply the amount of sodium per 100 grams by 2.5 to get the true salt content. In other words, 1g of sodium equals 2.5g of salt, which is almost half your recommended daily intake. You may be surprised by how quickly you reach the daily maximum.

A quick guide: I appreciate that few women want to take a calculator to the supermarket or do sums in the aisles, so, as a general rule, choose food that contains fewer than 0.1g of sodium per 100 grams.

Foods that are especially high in salt include:

- soy sauce
- yeast extract
- stock cubes
- ready-salted snacks, such as crisps and peanuts
- bacon, cheese and pickles tend to have large amounts too, because of how they are made

At home, don't automatically add salt to what you are cooking, and try to get out of the habit of reaching for the condiments before you have tasted your food. If you gradually cut down on salt you will soon adjust, in the same way as people who give up sugar in their tea. After a bit, you will find the flavour of too much salt a real taste-bud turn-off. Try using lemon juice, ginger, garlic or herbs to flavour food instead.

DIET AND ARTHRITIS

In your sixties, if you suffer from aching joints, you may have already encountered that dreaded phrase 'wear and tear' – a euphemism for arthritis.

Five million people in Britain suffer from osteoarthritis and it is responsible for one in five visits to GPs. Rheumatoid arthritis is generally more severe but less common, affecting about 1 in 100 people.

If you suffer from either of these conditions (see pages 421 and 268) and are too heavy for your height (see page 218), losing those extra pounds is the single most important thing you can do to minimize the pressure on weight-bearing joints (back, hips, knees, ankles and feet) when they are already damaged. Even losing a small amount of weight can make a huge difference.

You should also ensure your diet contains plenty of calcium and vitamins C and D to protect and maintain your joints and bones.

If you suffer from rheumatoid arthritis you may discover that eating some foods aggravates the condition. Keep a diary of everything you eat to see if there is a correlation between greater pain and particular types of food. Some people have found that eating more vegetables, bananas and cherries eases symptoms.

Research strongly indicates that consuming essential fatty acids

(EFAs), found in fish oils and plant seed oils, can reduce the inflammation associated with arthritis. Try to eat oily fish such as mackerel, pilchards, salmon and sardines three times a week, or, for veggies, linseeds or flaxseed oil.

DIABETES

About 1.4 million people in the UK are known to have diabetes – and possibly nearly as many again have not yet been diagnosed – see page 356. Around 85 per cent of diabetes sufferers have type 2, which does not require insulin injections and can usually be controlled either by diet alone or by a combination of diet and tablets. Diabetes is now so common that the chances are you will be faced with feeding a diabetic at some time or another – whether it's yourself or a family member – so it's helpful to know the 'rules'.

The diabetic diet
First, and most important, there is no need to buy special (and usually very expensive) 'diabetic' foods. What diabetics need is a healthy, balanced diet:

♦ **low** in saturated fat, sugar and salt
♦ **high** in fibre, fruit and vegetables

Carbohydrate intake should be spread throughout the day to avoid blood sugar peaks after meals. Try to eat the same amount of food at the same times of day to keep blood sugar stable.

Soluble fibres in fruits, vegetables and some seeds are especially beneficial because they help to slow down or reduce the absorption of glucose from the intestines. Legumes, such as cooked kidney beans, are one of the richest sources.

Try to have 6 servings of starches such as bread, cereals and starchy vegetables a day, and make sure you have your 5 daily portions of fruit and vegetables. A low GI diet is ideal for diabetics – for more information on this (see page 224).

Diabetics should never drink alcohol on an empty stomach because it can result in low blood sugar. Drink in moderation and always have something to eat with your drink or shortly before.

Diabetes

Diabetes is caused by a lack of insulin, the hormone that helps to move sugar from the blood into the body tissues, where it can be used to provide energy. Diabetes doesn't just make you unwell – it can cause a significant increase in atherosclerosis (furring and hardening of the arteries; see page 372), and this in turn can cause problems with the blood supply to the toes and legs, as well as increasing the chance of having a heart attack or a stroke. Diabetes can also damage the kidneys, nerves and eyes, and the longer it goes untreated, the greater the chance of long-term health problems.

Type 1 diabetes, where natural insulin production tends to stop altogether, usually starts early in life, and often has a dramatic onset. In type 2 there is some insulin production, but not enough to keep blood-sugar levels normal. It usually starts later in life, and people who are overweight are more at risk.

In type 2, symptoms can be quite vague; they are often mistaken for other illnesses or are missed altogether. Unfortunately, this means that thousands of people have untreated diabetes for years, with harmful effects on their long-term health.

Things to look out for include:

- feeling unusually tired

- feeling thirsty

- needing to pass urine more often than normal

- frequent minor infections, particularly thrush

- blurred vision

If you have any of these, then see your doctor. Diagnosis of diabetes is very easy – it just involves a blood test to check your blood-sugar levels. Treatment depends on the severity of the condition. For some, just losing weight and cutting back on sugary foods is all that is required. Others may need tablets to boost the production of insulin. Only those with type 1 and severe type 2 require insulin injections.

SUPPLEMENTS FOR THE OVER-SIXTIES

I'd be the first to admit that 'conventional' medicine hasn't got all the answers when it comes to an ageing body, and some supplements can be very helpful. However, what on earth do you choose from that vast range available at the chemist or your health-food shop?

The marketing people are clever: they know when they have a captive audience. There really are some women who will buy anything to hold back the advancing years, and some of the products available have very little solid scientific evidence to back their promising claims. So if you choose to go down the supplement route, read the labels before you buy. Some may look good value until you discover you have to take eight capsules a day. Supplements are expensive, especially if you are a pensioner.

Always tell your GP what you are taking because some supplements can be dangerous when taken with conventional medicine.

Here are some helpful supplements for the over-sixties:

Calcium: most women don't get enough from their diet. Opt for a product with a little added magnesium, which is also required for strong bones. Older women who get very little sunlight should choose a product that also has added vitamin D. Calcium can cause indigestion, but chewable versions are often better tolerated. It is best taken in the evening. If you are at risk from osteoporosis (see page 307) you should be able to get calcium and vitamin D free on prescription from your GP.

Cod liver oil: good for both the heart and the joints. It is rich in omega 3 fatty acids, which can help to reduce the activity of enzymes that damage cartilage. They also switch off the chemical process that causes pain and inflammation, making it ideal for arthritis sufferers. It is high in vitamin D as well, so is good for bones. Not everyone can tolerate fish oils – you can find yourself tasting them for hours afterwards. There is no need to buy a brand that claims to have lots of omega 6 and 9 as well – you should be getting enough of those from your diet. It's the omega 3s that will do you good.

Flaxseed (or linseed) oil: a good alternative source of omega 3s. It is available in capsule form, for veggies or those who cannot tolerate fish oils.

Garlic: there is plenty of research to indicate that garlic can lower cholesterol, especially LDL, the bad type that clogs up arteries (see page 351). As you would need a clove a day to reap the benefits, you may prefer to take a supplement rather than risk losing your friends!

Ginkgo biloba: the ginkgo tree is known to have been growing for more than 150 million years. Ginkgo has a slight 'blood thinning' action, and can increase blood flow, particularly to the brain, so it may enhance memory as well as counteract other effects of ageing such as mental fatigue and lack of energy. Some tinnitus sufferers have reported relief too. It can cause nosebleeds, and watch out for interactions – you should not take ginkgo if you are on other blood-thinning medication.

Glucosamine sulphate: formed naturally in the body and involved in producing cartilage. There is now good evidence to show that taking a supplement of 1500mg a day can help to preserve cartilage, and in some people it can reduce arthritic pain as effectively as ibuprofen; it also has fewer side effects. Most brands, however, are derived from shellfish and contain sugar, so are not suitable for diabetics or people with shellfish allergy.

Chondroitin: found naturally in cartilage. Less research has been done on its benefits than on those of glucosamine, though people often take the two together. It prevents body enzymes from breaking down the building blocks of cartilage. Early results indicate that it can also act as an anti-inflammatory to reduce pain. It, too, is extracted from shellfish.

Ginger: this anti-inflammatory remedy has been used for centuries and can ease the pain of arthritis. It is often used for reducing mucus and pepping you up – hence the expression 'to ginger up'. It's also a good remedy for nausea. You can include it easily in your diet.

LIFESTYLE AND MENTAL HEALTH

It's easy to assume that retirement is all about freedom. At long last you have the time to do all those things you've always wanted to do, whether it's travelling, developing creative skills, learning a language, spending more time with the grandchildren or restructuring the garden. Sometimes it doesn't quite work out that way, though, and life in retirement can seem more like a bed of thorns than of roses.

After all, the changes are pretty huge. If your life has been focused around work, the days can suddenly seem very empty. Not only that, but it's not just men who feel that their work gives them status; suddenly losing that role can make a real dent in your self-esteem.

And then there can be loneliness. Your work colleagues may not have been your best buddies, but chances are you enjoyed daily chats about the goings-on in your lives. No matter what their age, most women need to talk. It's as essential to our well-being as a daily cuppa.

Sad to say, if you have a 'significant other', gossiping is unlikely to be one of his strengths. Actually, just having him around all the time can be a problem. The time he has spent at work has left you free to do your own thing, meet friends, eat the kind of lunch you want at a time that suits you. Perhaps now you are suddenly finding your lovely routine disrupted by someone who needs feeding at a certain time, and who – frankly – can get in the way.

PLANNING YOUR RETIREMENT

The key to a happy retirement isn't just financial planning. It's lifestyle planning as well. The happiest retired people I know are the ones who are busy.

Structure in your weekly diary can be beneficial, so try to make sure you have some set activities timetabled in, such as a keep-fit session, a book group or a class of some sort. This can be a great time to learn a new skill, such as computing, gardening or a foreign language. Spending time doing voluntary work can also be very rewarding.

Most women have the 'caring' gene written large in every cell in their body, and there is certainly nothing wrong with spending time looking after grandchildren, or indeed your husband. But don't get taken for a ride – make sure you have some 'me' time as well. There is nothing wrong with being a little selfish.

LOOKING AFTER YOUR PARTNER

Making sure you make some time for yourself can be particularly relevant to 'him indoors'. Unless he is ill, if he is retired the home should operate as a level playing field, with a sharing of tasks. You should not have to be doing everything for your partner – and in fact, you won't be doing him any favours if he never cooks a meal or loads the washing machine. He needs to be able to cope if something happens to you.

Men are getting better at looking after themselves, but even so, if there's one thing they hate even more than asking for directions, it's going to see their doctor. That means that it's often left to the women in their lives to keep an eye on their health and, as your partner may become more prone to illness with the advancing years, you need to be vigilant.

Just as there are particular illnesses that tend to afflict women of this age, there are also some problems to which men are especially vulnerable. These include heart disease, prostate cancer and impotence. If you see signs of anything amiss, one of the best things you can do is to persuade him to see his GP as soon as possible. On a daily basis, encourage him to stick to a healthy diet and to take plenty of exercise.

HORMONE PROBLEMS

Yes, it's that old thorny hormone issue again. In the years following the menopause, although women are not completely lacking in sex hormones, overall the levels are much lower and, very importantly, the balance between the different hormones changes significantly.

Before the menopause, the ovaries are the main source of the sex hormones oestrogen and progesterone, together with small amounts of testosterone.

After the menopause, the ovaries stop working, and the main source of sex hormones switches to the adrenal glands, which are two tiny knobs on the top of each kidney. Fat cells can also influence the hormone mix in the bloodstream.

Throughout life, the adrenal glands produce small amounts of androgens, which are hormones with a weak testosterone action. Before the menopause this amount is insignificant compared to the huge hormonal output from the ovaries, but after the menopause it's a different story. The adrenal androgens become dominant, and not only are they active in their own right, but some androgens are converted by aromatase enzymes in fat cells to oestrone, a weak form of oestrogen. So the fatter you are, the more oestrone you will have – which could be viewed as a good thing, though it is thought to be a reason why obese women are more at risk of breast cancer.

Overall, though, oestrogen activity in the body is very low, and androgens become very much the lead hormone players. This is why older women have a tendency to acquire facial hair (particularly on the upper lip and chin) and also to have thinning hair, especially around the temples and on the top – just like men.

VAGINAL DRYNESS

Oestrogen has a moisture-retaining effect on the skin, and this means that at this time in your life your skin is generally thinner, not only in the obvious places, but also in the not-so-obvious, particularly the genital area. Some women just notice that sex is dry and uncomfortable; others find their vulva feels a bit itchy and sore, and often mistake this for thrush. Sometimes the dryness can be so extreme that it leads to inflammation, which can cause slight bleeding or a vaginal discharge. An inflamed vagina is also at risk from infection with organisms from around the anus. The change in the genital tissues can also increase the risk of urinary problems, particularly urinary-tract infections (see page 196).

Tests and treatment
There's generally no point in measuring hormone levels, as the results are predictable. However, any woman with an uncomfortable vulva, or

who is finding sex uncomfortable, or who has a discharge, should have an examination, together with swabs, to determine the exact cause.

Occasionally other skin problems (see below) can be to blame. It is also essential that any woman with any vaginal bleeding, no matter how small, has full investigations, as occasionally this can be a sign of cancer of the lining of the womb (see page 366).

A number of lubricating agents available from chemists can give some relief from vaginal dryness. Bio-adhesive products, such as Replens and Senselle, aim to replace moisture in cells and are generally more effective, easier to use and longer lasting than KY jelly, which is water-based and more slippery.

The most effective way of correcting the low oestrogen levels responsible for vaginal dryness is to take HRT (see page 300). This also balances out the dominance of androgens, and can help to stop the growth of facial hair, and also thinning scalp hair. However, the increased risk of breast cancer means that HRT is no longer recommended, even though it can be good for older bones. That doesn't mean you can't use it if you want to – it should be a matter of personal choice, though finding a doctor willing to prescribe it may be difficult.

The other option is to apply the oestrogen where it is needed, in the vulva and vaginal area, via pessaries or cream (which is available only on prescription). Several different brands are available, and though they can be messy, they do work. The usual practice is to apply your preferred treatment daily for a couple of weeks, to 're-oestrogenize' the area, then use a maintenance dose a couple of times a week. How long you use this type of treatment depends very much on personal circumstances – some women need a couple of courses a year, others need to use it most of the time. It can also be a very good way of preventing recurrent urinary-tract infections.

Very little of the oestrogen from these treatments is absorbed into the blood stream, and there is no evidence that they can increase the risk of breast cancer or DVT (deep vein thrombosis – blood clot in the legs). However, enough may reach the womb to stimulate growth of the lining, and eventually this can lead to thickening, which could, theoretically at least, increase the risk of abnormal cells developing. It could also lead to bleeding, which could be alarming. For this reason any woman using a vaginal oestrogen preparation for more than 3 months should take a course of progesterone tablets for a couple of weeks. This will trigger shedding of any lining build-up at the end of the course.

The drier skin of older women is also more prone to irritation from other chemicals, such as enzymes found in biological washing powders, and perfumes in bubble baths and soaps. A 1 per cent hydrocortisone cream can ease itching, but prevention is all-important, which means using plain, non-perfumed products.

LICHEN SCLEROSIS

This is a skin condition that can affect the vulva at any age (including in childhood), but is more common in older women. The inflammation caused by the condition can lead to extreme itching and soreness, discomfort on passing urine, and can make sex very painful. The skin can become so dry that it cracks, and scarring can lead to fusion of the labia, the small folds of skin around the clitoris. It is thought to be an 'auto-immune' condition, with the skin being attacked by the body's own immune system, and is more common in those with other auto-immune disorders, such as thyroid disease (see page 264).

A GP with knowledge of the condition can usually spot it immediately, but many women go through years of the wrong treatment for thrush or eczema before they finally see a dermatologist. The condition can be confirmed by a tiny biopsy, and treatment is with very strong steroid cream, usually Dermovate, which needs to be used twice daily for 3 months or so initially until the inflammation settles.

Lichen sclerosis is a long-term condition, which tends to flare up from time to time, so maintenance treatment with Dermovate once or twice a week is usually recommended. This is important, as the condition can increase the risk, very slightly, of vulval cancer; however, this risk is vastly reduced if the inflammation is kept under control.

PROBLEMS OF THE REPRODUCTIVE SYSTEM

Sadly, even though they are no longer performing any useful biological function, the womb and ovaries cannot be ignored. This is an age where they can, and sometimes do, cause serious problems.

CANCER OF THE WOMB

This usually refers to cancer of the lining of the womb, known medically as the endometrium. It affects about 6,000 women a year in the UK. It is rare in women who have not yet reached the menopause, but in 1 in 5 cases it starts around the time of the change. It is most common in women aged 60–69.

Tell-tale signs

The most common sign is abnormal bleeding. In slightly younger women this may be bleeding between periods, or unusually heavy, prolonged periods. In older, post-menopausal women it can be any bleeding – just light spotting, or heavy, with clots – and this is why any vaginal bleeding after the menopause should always be checked out.

Why has this happened?

The exact cause isn't known, but it does seem that exposing the womb to unopposed oestrogen – that is, oestrogen without the balancing contribution of progesterone – can increase the risk. It is more common in:

♦ women who are overweight (as fat cells can convert other hormones to small amounts of oestrogen)

♦ women who have had no children

♦ those with PCOS (see page 186)

♦ women who have taken tamoxifen for treating breast cancer, or have taken oestrogen-only HRT (see page 300)

♦ women with BRCA 1 or 2 gene mutations (usually identified because of a family history of breast cancer)

Tests and treatment

An ultrasound scan usually reveals a thickening in the womb lining, and the diagnosis is confirmed by a biopsy.

Treatment usually involves removing the whole womb, together with the ovaries, fallopian tubes and the lymph nodes from the pelvis. For cancers that are caught in the early stages, and are localized to the womb, this is the only treatment that is required. More advanced cancers, which have spread through the womb wall, may also be treated with radiotherapy to the pelvic area; additional chemotherapy may also be given to help stop further tumour growth.

As with so many cancers, how well you do afterwards depends on how early the tumour was diagnosed and treated. Fortunately, womb cancer does tend to cause symptoms from an early stage, and this means that many women are diagnosed with stage 1 disease, where the cancer is localized inside the womb, and overall 74 per cent are alive and well after five years. The outlook is not so good for those with more advanced disease, but this is much less common.

OVARIAN CYSTS

Fluid-filled sacs can develop in the ovaries at any age. In the vast majority of cases they are benign – that is, non-cancerous – especially in younger women. They can occur at any age, from the teenage years onwards.

The increased use of ultrasound for investigating gynaecological problems has revealed that small cysts often form in developing egg follicles, then disappear of their own accord. Sometimes, however, these cysts continue to grow to the size of a grapefruit, and occasionally larger still. Most ovarian cysts contain just fluid, but others, known as dermoid cysts, may contain structures such as hair, bone or even teeth. This is because, in the embryo, the ovaries develop from the same cells that go on to form the skin and its associated structures. Some ovarian cells still appear to retain their ability to form other tissues.

Many ovarian cysts produce no symptoms and are found by chance at a routine pelvic examination. However, they can twist or rupture, causing acute, severe abdominal pain. Some can cause a vague lower abdominal ache or discomfort, which is worse during sex. Some cysts produce hormones and can cause irregular periods, while larger cysts may cause a bulging lower tummy.

Diagnosis is by ultrasound scan. Immediate treatment isn't always necessary, as many smaller cysts go away of their own accord. However, larger cysts should be removed, especially if there is any suspicion of a malignancy. Often it's possible to remove just the cyst; the ovarian tissue that is left behind then continues to function normally. Removing larger cysts, though, may involve removing the whole ovary.

OVARIAN CANCER

Ovarian cancer affects just under 7,000 women a year in the UK. It mostly affects post-menopausal women, and over half of all cases are in women over 65.

Why has this happened?

It's the usual tale – any woman can get cancer of the ovary, but there are some things that can increase the risk.

Your genes are important – those with a first-degree relative affected by the disease (especially at a young age) are at increased risk, and those who carry the BRCA1 or 2 genes are at increased risk of both ovarian and breast cancer. There is also a link with some types of colon cancer. Screening is now available for these women.

Women who have not had children, or who start their periods early, or who have a late menopause, are also at slightly increased risk. A link has also been reported with the use of fertility drugs, but this risk appears to be confined to those who do not conceive – if the treatment is successful, there is no increased risk, so it may be childlessness, rather than the fertility drugs per se, that is the real risk.

On a more positive note, younger women taking the combined contraceptive pill have the risk of getting ovarian cancer reduced by as much as 50 per cent. This reduced risk continues for up to five years after the pill is stopped.

Tell-tale signs

Unfortunately, ovarian cancer does not generally cause symptoms in the early stages. Symptoms only tend to occur when the tumour is quite large, causing pressure, pain or bloating in the lower abdomen and an increased need to pass urine. But even then symptoms can be vague and the diagnosis easily missed. Younger women may occasionally complain of irregular periods.

Diagnosis and treatment

A pelvic examination may reveal an enlarged ovary, but the diagnosis is better suspected by a pelvic ultrasound scan, as cancerous cysts usually have a different appearance from benign ones. A high blood level of the chemical CA 125, which is produced by the cancer cells, also raises the suspicion of ovarian cancer.

Confirmation of the diagnosis can only be made by directly examining the ovary and removing the cyst. If cancer is confirmed, it's normal then to remove the entire ovary, and often the other ovary and the womb as well. Checking whether the cancer has spread – 'staging' – should be done using either CT or MRI scans; this can be helpful in determining what further treatment should be given. Most ovarian cancers respond to chemotherapy – usually either a platinum-based drug or taxol, or both.

Afterwards, all women should be routinely monitored by checking levels of CA 125 and using pelvic ultrasound scans. CT scans or MRI scans can be used to check on any distant spread.

Outlook

If the disease is caught early, the outlook is good – 9 out of 10 women will be alive and well five years later.

Unfortunately, many women are diagnosed when the disease has already spread to other parts of the body. Though new drug regimes have made huge improvements in the prospects for ovarian cancer patients, the overall outlook is still not good and five-year survival rates are much lower.

PHYSICAL ILLNESSES

For those women used to a busy life, perhaps not taking much notice of their own health, the sixties can come as a bit of a shock. This is a time when many women first get an inkling that they are not as young as they used to be. Odd aches and pains can become a problem; exercise makes you a little more breathless and stiff. Depressing, isn't it? Not only that, but the effects of smoking – a chronic cough and shortness of breath – can affect quality of life, even if you gave up some years ago. Worse still, cancer becomes a real health threat, along with diabetes and the biggest killer of all for women, heart disease.

HEART DISEASE

Look at any survey about what women worry about, healthwise, and cancer invariably comes out at the top of the list. But cancer is not the biggest threat to a woman's health. Instead, it's your heart.

Heart disease – or more specifically, coronary heart disease – claims the life of 1 in 6 women in the UK. This means more than 54,000 women die of heart disease every year, which is four times the number that die from breast cancer.

Far too many women think that heart disease only affects men. Not only does it affect women too, in huge numbers, but it affects them differently from men. The symptoms are often slightly different in men too, and these two factors together can mean that the diagnosis is missed: many women have heart disease that (very dangerously) goes untreated for years.

Most heart disease in women is caused by thickening and hardening of the arteries that supply blood to the heart muscle – atherosclerosis. This reduces the supply of both nutrients and oxygen to the heart muscle, making it weaker and less efficient. If one of the arteries is blocked completely, it prevents any oxygen reaching a portion of the muscle and results in a heart attack.

It is true that up until the menopause the rate of heart disease is lower in women than in men, because oestrogen has a protective effect on the heart and arteries. However, after the menopause, when oestrogen levels plummet, the rate of heart disease in women rises rapidly to match the rate in men. Not only that, but lifestyle changes in women mean that many are putting themselves at increased risk of heart disease in the future.

Why has this happened?

Heart disease can occur in any woman, at any age, but there are certain things that can put you at increased risk – and you may not even know you have some of these risk factors.

♦ **Smoking**. This is the number-one risk factor. Smoking is even more dangerous for women than for men, carrying almost twice the risk of developing coronary heart disease. Yet 25 per cent of women still smoke, and the smoking rate is going up among young women.

♦ **High blood cholesterol level**. This too is a major risk factor for atherosclerosis, and nearly half of all deaths from coronary heart disease can be blamed on a high cholesterol level. As we have seen (page 351), there are two types of cholesterol, high-density lipoprotein (HDL) and low-density lipoprotein (LDL). HDL can help to protect against heart disease; it is LDL that is the baddy. The recommended levels are a total cholesterol level of 5mmol/l or below, with an LDL of 3 mmol/l or below. Yet at least two-thirds of women over the age of 50 have cholesterol levels higher than these.

♦ **High blood pressure**. Your blood pressure should be no more than 135/85, but 40 per cent of women have levels above this.

♦ **Diabetes**. If you are diabetic you have a three times increased risk of heart disease, especially if it is untreated or poorly controlled. Diabetic women who have a heart attack are eight times more likely to die of it than those without diabetes. There are probably half a million women in the UK with undiagnosed diabetes. (See page 355.)

♦ **Being overweight**. The more overweight you are, the greater the risk of heart disease. Approximately a third of women are overweight, and one-fifth are obese, thus putting themselves at an even greater risk. You are more at risk of heart disease if you are 'apple' shaped, with most of your excess fat around your middle, compared to 'pears', who have most of their excess fat around their hips and thighs. 'Apples' are also at increased risk from diabetes – see the section on metabolic syndrome (page 377).

♦ **Lack of exercise.** Three-quarters of all women fail to meet the recommended guidelines for physical activity – at least half an hour of exercise, energetic enough to make you feel slightly puffed, five times a week.

♦ **A poor diet.** Fats aside (see page 351), a lack of fresh fruit and vegetables and oily fish, eating too much salt and drinking too much alcohol can increase the risk of arterial damage.

♦ **Family history.** If any members of your immediate family (parents or siblings) developed coronary heart disease at a young age (men under 55, women under 65), then you could be at increased risk. Genetic factors mean that heart disease can run in families, even if there is an obvious reason why a family member was affected – for instance due to heavy smoking.

♦ **Stress.** There is increasing evidence of a link between stress and heart disease. Those at particular risk are women in high-intensity jobs, with little variety and little control over what they have to do.

Tell-tale signs

Women do not generally perceive themselves as being at risk from heart disease, often attributing the symptoms to something else – indigestion or a muscle strain. This means the diagnosis is often made months or years after signs of heart disease first appear.

For some women, the first sign that they have heart disease is the sudden, severe pain in the chest of a heart attack. But more commonly there are early-warning signs, usually an ache in the chest while exercising, which feels worse in cold weather.

In the early stages, heart disease does not tend to cause what anyone describes as pain; rather it's a heavy or tight feeling in the chest, as if someone is pressing on it. It lasts typically for 10–15 minutes, and may spread to the arms, neck, back or jaw. Being short of breath and having swollen ankles can also be signs of problems with the blood supply to the heart.

Tests and treatment

Early diagnosis and treatment of heart disease really can be lifesaving. The first test is usually an electro-cardiogram, or ECG. This is best done during exercise – an ECG done at rest is likely to be normal unless the person has already had a heart attack.

Further tests may include:

◆ an ultrasound scan of the heart (an echocardiogram)

◆ checking the heart-muscle blood supply using radioactive markers (thallium scanning or positive electron tomography)

◆ a cardiac catheter test, usually known as an angiogram. This involves passing a tiny tube up from a blood vessel in the groin to the arteries of the heart, and then injecting a radio-opaque dye. Any narrowing of the blood vessels can be seen on an X-ray.

Which of these you have done depends on your symptoms.

The aim of treatment is to improve the blood supply to the heart muscle. This can be done in two ways – either by widening narrowed areas of the coronary arteries using a balloon and inserting tiny metal stents (angioplasty procedures), or by surgically creating a bypass using vein grafts – a bypass operation.

Again, the type of treatment depends very much on individual circumstances, but generally angioplasty is used where only small areas of the coronary arteries are narrowed; bypass operations are done where larger areas are affected. Both of these procedures can be very successful, but they are not a cure – drug treatment and lifestyle alterations are also important in maintaining a more healthy heart in the long term.

Self-help

As always, the right lifestyle really can make a huge difference to your heart. It can help to prevent heart disease developing in the first place, and also to maintain your heart even if you are already affected.

There are five steps to keeping your heart as healthy as possible:

♦ **Eat healthily**. This means eating a low-fat, low-salt diet (the less, the better) with at least 5 portions of fruit and vegetables a day, and also two portions of oily fish a week (see page 352).

♦ **Be more active**. Just half an hour's exercise a day can make all the difference, not just to your health, but also to your general well-being. Aim to do at least 30 minutes of an activity that makes you slightly puffed, at least 5 days a week.

♦ **Reduce your alcohol intake** to recommended limits. A little alcohol can help reduce the risk of heart disease, but too much is definitely harmful. And despite what you may have heard, red wine isn't that much better for your heart than any other form of alcohol.

♦ **Get your weight down** to a BMI of 24 or less (see page 218), and a waist of 80cm (32inches) or less.

♦ **Stop smoking**.

Metabolic syndrome

It's not just how heavy you are that can affect your risk of heart disease. Where you store those excess pounds is important too.

It's now known that women who store their excess weight around the middle – 'apple' shaped – are at increased risk of both heart disease and diabetes. The link is through a disorder known as metabolic syndrome. People with this condition are not only overweight; they also have abnormal blood-lipid levels (with high cholesterol, high triglycerides and low HDL levels), and often have high blood pressure. In addition, they have 'insulin resistance'.

Insulin, which is produced by the pancreas, is needed to move sugar from the bloodstream into cells, where it can be used to produce energy. However, the fatter you are, the more the cells become resistant to the action of insulin. The pancreas tries to correct this situation by producing more insulin, but often in the end simply can't make enough. Blood-sugar levels rise, resulting in diabetes.

Drug treatment can help reduce insulin resistance, reduce blood pressure and correct abnormal blood-lipid levels. But the best way of treating metabolic syndrome – and reducing the risk of both heart disease and diabetes – is to lose weight.

BOWEL CANCER

Though it is slightly more common in men, I've included bowel cancer because it is the second most common cancer in women (after breast cancer – see page 318). One in 20 women is diagnosed with bowel cancer at some stage in her life, and there are over 16,000 new cases in women in the UK every year. Though overall more people are surviving bowel cancer than ever before, it still claims the lives of over 7,500 women in the UK every year.

Tell-tale signs

The most common symptom of bowel cancer is a change in bowel habit – when you find you have persistent constipation, diarrhoea or a mixture of the two. The other common symptom is bleeding from the back passage, or blood mixed in with motions. Bowel cancer can also cause abdominal discomfort. Unfortunately, many people attribute these symptoms to either a tummy upset, irritable bowel syndrome or piles; this means that all too often they go to see their doctor only when they have developed symptoms suggesting that the cancer is more advanced – weight loss, and tiredness caused by anaemia.

Why has it happened?

Bowel cancer can occur in any women but, as with so many diseases, there are things that can increase individual risk.

♦ **Diet**. It is reckoned that at least 2 out of 3 cases of bowel cancer could be prevented by dietary changes alone. A diet low in fibre, fruit and vegetables and high in meat is linked with an increased risk of the disease. You can help reduce your risk by eating more fibre from cereals, beans, fruit and veg, eating fewer red, cured or processed meats, and more fish instead.

♦ **Age**. The older you are, the bigger the risk. More than 80 per cent of bowel cancers are diagnosed in those over the age of 60.

♦ **Family history**. Having a first-degree relative affected by bowel cancer before the age of 45, or two first-degree relatives affected at any age, or a family history of breast, ovarian or bowel cancer increases your risk. There is a large increased risk where a particular type of bowel polyp runs in the family.

♦ **Other illnesses**. People with diabetes, and also those with an inflamed bowel due to ulcerative colitis, have a very slightly increased risk of bowel cancer.

Tests and treatment

Bowel cancer is usually diagnosed via colonoscopy – using a flexible camera to view the lining of the bowel directly. Barium X-rays are used much less commonly now than in the past. Further tests may include either a CT or an MRI scan of the abdomen and liver to check if the cancer has spread. Treatment is usually by surgically removing the affected part of the bowel. Chemotherapy is also now usually offered to all patients, apart from those with very early tumours, and new drugs such as irinotecan and bevacizumab are improving the survival rates for those with advanced tumours.

BLADDER INFECTIONS

Throughout their lives women suffer from far more bladder problems than men, simply because of their anatomy. The urethra, the tube from the bladder to the outside, is much shorter in women, and both the urethra and the bladder sit just in front of the vagina. This means they are often affected by the changes that happen after childbirth.

Urinary-tract infections (cystitis; see page 196) can occur at any age, but there are two peaks – one when a woman is being very sexually active ('honeymoon cystitis') and another in later life. Older women become more prone to infections because the tissues around the genital area are more fragile, and also because there are fewer natural secretions, which act partly as the body's self-defence mechanism against invading bacteria.

Sometimes the symptoms of extreme pain on passing urine, and a need 'to go' more frequently, come on dramatically, as is usually the case in younger women; however, in older women the symptoms of a urine infection can be much more subtle: slight discomfort and going slightly more frequently, especially at night, and slight incontinence – needing to go to the loo suddenly, but not quite making it.

Straightforward infections can usually be cleared with a short course of antibiotics, but in many women they can become a recurrent nuisance. Applying oestrogen cream to the vulva can help, and some women require long courses of low-dose antibiotics (3 months or more) as a preventative measure.

INCONTINENCE

I'm not just talking here about the severe urinary incontinence that affects a few of the elderly and infirm. I'm talking about accidentally passing urine – often just a little – at any time. Bladder weakness happens just as often as hayfever. A survey by the Royal College of Physicians revealed that 24 per cent of older people suffer from accidental leakage of urine.

Incontinence affects people of all ages, but in older women it's a particularly common problem, affecting up to 20 per cent of women over 65. It can cause huge distress, embarrassment and loss of dignity. You don't need to leak a large amount of urine to feel wet and dirty. Just a few drops is enough.

Far too often, incontinence is viewed as 'just part of ageing'. But I'm here to tell you 'No, it's not!' There is plenty that can be done about incontinence and, with the right treatment, most women can be cured, or at the very least have the problem vastly improved.

If you do have to resort to pads (and hopefully you won't), those specifically designed for the purpose, such as Tena, are far better than sanitary towels. They have much better absorbency and are less likely to cause skin irritation or rashes.

There are two main types of incontinence in women – stress incontinence and urge incontinence. It's important to sort out which you have, as the treatments are very different. Some women have just one type, others a mix of the two. Urodynamic testing can help to distinguish between them. This involves drinking a large amount of water and then having the pressure inside the bladder tested as it fills. It is a way of checking the volume of the bladder to determine the point at which incontinence occurs.

STRESS INCONTINENCE

This is accidentally leaking urine when you cough, sneeze, run or even just laugh. It's caused by weakness of the muscles around the base of the bladder and the urethra – the pelvic-floor muscles – which help to control the valve that holds urine inside the bladder.

The usual cause in women is having a baby. Both pregnancy and, especially, childbirth put an enormous strain on the pelvic-floor muscles; the more babies you have, and the bigger they are, the greater the risk of stretching those all-important muscles. The changes in the genital tissues at the menopause can aggravate the problem, along with being overweight or having a chronic smoker's cough.

Self-help

There is a lot you can do to help stop stress incontinence. For many, there is just one answer – pelvic-floor exercises (see page 383). As with any other muscles, the more you exercise them, the stronger they will become. All women are advised to do pelvic-floor exercises after they have had a baby, but, frankly, who has the time? When you are younger the muscles often recover a little – it's only a couple of decades later that the damage is revealed.

But it's never too late to start. You can teach yourself pelvic-floor exercises, though some women find it helpful to see a physiotherapist or continence nurse specialist. The exercises don't work instantly; you need to keep at them, regularly, for at least a month before you notice any difference, but 3–6 months of dedication really can pay off.

If they don't do the trick, then there are other treatments that can help.

Medical treatments

♦ Duloxetine is a relatively new medical treatment that can strengthen the muscle at the base of the bladder. It doesn't work for everyone, but it's worth a try. It's most effective if combined with pelvic-floor exercises.

♦ There are a number of well-established surgical techniques for stress incontinence, all of which aim to improve the closure at the base of the bladder, particularly when it is under pressure (which is what happens when you cough or sneeze). The two most popular involve either hitching up the base of the bladder to the back of the pubic bone (a colposuspension) or creating a hammock for the urethra using tension-free vaginal tape (TVT), which is inserted through the top of the vagina.

♦ Laxity of the front wall of the vagina (which is often found in women with stress incontinence) can also be corrected via an 'anterior repair' procedure.

♦ More recently, injecting 'bulking agents', such as silicone or collagen, have been used to strengthen the bladder base; this can be done as a day-case procedure under a local anaesthetic. However, the long-term success rate of this is not known.

♦ Stem cells from muscles in the arm have also been successfully used to strengthen the bladder base, but this is still only done in research trials.

As with so many things, there is no single best option – it depends on each individual patient, but it is important to know why your gynaecologist suggests a particular procedure.

Pelvic-floor exercises

First, a word of caution. Toning up your pelvic floor is not something that can happen overnight. As with all other muscles, to make a real difference you have to do the exercises regularly, several times a day, and stick at them for at least 3 months. And if you want your intimate parts to stay toned, then some maintenance work will be required after that.

But it can pay dividends. A good pelvic floor can both put an end to stress incontinence and improve your sex life.

1. First you need to identify the right muscles, and the best way to do this is to try stopping, then starting again, the flow of urine as you pee. Do this until you feel you have really good control of the flow; this will mean you are working the muscles at the base of the bladder.

2. Once you can do this, switch to practising when you are sitting down anywhere, even when you are just watching TV. Hold for a slow count of 5, then relax. Repeat as often as possible – aim for at least 30 times a day.

3. The next step is to work on the muscles further back, around your vagina and anus. Squeeze the muscles as if you are trying to stop yourself passing wind or a motion. Again, hold and repeat as above.

4. Next you need to combine the two. Get into the habit of working one set, then the other, then both.

Special weights for the vagina – 'vaginal cones' – are available that can help train the pelvic-floor muscles, but don't use them until you have done some preliminary exercises first, otherwise it's too depressing. They just fall out.

URGE INCONTINENCE

This is when there's a sudden uncontrollable urge to pass urine, and holding on till you get to the loo is nigh-on impossible. Affected women get very little warning that they need to pass urine (medics call this 'urgency') and often have to urinate very frequently, sometimes as often as every half an hour.

Normally, the bladder fills slowly, and the muscles in its walls send a signal to the brain, in good time, that it's full. But in some people, the muscles contract at the wrong time, often when there is very little urine inside the bladder. It's called an overactive bladder, and at its worst it can lead to urge incontinence – the muscles contract so much that the bladder empties, no matter how hard you try to stop it happening.

How often a 'normal' person empties their bladder depends a lot on how much they drink, and also on the weather – if it's hot then you lose a lot of water through sweat and don't need to go to the loo so often. On the other hand, if you drink fifteen cups of tea or coffee each day you are bound to be a frequent visitor to the girls' room. But, as a general rule, it's normal to go to the loo to empty your bladder up to eight times a day, and once or twice a night; if you are consistently going more than this, you may have an overactive bladder.

It can occur at any age, but is especially common in older women. Usually there is no obvious cause, though lack of oestrogen may play a part, and being overweight makes it worse, as this puts extra pressure on the bladder.

Self-help

Losing weight can help; so can avoiding caffeine and alcohol, as these may irritate the bladder. The stronger they are, the worse the effect, so if you need that morning boost, get it from a cup of instant, not a double espresso. And from what my patients tell me, gin is notoriously bad news for bladders.

However, it's not a good idea to cut down on the amount of fluid you drink (as many women do), as this can make your urine very concentrated and increases the risk of developing a bladder infection. Aim to drink about 2 litres a day.

Bladder retraining can also be very helpful – which means, as its name suggests, training your bladder to hold more urine. Your bladder is like your stomach – it gets used to holding a certain volume, and in the same way that people who eat small meals have a small stomach, the more often you go, the more often you'll need to go. So what you need to do is learn to suppress or ignore the desire to pee, and then you can get back to a more normal pattern of going to the loo.

What you are actually doing is getting the bladder used to holding more urine. This means making yourself 'hold on' just a little bit longer when you first feel the need to go, and avoid going 'just in case', unless it's really necessary.

To do this well, you need to keep a diary of how often you are going, and ideally measure out how much urine you pass each time. You can then chart your progress week by week, and hopefully see that you are going a little less frequently, and passing more urine when you do go.

Set yourself targets. Aim initially to hold on an extra 10 minutes, then gradually work it up to half an hour, and so on. Squeezing your pelvic-floor muscles can help you to hold on (see page 383). A specialist continence nurse can help with bladder retraining – see your GP for a referral.

Medical treatments

There are a number of drugs that can help with an overactive bladder and urge incontinence, such as tolerodine, oxybutynin and solfenacin. They work by relaxing the muscles of the bladder, and they can be very effective, though side effects such as a dry mouth and constipation can be a problem. If one doesn't suit, try another, but be patient: these drugs take several weeks to be really effective.

Surgery is not generally used for urge incontinence, but more recently botox injections have been used with some success, as they can help to relax the bladder wall. However, the long-term effects of this are not yet known.

SKIN AND HAIR

AGEING SKIN

The biggest change that most women notice at this age is that their skin becomes a lot drier. It may feel taut, uncomfortable and itchy, and there may be visible dry, scaly patches.

Self-help

♦ Water can make dryness worse, so don't wash more than once a day, unless you have good reason to.

♦ A quick shower is generally better for a mature skin than a long soak in the bath.

♦ Most soaps are alkaline and can disrupt the skin's normally slightly acidic secretions, making dryness worse. Special moisturizing soaps or cleansing bars, which are less alkaline, are more suitable for mature skins.

♦ Better still are cleansing lotions, especially those formulated for people with dry skin or eczema, such as E45, oilatum or balneum. They don't lather up like soap, but they will remove all but very stubborn dirt and won't strip your skin of the little moisture it still has.

♦ Get into the habit of applying a moisturizing cream or lotion, all over, after you have washed, when the skin is still slightly damp and warm, as this aids absorption of moisture into the skin.

One of the less attractive aspects of ageing is the tendency for small coloured lumps and bumps to appear. Skin tags can crop up anywhere, but are especially common in skin folds around the neck and armpits.

Seborrhoeic warts (which confusingly have nothing to do with other types of wart) are raised areas, with a slightly waxy appearance, that look as if they have been stuck on the skin. Their colour can vary from light to dark brown and, if left, they can grow quite large. They can look alarming and as with any changing skin mark, they should always be checked out by a doctor.

Both seborrhoeic warts and skin tags are harmless, but they can look unsightly and catch on clothing. They can be removed by cryotherapy, or by 'shaving' under local anaesthetic.

SKIN CANCER

Anyone can get skin cancer, but women's love affair with the sun, and with acquiring a tan, means they are more at risk. Unfortunately, damage from the sun – the main cause of skin cancer – is cumulative, which means that the older you are, the greater the risk.

There are two main types of skin cancer – malignant melanoma and non-melanoma.

Non-melanoma skin cancer (NMSC) can usually be easily treated, and though this may result in some scarring, it is rarely fatal.

Malignant melanoma is very different. It can kill, and it does – in 2003 it claimed more than 1,700 lives.

There are over 8,000 new cases of melanoma in the UK each year, and the number is rising at a horrific rate. The female:male ratio of those affected is 3:2, with at least 1,000 more women than men affected each year.

Melanomas can occur at any age, but are most commonly diagnosed in the 40–60 age group. Non-melanoma skin cancers, though, are more common in the over-sixties.

Why has this happened?

The main risk factor for skin cancer (both melanoma and NMSC) is excess exposure to the UV rays in sunlight; this causes at least 80 per cent of melanomas in women.

The greatest risk of developing melanoma comes from short, sharp bursts of strong sunlight, and though the risk is even greater if you 'lie and fry' on a continental beach, you don't have to go abroad to damage your skin enough to cause cancer – going out into the park at lunchtime on a sunny day in the UK may be all it takes to give your skin a lethal dose of rays.

Excess exposure to UV light in childhood is especially dangerous. Getting burnt, wherever you are, is particularly risky.

By contrast, NMSC is related more to long-term sun exposure, and is more common in people who spend a lot of time outside, such as those keen on gardening, hiking, tennis or cycling.

There are two types of UV light in sunshine – UVA and UVB. Though UVB is the more damaging and carcinogenic, there is increasing evidence that UVA can also cause skin cancer. This means that sunbeds, which emit UVA, can cause skin cancer, especially in those with susceptible skins.

Anyone can get skin cancer, but people with fair or red skin, with blue eyes, who tend to burn easily, are more at risk. Having freckles can also increase the risk, along with having lots of moles. The more moles you have, the greater the risk – those with more than 100 ordinary moles have a seven times increased risk compared to those with 15 or fewer. Those with larger (greater than 3mm), slightly odd-looking moles, with a variable colour and irregular edge, have a higher risk.

Melanoma can run in families, and those with an affected family member have double the normal risk. A gene defect has now been identified, and is thought to account for about 10 per cent of cases of melanoma.

The risk of NMSC is doubled by smoking, and it's also more common in areas of skin that have been exposed to radiotherapy treatment.

Tell-tale signs

Skin cancer can occur anywhere on the skin, including under nails. The most common site for melanomas in women is the lower leg (on men it's the back). They can occur either in a pre-existing mole, or arise in an area of normal skin.

Signs to look out for are any mark or mole that is:

♦ increasing in size

♦ changing colour, especially if the colour is uneven, with an irregular edge

♦ itching

♦ crusting or bleeding

Prompt treatment of melanomas really can be lifesaving. The diagnosis is usually confirmed by a biopsy, and in the early stages removing the lesion, together with a wide margin of skin, may be all that is required. More advanced melanomas may require treatment with chemotherapy or immunotherapy.

Non-melanoma skin cancers do not tend to look like abnormal moles. They tend to occur in areas of skin that have had a lot of exposure to the sun, such as the face (especially the nose and forehead), the backs of hands and the lower legs. Watch out for:

♦ spots or sores that don't heal in 4 weeks

♦ spots or sores that itch or hurt, or have a persistent scab or scaly surface

♦ lesions with a slightly pink or pearly appearance and a raised edge

Usually the only treatment required is to remove the lesion with a small area of surrounding skin. Small, very superficial lesions may be treated with a special type of chemotherapy cream, while larger lesions may be treated with radiotherapy.

Once you have had one NMSC, you are at increased risk of another, so it is vital to keep a close eye on your skin.

Prevention

The vast majority of skin cancers can be prevented by protecting the skin from UV light. A little sunshine can be good for you – it boosts your mood, and it also helps to boost the skin's production of vitamin D, which can be important in older people. It's getting too much that is so dangerous, especially burning. To avoid skin damage:

- Keep out of the sun when it is at its strongest, between 11a.m. and 3p.m.

- Cover up areas prone to burning, such as shoulders, with opaque fabric (UV light can go through flimsy voiles and cottons) and wear a wide-brimmed hat to protect your face.

- Vitally, always wear a sunscreen, factor 15 or more, whenever you are going to spend more than 15 minutes outside (half an hour in the winter). This doesn't just mean when you are going out to read on a lounger – it includes gardening, shopping outdoors, or having a coffee on the pavement café. (For more about sunscreens, see page 42.)

- Don't use sunbeds – the UVA they emit can cause cancer, and is a fast way to accelerate skin ageing. If you want a tan, get it from a bottle!

HAIR CARE

Our hair is so bound up with our femininity and sexuality, it's little wonder that women can begin to despair when they notice they are having more bad hair days in middle age. What's more, they also seem to have less hair.

The main culprit is usually diminishing oestrogen, which leads to a higher activity of androgens (male hormones). These are bad news for hair. Not only can they cause loss of hair in a male-pattern baldness, they can also cause each hair to have a smaller diameter and prevent it growing as long as it used to.

Hair thinning

Throughout life, each hair goes through a cycle of growth, then resting, then finally falling out, which overall takes about 4 years. As you grow older, the chances are that as you naturally lose a hair, it will be replaced by a thinner and weaker descendant. The result is less overall volume.

How badly you are affected will depend on your genetic susceptibility to androgens – you may be one of the lucky ones and hardly notice at all. It's reckoned that half of all women aged over 60 will suffer some hair loss because of androgens, but it's only when you've lost 15 per cent of the average 120,000 hairs on your head that you'll even notice.

There are plenty of things you can do to minimize thinning, such as adopting a good hair diet, treating your hair kindly and picking the best products for your hair type. HRT (see page 300) can help address the hormone imbalance responsible for thinning hair, but it's using a sledgehammer to crack a nut if this is the only reason you are taking it (and most doctors would be very reluctant to prescribe it solely for hair loss anyway). Minoxidil lotion was originally developed as a treatment for baldness in men, but it works in women too. However, it's not a permanent cure – as soon as you stop using it your hair will thin again, and it does need to be applied every day. It's also not available on the NHS, so using it adds up to quite a time and money investment.

Diet for healthy hair

You may think you have the perfect diet, but it may not be perfect for your tresses. Hair consists of protein and it needs plenty of protein to look its best. Give it some protein for breakfast (the best time to feed hair) and lunch, too. Boost the energy in your follicles by snacking on something healthy if you go for 4 hours without eating. Hair needs plenty of iron; if it is lifeless, low iron levels may be to blame, especially if you eat very little red meat.

Sometimes a mineral supplement which will give you other essentials such as zinc, magnesium and copper will help, but don't expect a quick fix. As with all supplements, time is needed to make them work and it may take 6 months for the results to shine through in your hair.

Look after your hair

Treat your hair like porcelain and be gentle with it at all times. It may help if you visualize how your hair actually looks under a microscope. Its outer layer (the cuticle) comprises overlapping cells which resemble fish scales. They are easily snapped off with rough handling, especially when wet. Once damaged, the hair is weakened and loses its lustre.

How often you shampoo is a personal choice, and though some experts say it doesn't matter if you give it a daily wash, others say that too much washing, and particularly styling, can traumatize hair. Tugging at tangles certainly causes damage, so always use a conditioner, and comb through with a wide-toothed comb to ease out knots before you start with a brush. Know your hair type and pick a shampoo and conditioner that suit it. Despite manufacturers' claims, protein and collagen in hair sprays and shampoos cannot be incorporated into the hair shaft to enhance strength, but they do leave a coating on the hair which makes it appear thicker.

Dealing with the grey

There's no such thing as grey hair; it's the overall effect of hairs that have lost their pigment (melanin) being interspersed with those still making colour.

Diseases such as diabetes, pernicious anaemia or thyroid problems can turn hair prematurely grey, but by the age of 50 most women will find half their hair is grey unless they have been particularly genetically blessed. You may be in denial, but don't pull it out. You'll damage the follicle, which may make its replacement undesirably crinkly – and it will still be white! Although there's some evidence that lack of vitamin B reduces hair pigment, the jury is still out on this.

If being grey suits you, protect your hair from the sun because the absence of melanin will make it more prone to damage. Although grey hair is not coarser than coloured hair, it may be drier because oil glands in the scalp may work less efficiently.

If you want to colour your hair, don't let the scare stories put you off. There is no concrete evidence that dying your hair causes cancer. Colouring actually swells the hair shaft and makes it look thicker. It won't make your hair fall out or damage your scalp as long as you stick to the instructions on the packet or have it done professionally, use the conditioner provided and always do a patch test. This involves putting a small amount of dye behind your ear and waiting for 24 hours before colouring to see if there are any adverse effects.

Going a lighter shade than your own involves bleaching and this will make hair dry, brittle and prone to breaking. Ideally, have it done professionally, but if you decide to DIY be absolutely sure you follow all the instructions on the packet.

Any chemical process will reduce the hair's elasticity, so treat your hair to deep conditioning a couple of days before and a couple of days after colouring to smooth down hair cuticles that have been ruffled by the chemicals.

IN SUMMARY

The sixties are a time of consolidation for many women; for others they are the beginning of a freedom that they have been looking forward to for many years. It's time at last to branch out into something new without the constraints of family and work.

The physical concerns of older women are different from those of the reproductive years. Many women find it hard to accept the inevitable changes in their appearance and energy levels. The best advice I can give is to make the most of what you have, and while you don't want to try to be a 20-year-old again (heaven forbid!), keeping a youthful outlook is vital for your mind and body.

Some of the medical check-ups you have had in your earlier years will no longer be necessary. However, there are others mentioned in this chapter which you will need to undertake, particularly those to do with heart disease and osteoporosis. No woman wants to become incapacitated just when she is planning to have a good time gardening, holidaying, looking after the grandchildren or studying for a degree.

With an informed, healthy mind in a healthy body, the woman in her sixties can plan to make the most of her later years.

CHAPTER SEVEN

LATER LIFE:
75 ONWARDS

In 2006, at the time of writing this book, an average woman's life expectancy in the UK is just under 80. Owing to advances in medical science and a general improvement in living conditions, however, this is rising all the time. By 2085 the life expectancy of the average woman in the UK will be over 100. Although, of course, some women do sadly die young, increasing numbers will now have many years of good health well into their eighties and beyond.

Realistically, though, this is a time when the human body does show signs that it is not in the first flush of youth, and medical problems and chronic illness become much more common. You can't, and shouldn't, expect to be running around like a 20-year-old in your eighties, even if you feel like the same person inside. It's time to pay attention to your body's needs.

By looking after yourself, and with good care from the medical profession, you should be able to enjoy a happy, fulfilling old age.

In this chapter you will find:

- **Staying healthy**
  - essential health checks
- **Diet and nutrition**
  - adapting your diet to your lifestyle
  - important nutrients

- **Staying active**
  - what kind of exercise?
  - after-effects and benefits
- **Lifestyle and mental health**
  - travelling in later life
  - bereavement
  - depression
  - wills and power of attorney
  - sexuality in later life
- **Physical illnesses**
  - arthritis
  - loss of memory and dementia
  - common eyesight problems
  - hearing problems

STAYING HEALTHY

This is a time when regular health checks are of paramount importance, so that any health problems can be detected and dealt with as soon as possible.

Essential health checks

Every woman over 75 should have:

♦ **Every year:** a blood-pressure check.

♦ **Every 3 years at least**: a blood cholesterol and glucose check, more often if it is borderline or raised.

♦ **Every 3 years**: a mammogram; ask your GP to make sure you continue to receive regular invitations for these.

♦ **Every 2 years at least**: an eye test by an optician.

Other checks

In addition, you should see your doctor at least once a year if you are on any regular medication.

If you have lost more than an inch in height, or broken a bone (particularly after a fairly trivial fall), you should discuss whether you need a bone-density scan.

You should check your skin at least once a month for changing moles, lumps or bumps, and practise regular breast self-examination (see page 314) – breast cancer becomes more common with increasing age.

You should also be on the look-out for any changes to the way your body is functioning. This should include:

♦ any change in your weight that cannot easily be explained

♦ breathlessness

♦ swelling of the ankles

♦ a change in bowel habit, or blood in your motions

♦ blood in your urine, or anywhere from the genital area

♦ pain in any part of your body that is severe or persistent

However, don't be too alarmed or frightened. These symptoms may relate to things that are perfectly treatable, for instance a thyroid problem, a urinary-tract infection or gastro-enteritis. Common problems like these can, and do, occur at any age. Even so, if you do develop unusual symptoms, you should see your doctor – the sooner any ailment is treated, the better.

DIET AND NUTRITION

At this age, nutrients from food are not as well absorbed as they once were. Yet a healthy, balanced diet is more important then ever to support, repair and regenerate cells which in turn stave off degenerative illness.

However, it's very easy to eat too much. In later life the average woman requires only 1,500 calories a day – even less if you have a sedentary lifestyle due to illness or arthritis. Nature does compensate for this: many older women have fairly small appetites, but that means it's especially important to make sure that what you do eat is nutritious. If you are living alone it can be tempting not to bother to cook and to snack on convenience foods, but there really is no substitute for fresh, home-prepared, balanced meals. Preparing several portions and freezing them can make life easier and is more economical than buying single portions.

The basic rules for healthy eating are the same as ever:

On top of this, particular care should be taken at this age to include certain nutrients in your diet:

Fibre: plenty of fibre is particularly important, as the bowel often becomes sluggish in later life, leading to constipation. Fibre can also help prevent problems from diverticular disease, where pockets develop from the wall of the lower bowel.

Calcium: 1 in 3 older women has osteoporosis, and trying to maintain strong bones by eating plenty of calcium should be a priority. Good sources are dairy food, such as milk, yogurt and cheese. Green leafy vegetables also contain useful calcium. However, it's quite difficult to manage to eat the recommended 1000 mg a day, and in practice this means that most women will benefit from a calcium supplement. Vitamin D, found in margarines and oils, and added as a supplement to some cereals, is also needed for calcium to be absorbed into bone. Dietary vitamin D is important, but much of the daily requirement is made in the skin, under the action of sunlight, and in the winter especially many older women do not get enough. Again, taking a supplement is often the best solution.

Iron: although you need less iron in old age, iron deficiency is prevalent among the elderly and can lead to anaemia. This is usually caused by poor absorption of iron, blood loss through ulcers or disease, or medication such as aspirin and non-steroidal anti-inflammatory drugs, which can irritate the lining of the stomach and cause bleeding. If you feel tired and listless, ask your GP to check out your levels.

Folic acid: medication can interfere with the uptake of folic acid, which is also needed to make red blood cells, and this is a common deficiency in the elderly. You get folic acid from green leafy vegetables and liver. Supplements are available too.

Antioxidants and vitamin C: the antioxidants in the recommended 5 daily portions of fruit and veg will boost your body's defences against the free radicals that damage cells. Moreover, vitamin C will ward off cataracts and skin disorders.

Liquid intake: drink at least 6–8 cups of liquid a day – preferably water and fruit juices – to give your body a chance to deal with toxins.

Oily fish: eat oily fish such as mackerel or kippers a couple of times a week because they contain omega 3 oils which will keep your joints supple and help to keep arteries healthy.

In general: try to include raw vegetables, fruit, grains, seeds, nuts, garlic, onions and quality protein in your diet.

STAYING ACTIVE

It's a simple truth that the more active you are, the younger you will feel. It's now thought that up to half the physical decline associated with old age may be due to lack of physical activity.

Without some form of exercise to keep your muscles and joints active, you may not remain strong enough to carry out necessary daily tasks. No matter what operations you have had, or aches and pains you cope with, try to build some gentle exercise into your daily routine. It will help decrease muscular tension and joint pain, increase your circulation and build muscle and bone density, which protects against fractures.

Exercise will also release feel-good endorphins in your brain. This means it is a powerful protection against depression, which can undermine the well-being of elderly women, especially if they are widows coping with bereavement and the daunting experience of living alone for the first time. It can also help you to sleep better.

WHAT KIND OF EXERCISE?

Swimming is excellent for older women because the water takes the strain off joints, enabling you to be much more mobile than normal. If you have arthritis, find out if there is a therapeutic pool in your area that offers aquatic aerobic training. It will be kept much warmer than normal pools – 78–83 degrees (25.5 Celsius) – and will have special access ramps.

Getting out of the house is therapeutic in itself. Walking in the fresh air will be good for your heart and lungs, while a bit of sunshine will boost your vitamin D intake. Choose an exercise activity that you enjoy: you will be more likely to stick with it. Even better, attend a class with a friend, because you will not want to let each other down. Try to build up to being physically active for at least 30 minutes a day.

There are three main types of exercise that you should build into your routine:

- ◆ aerobic workouts to condition the heart
- ◆ strength training to build muscle
- ◆ stretching to make muscles and joints flexible

Before you start exercising, warm up for 5 minutes by walking slowly or doing a few stretches (see page 407). When you have finished, cool down in the same way for 5 minutes – longer in warmer weather.

Wear loose-fitting clothes and comfortable shoes. If it's cold, wear layers of synthetic clothing because they absorb less moisture. Peel off the layers as you get warmer.

Many older people do not drink enough to replace lost fluids; this is particularly important when exercising. Have a drink of water 10 minutes before you start and drink during and after your workout, even if you do not feel thirsty.

Aerobic exercise

Aerobic exercise, such as walking or swimming, will raise your endurance and energy levels and give your heart a workout. It improves your ability to use the oxygen in your blood and can lower risks of chronic diseases such as diabetes and heart disease (see pages 355 and 372). Try to do 30 minutes every day.

You don't have to join a class or wear a leotard to get your aerobic workout. There are many everyday tasks that qualify as aerobic exercise

– gardening, playing with your grandchildren, walking to the shops and, of course, housework. Washing the car, gardening or dancing burn as many calories per minute as walking briskly.

You don't have to do the 30 minutes all in one go either. Breaking it up into three 10-minute stints every day will be just as good for you.

Muscle-strengthening exercise

If the thought of lifting weights seems intimidating, you should know that it's not necessary to head for the gym or buy expensive dumb-bells – a couple of baked bean tins will do. However, to perform leg exercises you may consider investing in weight cuffs that wrap round your ankles.

Strength training will increase muscle mass and bone density, reducing the risk of fractures. It will also increase the fluid in your joints, which will improve your flexibility, making falls less likely in the first place.

Try doing the following muscle-strengthening exercises, slowly and gently, twice a week. If possible do two sets of 8–12 repetitions.

Arms Sit on a chair and hold one weight (baked bean tin or small bottle of water will do) in each hand with your arms straight down at your sides. Bending your elbow, with your palm facing your shoulder, lift one weight at a time to shoulder height or as far as you can without hurting. Then return it to your side.

Shoulders Still seated and holding your weights, lean forward slightly and, with a straight back, stretch out your arms to the sides, palms down, raising them to your shoulders or as far as you comfortably can. Then lower them slowly.

Hips and bottom. Wearing ankle weights, stand behind a chair and hold on to the back. Lean forward a little, lift one leg, bend your knee slightly and lift the bottom half of your leg as far as you can without hurting. Then lower and switch legs.

Thighs. Still wearing the ankle weights, sit on the edge of the chair and slowly extend and lower the bottom half of each leg in turn.

Back. Lie face down on the floor with your arms extended along the floor in front of you and a pillow beneath your hips. Try to lift your upper body and arms towards the ceiling and hold for a second before lowering.

Stomach. Lie on your back, knees bent and feet 12 inches apart. Tuck your chin into your chest, place your hands on your thighs and raise your shoulders off the floor for a moment before gently lowering. Having strong tummy muscles isn't just good for your figure – they provide essential support for your body and can help prevent back pain.

One word of warning: if you think you might have problems getting up from the floor, don't do these alone. Do them with a friend who can help you up if required!

Stretches

It's important to do a few stretches before and after any exercise. This helps to keep muscles supple and flexible, increases body temperature and blood flow to muscles and helps prevent injury. Do stretches in a slow, relaxed fashion; do not 'bounce' or you may pull the muscle you are trying to stretch. Aim for mild tension and do not hold your breath. Stretching should feel good – it should never be painful. Repeat a stretch a couple more times if you can, trying to stretch a little further without straining.

Neck. Sitting or standing, arms at your sides, slowly turn your head to one side until you can feel a stretch. Hold. Then turn and stretch the other side. To stretch the side of your neck, tilt your head to the right. Hold. Then tilt to the left. To stretch the back of the neck, lower your head forward towards your chest. Hold. Maintain each of these stretches for 5 seconds.

Side of shoulders and back of upper arms. Standing or sitting, place your right hand on your left shoulder. With your left hand, pull your right elbow across your chest towards your left shoulder. Hold for 10–15 seconds. Repeat on the other side.

Shoulders, middle back, arms, hands, fingers and wrists. Interlace fingers and turn palms out. Extend arms to shoulder height. Hold for 10–15 seconds.

Triceps, top of shoulders, waist. Stand or sit with knees slightly flexed. Raise one elbow and gently pull it behind your head with your other hand until you can feel a stretch. Hold for 10–15 seconds. Change arms.

Middle back. Stand with hands on hips and twist your body at the waist until you can feel a stretch. Hold for 10–15 seconds.

Ankles. Standing and holding on to something secure, lift one foot and rotate both foot and ankle 8–10 times clockwise, then do the same anticlockwise.

Calves. Stand a little way from a wall and lean on it with your forearms, with your head resting on your hands. Place your right foot in front of you, leg bent, your left leg straight out behind you. Slowly move your hips forward until you feel a stretch in the calf of the left leg.

AFTER-EFFECTS AND BENEFITS OF EXERCISE

If your muscles or joints are sore the day after exercising, you have done too much. Exercise only when you are in good health. If illness makes you inactive for a couple of weeks, ease yourself in gently when you start exercising again. If any pain persists afterwards, see your GP. Also, seek medical advice if you experience chest pain, excessive shortness of breath, light-headedness or dizziness, difficulty in balancing or nausea.

If you continue to exercise you will experience physical improvements which will spur you on. After 6 weeks of lifting weights, you will find it easier to carry the shopping, and in 3 months your muscles will be more toned. After 8 weeks of aerobic exercises you will have more energy. You may lose some fat and lower your cholesterol too.

LIFESTYLE AND MENTAL HEALTH

TRAVELLING

Getting out and about is a vital part of leading a fulfilling and healthy life, but it can present challenges when you are older. However, there are plenty of women who are still travelling the world in their nineties – don't let age defeat your sense of adventure!

The key to healthy travel in later life is careful preparation, not only in your destinations but also in the way you travel. For instance, going on a long journey by train may be a better option than a coach if you have a weak bladder.

Medical insurance is essential if you are going abroad. Go through the small print carefully to check whether there are any exclusions, especially for pre-existing medical conditions. Carry a notification card if you have a condition such as diabetes or epilepsy and take your GP's phone number with you.

Always make sure you have a good supply of your regular medications, and if these include strong painkillers it may be advisable to have a covering letter from your doctor if you are taking a large quantity. Granny drug smugglers are a rare breed but they do exist!

Driving

Your car can be your greatest mobility asset, vital for independence. All drivers must renew their licences and declare any medical conditions at the age of 70 and every three years after that. That means it's up to you to decide whether you are fit to drive or not; in fact, most women are very sensible about this and most are safe drivers.

The biggest mistake that women make is letting their husbands do the bulk of the driving, especially on long journeys. That's fine as long as he stays fit and well, but if something happens to him, just driving 30 miles can seem daunting to you. Don't let yourself become de-skilled behind the steering wheel – give him your reasons, and take turns.

With increasing age, reaction times slow down, it takes longer to spot potential hazards, and road signs and layouts can seem more confusing. Research by the Institute of Advanced Motorists has indicated that elderly drivers are more likely to be involved in collisions causing death or injury. Many of those involved have had 'near misses' previously, and if this has happened to you, or if your family and friends have expressed concern about your driving, then it probably is time to consider hanging up your driving gloves.

Before you do so, it may be worthwhile having a couple of refresher sessions with a driving instructor or the Institute of Advanced Motorists – you might just need a little more confidence, and probably all of us could benefit from a refresher course on the latest edition of the *Highway Code*.

There is no independent assessment of ability unless you have a specific medical condition, such as diabetes, or a relative or doctor contacts the DVLA and informs them that you may be no longer fit to drive. The DVLA wants over-75s to sit driving exams and have eye tests every 5 years, but at present there are no government plans to make them do this.

Air travel

There are very few medical conditions that mean you cannot fly. However, the air pressure in a standard commercial plane is equivalent to that at an altitude of 2,000 metres – a third less than at sea level. This can cause problems for people with breathing problems or with heart disease. If you are not sure about your own fitness, discuss it with your doctor before you make your booking.

Arthritis can also present problems – the average airline seat is a bit cramped, even for a person with normal joints. However, some seats do have more room and you can request these when you make your booking. You can also request a seat near the loo.

Airlines generally take a lot of care over their elderly passengers, especially if they have difficulty walking. Today's airports are the size of small towns, so there are motorized carts to whizz you to your departure gate if you have mobility problems. You are allowed to board the plane first, so that you don't feel hurried, and you will disembark last to avoid holding up others. In some cases, staff will physically lift you up and down the steps of the aeroplane. Before you buy your ticket, tell the airline you need help and check out the facilities they offer.

Short flights do not usually pose health risks, but if you are going long-haul you can maximize your well-being in the air.

♦ Pack your medication in your hand luggage so that it is easily accessible and take extra supplies in case your flight home is delayed.

- Ask your GP for advice on when to take medicines at your destination if you are crossing time zones.

- Air in a plane's cabin is very dry, so drink plenty of water and non-alcoholic drinks while flying to avoid dehydration. (Alcohol will make the problem worse.)

- Slap on plenty of moisturizer in advance to protect your skin.

- If you suffer from sensitive ears, taking a puff of a decongestant nasal spray an hour before landing can be helpful.

- If you have had eye surgery, especially a detached retina, ask your doctor about the advisability of flying. Eyes get dry in a pressurized cabin, so wear spectacles rather than contact lenses and use artificial tears if your eyes feel uncomfortable.

- Anyone, irrespective of age, can get deep vein thrombosis (DVT – a blood clot in their legs) during a long plane journey. You can buy special support stockings from pharmacies to prevent this. In addition, try to walk around as much as feasible when you are airborne and flex your calf muscles and wiggle your feet from time to time when you are seated to stop the blood pooling.

BEREAVEMENT

On average, women live 5 years longer than men and, because of their longer life expectancy, it's a sad fact that many women spend the last years of their lives as widows. Losing a partner is a bitter blow, especially if you have never coped alone before. Not only that, but at this stage in life inevitably you start losing your friends too.

Initially, women have to deal with the bereavement itself. Although there is no timescale for grieving, it's generally accepted that coming to terms with the death of someone you love, or have been very close to, can take up to two years. Everyone negotiates this emotional minefield in their own individual fashion: there is no 'right way' to behave. However, grief does go through distinct stages.

♦ A common first reaction is emotional numbness, which can last from a few hours to several days. This can help shield you from all the emotional pressures you will face at this time, including making funeral arrangements.

♦ This wears off to be replaced by feelings of supercharged intensity. You long for the person who has died. You may feel furious that they have left you and find it difficult to relax, sleep or concentrate. Guilt may kick in, too – remorse for the arguments you had or for the things you left unsaid.

♦ Then comes the time when you retreat into yourself like an animal licking its wounds. You want to deal with your sadness alone, perhaps even avoiding family and friends. Anything that reminds you of the person who died will make you cry.

♦ The final stage of grief is to accept the finality of death and move on. The crushing weight of sadness lightens and your appetite, energy and sleeping patterns return to normal. You may never completely get over losing someone you love but, with time and normal grieving, the pain becomes more bearable and you will start to take an interest in life again.

While you are grieving, do not be afraid to ask your family and friends for support, and try to express what you feel rather than bottling it up. Your judgement may not be reliable, so do not make any major decisions such as moving home. If you give yourself time and space to mourn, you are more likely to avoid mental-health problems later.

Some people get stuck in the grieving process, unable to move on or to acknowledge and deal with their feelings. Women most at risk are those with a history of mental illness, those who have experienced several other bereavements or those with negative feelings about the person who died. Also vulnerable are women with low self-esteem, those who were over-dependent on the deceased person or who lack support from family and friends.

The manner of death, especially if it was totally unexpected, can also make grieving more difficult to negotiate. Particularly hard to bear are sudden deaths, for example from road accidents (especially where the deceased was responsible) or heart attacks, suicides, death involving relationships that are not easily recognized by society – for example, a married or same-sex lover – murder, or a fatality where a post mortem or inquest is required.

Consider bereavement counselling, psychotherapy or attending Cruse meetings (the organization for the bereaved), where you will meet other people coping with loss.

If someone in your family is bereaved, the best thing you can do is to give them time and listen to them express their feelings. Offer practical help, too, such as doing the shopping or cooking a few meals, because they will initially find it difficult to cope with life's daily chores. If they do not seem to be coming out of the trough, encourage them to see their GP and get help.

DEPRESSION

Loneliness, chronic pain, loss of mobility or general ill health all mean that depression is very common in older people. Life simply isn't much fun when you can't do the things you want to do, if you have no one to talk to, your family are miles away, and you have lost your husband and several of your friends.

Sometimes there seems to be no particular reason for depression. However, traumatic events such as bereavement or physical illness – suffering a stroke or being diagnosed with Parkinson's, for example – can trigger it.

Just because you are older does not mean that you have to put up with feeling this way, especially if you sometimes think that life is not worth living any more. Warning signs that you need help are:

- ♦ feeling 'down' for weeks
- ♦ not wanting to be bothered to go out or meet friends
- ♦ a change in your appetite or sleeping habits

Depression is an illness, every bit as serious as a physical complaint, and your doctor will take it just as seriously. Luckily, there is plenty that can be done, whatever your age, to lift your mood.

Antidepressants

Antidepressants can help between 50 and 60 per cent of people who take them. There are two main types – tricyclics and SSRIs (see page 235). Which type you are given depends on your individual symptoms.

- ♦ **Tricyclics** can be especially helpful if you are sleeping badly, and if chronic pain is adding to your low mood; side effects, however, especially constipation and a dry mouth, can be troublesome.
- ♦ **SSRIs** work more quickly, but in the elderly can sometimes cause agitation.

Often it's a case of 'try it and see', and if your doctor gives you tablets that do not agree with you, tell her. There is plenty of choice.

Taking antidepressants will not turn you into a drug addict and can help you cope during a particularly tough time. Although your sleep patterns may quickly become more normal, it usually takes 1–2 weeks for antidepressants to start working, and it may be as long as 8 weeks for them to improve your life significantly.

If this is your first bout of depression, you may need to take the tablets for 6–12 months. If you have had depression before, your doctor may recommend that you stay on them longer. You need to come off antidepressants slowly to avoid mild withdrawal symptoms.

Other ways to combat depression

There are also things you can do yourself to ward off depression.

♦ Try to get out of the house every day, even if you have a condition like arthritis that makes mobility difficult.

♦ Let people help you if they offer, and find out if there are any local day centres or lunch clubs that will give you the chance to meet new friends. Often, transport is laid on.

♦ Try to eat properly. If you neglect your diet your health will suffer.

♦ It's also important not to try to blot out your feelings with alcohol. Not only is it a depressant, but it will rob your body of the vitamins and minerals it needs.

The natural antidepressant St John's Wort, which you can buy over the chemist's counter without a prescription, can be effective for mild depression. However, tell your GP if you are going to take it as it may react with other medicines you are taking. Some people prefer to go down the psychotherapy route (see page 237); again, your GP can arrange this.

If drug treatment or talking cures do not work, you may be referred to a psychogeriatrician (psychiatrist for the elderly) who specializes in treating depressed older people. If you are depressed, you might find it difficult to remember when your symptoms first began, or you may be vague about other details, so take a friend or family member with you to the initial interview so that the specialist can build up a clear picture of your life.

A woman's family can do much to help her if she is depressed. Older people with this condition tire easily, so offer practical help. Don't force someone to talk and don't bully them. Above all, be patient. Caring for someone with depression can be exhausting. Your Community Psychiatric Nurse can arrange for your relative to go to a day centre or day hospital to give you a break.

BEING PREPARED

None of us is immortal, and you can save worry for yourself, and heartache for your nearest and dearest, by thinking ahead to when the inevitable occurs. This may sound a bit gruesome, but this type of planning is best done when you are still fit and well, rather than when you have become terminally ill.

Around half the population dies without having made a will and by neglecting to do so they subject their families to a lot of problems. A will does not have to be written or witnessed by a solicitor to be legally binding but it does have to be witnessed by two people who are not beneficiaries or directly related to beneficiaries. Don't put off making a will unless you want the taxman to take all your money after your death.

Living Wills

Every mentally capable adult has the right to accept or refuse medical treatment. Making a Living Will enables you to ensure your feelings about this are known. You sign the will when you are mentally competent. It sets out the circumstances under which you would not want to receive life-prolonging medical treatment if you became incapable of making this decision.

Although Living Wills are not legally enforceable at present, the law may well change. This document can be helpful to medical staff responsible for your future care and family and friends can use it as evidence of your wishes.

In your Living Will you can set out treatments you would be happy or unhappy to have under particular circumstances and name someone you would like to be consulted at the time. When you do this, bear in mind that medical science does not stand still. You can cover yourself by saying that although you would prefer not to receive current treatments you might consider new ones.

Your Living Will should be in your medical notes, so tell your GP about it and give her a copy so it can be acted on in an emergency. Most GPs positively welcome Living Wills, and are very happy to discuss the contents and check that you have covered everything properly. It is advisable to send copies to the hospital treating you and to your nearest relatives.

Power of attorney

This is a legal document that authorizes one or more people to handle your finances if you are unable to do so. There are two types:

◆ Ordinary Power of Attorney
◆ Enduring Power of Attorney

Ordinary Power of Attorney. If you want someone to look after some, or all, of your financial affairs because of physical illness or injury, you can grant an Ordinary Power of Attorney. You should not do this if you have been diagnosed with mental illness or have a disease which will lead to mental degeneration, such as Alzheimer's (see page 429), because an Ordinary Power of Attorney automatically ends if you lose your mental faculties.

Enduring Power of Attorney. If you have been diagnosed with a mental illness or have a disease likely to lead to mental impairment, you should opt for an Enduring Power of Attorney. This can come into effect or continue after you lose your ability to make decisions.

If you have not already drawn up an Enduring Power of Attorney and you lose your mental capacity, a court application has to be made regarding your affairs. This means a court decides who will deal with your finances, not you. The process is usually time-consuming and costly. As with making a will, addressing this issue before you become too ill to do so can save your family much unnecessary grief and expense. In both cases it is highly advisable to seek expert advice from either a solicitor or the Citizens Advice Bureau so your interests are safeguarded.

SEXUALITY IN LATER LIFE

It is unfortunate that the media tends to equate sex with youth and vigour, and there is a popular assumption that once you are older you are 'past it'. Nothing could be further from the truth. A woman's sexuality is an essential part of her human nature, and there is no reason why you should have to give up having sex or intimate relations just because you have been alive a little bit longer than others. No matter what your age, a warm, loving sexual relationship can help to bring happiness and contentment, and there is evidence that older people who are sexually active live longer, and stay healthier, than those who are celibate.

However, there is more to 'sex' than just having penetrative intercourse, and though this is an essential part of a relationship to some women, others find more satisfaction just in physical closeness and emotional understanding, especially at an age when illness or physical infirmity can make actually having sex less enjoyable than before.

As mentioned in Chapter 6, very low oestrogen levels can lead to a dry vagina, and this in turn usually makes sex uncomfortable, and the vagina sore afterwards. Lubricating creams can help, but oestrogen cream is a more effective solution, and can also help prevent urinary-tract infections (see page 196).

Arthritis or back pain can also make having intercourse painful, and heart disease or breathing problems may mean that the exertion involved is inadvisable. Some drugs can also have side effects that reduce your sex drive, or your ability to have an orgasm.

However, you should never just assume you shouldn't have sex.

Pluck up courage and discuss it with your doctor. I suspect that most women would prefer to talk over this sort of highly personal problem with another woman, so if there isn't a female GP available, see your practice nurse. She won't be shocked, but will be happy to give you advice and help.

PHYSICAL ILLNESSES

Unfortunately, there's no getting away from it – as we get older, the body does not function as well as it used to.

Heart disease, especially, can sap energy levels. Most cancers also become more common with increasing age, along with failing sight and hearing, and memory loss can threaten your independence. However, for many women the biggest health problem they face is coping with arthritis.

ARTHRITIS

Arthritis – the term we all use for joint pain – can occur at any age, but sadly it does become much more common the older you are, and it's rare to find someone in their seventies who hasn't felt that at least one of their joints is a bit creaky at some time or another.

There are two main types of arthritis – osteoarthritis, which is caused by the joints becoming rough and worn, and inflammatory arthritis, caused by damage from the body's immune system. This section deals with osteoarthritis (OA); for information on inflammatory arthritis, see page 268.

In osteoarthritis, the cartilage cushions that protect the surfaces of the bone slowly become worn away. Though OA is often referred to as 'wear and tear', this is an over-simplification of the disorder. It seems that what is mainly at fault is the body's own ability to repair damaged cartilage and bone. In some areas the cartilage disappears, leaving the bone underneath exposed; it then grates on the other bone in the joint. This can result in the body trying to protect itself by forming new bone, but it grows in the wrong place, at the edge of the joint. This causes deformity and can lead to pressure in surrounding structures, such as nerves in the back.

OA is a condition that's far more common in women than in men, and the symptoms are more severe. Hand OA is twice as common in women, while knee OA is four times as common. The older you are, the more likely OA becomes. It does sometimes seem that the joints, more than other parts of the body, are not designed well enough to last a lifetime.

Osteoarthritis is a slow process that occurs gradually over many years. In some, just a small area of one joint is affected; in others several joints throughout the body slowly become very deformed. Most women over 75 will have symptoms of OA in at least one part of their body, and 25 per cent of women over 85 are disabled due to it.

Why has this happened?

It is often not clear why some women get OA while others don't; and why one hip, for instance, is affected more than the other one, or more than other joints in the body. However, there are some known factors that can increase the risk.

Top of the list is being overweight – the heavier you are, the greater the strain on your joints, especially the hips and knees. It is also more common in joints that have been subjected to a lot of heavy use, or have been injured. Normal activity and exercise are generally good for joints, and do not cause OA. But hard repetitive activity – for example, training and doing the marathon several times – can be damaging for the knees.

The tendency to be affected by OA can also run in families: eight genes have now been identified as playing a major part in the development of the disease. This familial tendency applies particularly to OA affecting the finger joints of middle-aged women.

Tell-tale signs

Though OA can affect any joint, it's far more common in weight-bearing joints – the hips and knees especially, and the joints in between the bones of the spine. In women it also tends to affect the joints of the hand, especially in the fingers and the base of the thumb.

The chief symptoms of OA are stiffness and pain, which tends to be worse on exercising the affected joint and at the end of the day. There may also be some stiffness after resting a joint, but this wears off once you get the joint moving. Joints may be creaky, and have a decreased range of movement, and when more severely affected may suddenly give way with no warning.

Symptoms can vary enormously, for no obvious reason, and a bad spell of pain and stiffness may be followed by a good spell lasting weeks or months when the joint gives little trouble.

Changes in the weather – especially damp weather associated with low atmospheric pressure – can make symptoms worse.

Progress of the disease

As OA progresses, affected joints become swollen, due either to an accumulation of fluid or to new growth of bone at the edge of the joint. The easiest place to see this is often in the fingers, where the joints become very knobbly. The joints may also appear to be larger as the muscles around them become thin due to lack of use.

As OA progresses, pain may become constant and more severe, occurring both at rest and at night. Just small movements of affected joints are difficult, and can make everyday activities troublesome – driving a car, using kitchen utensils or just getting out of the bath. Life isn't much fun if you can't walk, or even cook, without pain, so it's not surprising that many women with OA become very depressed.

OA in the spine can occur in the joints that are found between the individual bones. It can cause a slight change in the structure of the spine, which in turn can lead to spasm of the supporting ligaments and muscles, and together this can lead to severe back pain and stiffness. Though the lower back is often the worst affected, many women also have problems with their neck. Any new growth of bony spurs can cause pressure on the nerves leading to the spine, causing pain that radiates down the buttock and outer leg (sciatica) or pain across the shoulders and arms, with tingling in the fingers.

Tests and treatment

In the early stages the diagnosis is usually made by ruling out other causes of arthritis. There is no specific blood test for OA, and X-rays may be unhelpful, as they only reveal changes to bone, not cartilage. MRI scans are more helpful, as they do show what is happening to cartilage and to ligaments, but they are just too expensive to do on everyone who might have OA.

As OA progresses, changes are visible on a standard X-ray. As the cartilage thins, the space between the bones in a joint narrows, and in some cases the bones appear to be touching one another. Bony outgrowths, looking like spurs, can also be seen. However, X-ray changes do not necessarily correlate with pain, and an X-ray that looks pretty awful does not necessarily mean that the joint is causing a lot of discomfort or disability.

But it's important to remember that OA doesn't always progress, and thankfully most people with it are able to carry on a relatively normal life and don't become disabled. It's quite common for a joint to give trouble for a year or two and then to settle down. However, one or more joints, especially hips and knees, may continue to cause increasing pain and discomfort.

At the moment there is no cure for OA, so its treatment should be centred around relieving pain and maintaining mobility. Treatments include:

♦ Paracetamol, which is an excellent painkiller as long as you take enough of it (4g a day, which is 8 tablets). It is very safe, and generally does not cause any nasty side effects.

♦ Adding in codeine, and other stronger morphine-based analgesics, can give more pain relief but can cause constipation and also mental confusion.

♦ Non-steroidal anti-inflammatory drugs (NSAIs), such as ibuprofen, can also give relief from pain, but are best limited to short-term use as they can cause stomach inflammation and bleeding, and can also make any tendency to fluid retention worse. They can also increase the risk of heart disease.

- Locally applied creams, containing NSAIs or capsaicin, can also be helpful, but they need to be applied regularly each day to be effective.

- Physiotherapy can also be beneficial in helping to keep stiff joints moving and muscles strong.

- Osteopathy and chiropractic manoeuvres, done gently, can also help to re-align joints and relieve any associated muscle spasm.

Further treatment

More severe OA may be helped by a steroid injection into the affected joint, especially the thumb or the knee. Alternatively, a series of injections of hyaluronin may be given. This is similar to the fluid that is found within the joint capsule and can help to give extra lubrication.

Then there is surgery. Just tidying up rough cartilage and removing loose pieces of cartilage – an arthroscopy, which is done using keyhole surgery – can often bring a great deal of relief, particularly in knees.

The final option is to have the affected joint replaced. This is most commonly done for hips and knees, but can now be done for an increasing number of other joints, such as the elbow. Though the techniques are improving all the time, having a large joint replaced is a major surgical procedure and you should always discuss the pros and cons carefully with your surgeon beforehand. It's not something that should be undertaken lightly.

The enforced rest afterwards can lead to a significant risk of a deep vein thrombosis (DVT), and wound infections occur in about 10 per cent of cases. Sometimes pain can persist in the tissues around the joint, particularly after a knee replacement.

Unfortunately, false joints do have a limited lifespan, and some loosening of one of the components can start to occur after ten years, though some joints are now lasting twenty or more years. That said, having a new joint can give you a completely new lease of life, enabling you to move freely again without pain.

Self-help

The good news is that there is a lot that you can do yourself to limit the impact that OA has on your life.

The first thing to do is to reduce the stress on affected joints. You can do this by losing any excess weight – the heavier you are, the more load the joint has to carry.

It can be easier to lose weight if you combine dieting with regular exercise, but many people with OA feel they are in a catch-22 situation – they can't exercise because it makes their joints hurt. However, there are some exercises that you can do – see pages 405–409.

Wear flat shoes with thick soles that give a cushioning effect and act as shock absorbers for the knees and hips. High heels alter the angle of the hip and knee and can make OA worse, so wear them only when it's really necessary. And, reluctant though you may be to use one, a walking stick really can help to reduce stress on a painful leg. Make sure it's the right height though – your GP should be able to advise you on this.

It's also important to keep your joints moving, both for your general fitness and also to keep the muscles around joints strong. Muscles act partly as joint stabilizers; weak muscles will mean that the joint is more likely to give way and that you will fall over.

Many OA sufferers also find supplements helpful, especially cod liver oil, glucosamine and chondroitin (see pages 358–9).

Osteoarthritis and osteoporosis – what's the difference?

Many women get these two muddled up, but they are actually quite different conditions.

Osteoarthritis is a problem with the joints, specifically the cartilage covering the ends of bones, especially in the lower back, hips and knees. It causes pain and stiffness, which often starts in the early stages of the disease. It can be treated with painkillers or, if severe, by replacing affected joints.

Osteoporosis, by contrast, is a disease of the bones, which become weaker and more prone to breaking. It does not usually cause any symptoms at all until a bone either breaks or is crushed. Treatment is with calcium and drugs that help to strengthen bones.

Osteoarthritis is usually more severe in women who are overweight, while osteoporosis is more common in those of small, slight build. Many women do have both osteoarthritis and osteoporosis, but just because you have one does not mean you have, or will be affected by, the other.

LOSS OF MEMORY AND DEMENTIA

I think every older women has a dread of 'losing her marbles'. Unfortunately, some degree of memory loss is relatively common – 1 in 50 people between the ages of 65 and 70 have some form of dementia, and this increases to 1 in 5 over the age of 80. It's also a sad fact that dementia is more common in women than in men, though the reasons for this are unclear.

There are two main types of dementia:

♦ **Alzheimer's** is the one most people have heard of, and is caused by changes in the structure of the brain cells. In addition, there is a shortage of certain chemicals that are involved with the transmission of messages between the brain nerve cells.

♦ **Vascular dementia**, the second type, is caused by a decrease in the blood supply to the brain due to narrowed arteries.

Tell-tale signs

Everyone becomes a little bit more forgetful as they grow older, and just because you can't remember where you put your keys does not mean you are getting Alzheimer's. Dementia is more than being a bit absent-minded – it's a progressive change in mental function, losing the ability not only to remember, but also to reason, to understand and to communicate.

Early signs. Loss of memory can be an early sign, usually about recent events. However, there are often other minor changes in personality – slight confusion, a tendency to repeat what they have just said, difficulty making decisions and an unwillingness to adapt to change.

Later signs. Later, a person with dementia may become anxious or agitated, and get unduly distressed. She may blame others for lost items. This may progress to becoming confused about the time of day, 'wandering off', and behaving inappropriately, such as going outside in nightclothes.

There is a tendency for people with dementia inadvertently to put themselves at risk by leaving doors unlocked, or the gas on, or the bath water running. In the later stages there is a more marked personality change, with restlessness and aggression. The person may have difficulty eating, and may become incontinent. Inevitably, they become completely dependent on others to look after them.

How long this all takes varies enormously between different people, and cannot be predicted, but it is usually very slow, developing over the course of many years.

Why has this happened?

The exact reason why some people develop dementia and others don't is unclear, but, as with so many other diseases, a combination of genetic and environmental factors is thought to be involved.

Having an affected close family member does put you at a slightly increased risk, and this can be linked to your genes. It is now known that inheriting a particular type of the gene known as ApoE can influence the risk. ApoE comes in three forms: one type increases the risk, another decreases it and the third gives you an average risk.

Factors that increase the risk of atherosclerosis (furring and hardening of the arteries) also increase the risk of vascular dementia – so smoking, having a high cholesterol level, high blood pressure, being overweight and inactive are bad for your brain as well as your heart. A high alcohol intake can also damage brain cells.

Tests and treatment

There are many treatable illnesses in the elderly that can cause symptoms which may be mistaken for dementia. These include infections (often a urine or chest infection), constipation, an underactive thyroid, diabetes, stress and depression. These should always be excluded first. Many drugs used in the elderly can also cause a change in mental function, particularly sedatives and strong painkillers.

The diagnosis of dementia is usually made only after a series of memory tests, and often a brain scan as well.

Unfortunately, there is no cure for dementia at the moment, but drugs that boost the levels of the enzyme acetylcholine in the brain, such as donepezil, can slow down the progression of symptoms in some people. The drug memantine works in a slightly different way and can be helpful in those more severely affected. Currently, treatment on the NHS has to be commenced by hospital specialists.

Self-help

Much of the advice for keeping your brain functioning well is exactly the same as that for the heart:

- ◆ don't smoke
- ◆ eat a low-fat diet
- ◆ eat plenty of fruit and vegetables
- ◆ drink alcohol in moderation
- ◆ take regular exercise
- ◆ have your blood pressure and cholesterol level checked regularly
- ◆ there is some evidence that the omega 3 fatty acids found in oily fish are beneficial to nerve cells, so include this in your diet at least once a week

There is also increasing evidence that the old adage 'use it or lose it' really does have a ring of truth about it when it comes to brain function, so try to do something every day that is a mental challenge – a crossword, a sudoku, or learning a new skill, such as computing.

It has been suggested that caffeine, the herbs sage and lemon balm and extracts from Ginkgo biloba may have a protective effect on the brain, and it has also been claimed that vitamins A and E may be helpful for those with dementia. As yet, however, the research on these products is not conclusive one way or the other.

COMMON EYESIGHT PROBLEMS

Short-sightedness

For you to have perfect vision, your eyes must focus light directly on to your retina, the lining at the back of the eye which transmits images to your brain of what you are seeing.

Short sight happens when the eye focuses light in front of the retina, rather than on it. As a result, things that are further away become blurred, although objects that are close will look clear and sharp. Short sight usually develops when people are children or teenagers.

Long-sightedness

If you have this condition then your eye focuses light behind the retina. This forces the eye to work harder to re-focus, which can lead to headaches and problems seeing things that are near to. From the age of around forty, many people find that their distance vision becomes blurred.

Astigmatism

You are more likely than not to have this problem to some degree. It happens when the cornea (outer layer) or lens (light-focusing part) of the eye is not perfectly round. If it causes blurred vision or headaches then you may need to wear glasses or lenses at least some of the time.

Presbyopia (difficulty focusing the eyes)

This is something that happens to us all, and usually becomes noticeable around the age of 50. It occurs because the lenses in the eyes become less flexible with age, making it harder to focus on things that are near to.

Using reading glasses can help you focus on things that are close, but if you also have a degree of long-sightedness (which most older people do), then the answer is either two different pairs of glasses or, much more practically, bifocals or varifocals. Though you may not like having to resort to wearing glasses, they can stop headaches which are due to aching eye muscles, and they will not make your eyes lazy.

Age-related Macular Degeneration

This obscure-sounding condition is actually the most common cause of bad sight in people over 60 years old. It can lead to severe difficulties with vision although it only very rarely causes actual blindness.

The problem arises when the macula – a small part of the retina at the back of the eye, which is used when we look straight ahead – stops working properly. As a result, things that are straight in front can appear blurred or distorted, or, when the condition becomes advanced, they can be invisible. These changes are not painful but they can make daily life much more difficult. When they happen in older people they are known as Age-related Macular Degeneration (AMD).

The condition comes in two forms. The most common is 'dry' AMD, which gets worse slowly and for which there is no treatment. One in 10 people with AMD has the 'wet' form of the disease, which can become suddenly worse and can sometimes be helped by laser treatment in its early stages.

If you think your vision is changing slowly then ask your GP or optician to refer you to an eye specialist. However, if you notice sudden changes, go immediately to your doctor, or to a hospital accident and emergency department.

Glaucoma

Around 2 in every 100 people over the age of 40 in this country have some form of glaucoma. The condition involves damage to the optic nerve that carries signals from the eye to the brain, and this in turn damages your vision. Glaucoma can be caused by raised pressure within the eye (which has little to do with blood pressure) or by a weakness in the optic nerve.

The most common form is chronic glaucoma, which gets worse very slowly and causes no pain, although there is a gradual deterioration in quality of vision. Because the decline is so slow, there is a danger that people don't realize they have a problem. Early on, they may experience loss of vision in small arcs immediately above and below the central field of vision, but as the problem gets worse the 'blank' area spreads out, leaving the affected person with 'tunnel vision' – they can only see straight ahead. Even this last area of vision can eventually disappear.

Having a close relative with glaucoma puts you at greater risk of suffering it yourself, and this is why people whose close family members are affected are entitled to free annual eye tests to help detect any sinister changes early on. Being over 40 is another significant risk factor, so if you are in this group then have your eyes tested at least once every 2 years, and ask to have all three tests that are specifically for glaucoma.

Thankfully, if the condition is caught early and treated regularly (in hospital), then damage can be kept in check and good vision preserved.

Glasses

Wearing glasses can transform your experience of the world – where once you had only blurred vision, you will instead see shapes, patterns and faces in all their glory.

The eye test that shows you need glasses will determine the sort of lenses that you need to correct your vision. For example, people who are short-sighted will need concave lenses, and those with long sight convex ones.

Lenses are made with one, two or even three different corrections for your sight. Bifocals contain two distinct corrections and are most commonly used by people with presbyopia, with the upper part of the lens helping with distance vision and the lower part used for seeing things close up. Another, more attractive, type of lens is called varifocal, or progressive. There are no visible dividing lines between the different corrections; instead there is an invisible and smooth transition between one part of the lens and the next.

Experts recommend that adults have an eye test at least every 2 years to help pick up on any eye or other diseases. For those with certain medical conditions, including diabetes, they recommend a check once a year. People who get state benefits for those on low incomes, as well as everyone over 60 and those with medical conditions including diabetes and glaucoma, are entitled to free eye tests. Financial help towards the cost of glasses and contact lenses is also available to people on income-related benefits. Your GP or optician should be able to tell you whether you qualify.

Contact lenses

Another way to correct most common eyesight problems is to wear contact lenses, which are held naturally in place by the layer of tears covering the surface of the eye, though admittedly these can be fiddly to use, especially if you have arthritic hands.

These days there are two main types: rigid gas permeable and soft. The former are more rigid, easier to handle and usually longer lasting than soft lenses, but they do take longer to get used to. Rigid lenses are often used for people with more severe astigmatisms.

Soft lenses are more pliable and easier to adapt to wearing; they are often suitable for people with astigmatism or presbyopia.

Contact-lens wearers also have a choice between daily disposable lenses, lenses that are removed at night for disinfection, and extended-wear lenses which can be kept in overnight.

One thing to bear in mind is that people who wear lenses face a greater risk of eye infections than non-wearers. The risk is greatest among people who leave their lenses in overnight, although relatively new silicone hydrogel lenses may be less risky than traditional extended-wear lenses. Other problems arise when people fail to clean or look after their lenses properly; if you tend to cut corners then daily disposable lenses, or glasses, may be a safer bet.

Cataracts and how they are treated

A cataract is a clouding of the lens of the eye. It causes blurred vision, because it prevents the lens from properly doing its job of focusing light on the retina at the back of the eye and producing a clear image there. Cataracts produce symptoms, including blurred or misty sight, being dazzled by bright lights and seeing colours as faded, although all of these can also be symptoms of other eye problems.

Experts are unsure about what causes cataracts, although it is thought that contributory factors may include smoking, eating a poor diet and too much exposure to sunlight. Although they can form at any age, most cataracts occur as people get older. Of the 300,000 people a year who have NHS operations to remove their cataracts, the vast majority are over 80 years old.

The good news is that the operation is highly effective. It has a success rate of at least 95 per cent and is normally done under only a local anaesthetic, with most patients leaving hospital the same day. Most people enjoy an instant improvement in their sight, although full healing may take a few months. Complications are unusual.

Any NHS patient whose sight is significantly affected by a cataract can have the operation done free. The NHS waiting list is around 2–3 months. Private hospitals charge roughly £2,500 for the operation.

How to register as blind or partially sighted

If you are living with a significant sight problem, consider registering with your local council as partially sighted or blind. The register is confidential, and being on it will make you eligible for particular concessions, benefits and services. To sign up, you need a certificate from a consultant ophthalmologist (an eye specialist) – ask your GP to refer you.

HEARING PROBLEMS

It's a difficult thing for most people to admit, but struggling to hear may simply be a sign that you are getting older. There may be causes other than age, such as that your hearing is being damaged by loud noise (maybe from an iPod turned up too high) or that you have a medical problem. However, it's a fact that 4 in 10 people aged over 50 have some hearing loss, and among the over-70s this rises to 7 in 10.

Signs that you may have lost some hearing include:

♦ having difficulty hearing what's being said in noisy environments or on the telephone

♦ other people seeming to mumble

♦ other people thinking that you have the TV or music playing too loud

Reduced hearing can also be caused by ear conditions such as wax build-up, and less commonly by bacterial infections, which your GP will be able to help with. More rarely, a more serious medical problem is to blame, such as damage to the eardrums, or to tiny bones that help conduct sound through your brain. Treating these is a job for a specialist, and sometimes surgery can be helpful.

For most people, though, the way to improve hearing is a hearing aid. These can't restore precious natural hearing ability, but they can make a great difference to everyday life.

Hearing aids

Hearing aids help people to hear things by making sounds louder, and these days there is a wide range of models from which to choose. They won't suddenly give you perfect hearing, but they will make conversations easier and help you to feel more confident with other people. The strange thing about hearing aids, though, is that only about 1 in 3 of the people who would benefit from using them actually have one.

People can get used to having reduced hearing, and then find everything too noisy when they first try a hearing aid. Persistence is vital – it's really worth it to avoid losing touch with the world around you.

Digital or analogue?

The newest hearing aids are digital. Many of them help to reduce constant background noise such as traffic, and the better ones can be precisely adapted to your ears and your needs. Some also reduce the whistling that can be a problem with older types of hearing aid.

Analogue hearing aids have been around for longer and have fewer features than digital aids, but they are less expensive.

Hearing aids also vary in size and in the way they are worn; the most widely used rest behind the ear and have a tube which extends into the ear.

Many people find that wearing an aid in both ears is more helpful than in only one, but it may take 2–3 months to get used to wearing a hearing aid for most of the day.

How to get a hearing aid

To get an NHS hearing aid, you need your GP to refer you to an ENT (ear, nose and throat) consultant, or to the audiology department of a local hospital. They will test your hearing. If you've never had an aid before and the tests show you would benefit, then you are entitled to one or two digital aids. If you already use a hearing aid which was fitted within the last 3 years, then you probably won't be eligible. You may have to wait several months for your first appointment with a specialist, and then a further few weeks before your aid is fitted.

You can also buy a digital hearing aid privately, although each aid can cost up to £2,500, leaving a bill of £5,000 if you want one for each ear. Bear in mind that on average a hearing aid lasts for about 5 years.

IN SUMMARY

A woman's health in later years is just as important as in her first years. Her responsibilities to others may or may not have decreased. She may now be looking after an elderly partner, or 'babysitting' teenage grandchildren or even great-grandchildren. Alternatively, she may find herself on her own for the first time in her life. No longer does our image of 'granny' consist of a toothless little old lady dressed in black, eating soup from a bowl; instead she may well be happily spending the winter months in a warm climate, or helping in her local charity shop, or walking her dog through wind and rain.

This is a time when many women find it difficult to accept the constraints of slowing down, of aching joints and physical decline.

Some change is inevitable, but a strong mental attitude can make all the difference. As ever, dealing with a problem before it becomes overwhelming is vital, although this may be harder at an age when getting about is more difficult. Make use of your friends and relations, take them up on offers of help, and don't be too proud to accept their invitations.

CONCLUSION

I t used to be said that a woman's greatest asset was her looks. In the twenty-first century, I'd be more inclined to say that a woman's greatest asset is her health.

THE CARING ROLE

Despite the many advances in equality between the sexes, it is still true that women bear the greatest burden when it comes to caring for others. It would be a rare woman who never experienced any caring duties.

Women have so many roles to fulfil in life. They are mothers, sisters and partners; they are cooks, teachers and nurses; they are bankers, farmers and charity workers; what's more, all these roles are often expected to run concurrently, and an incredible amount of juggling goes on behind our front doors to make sure that our personal and family lives flow smoothly.

When you think what demands are placed on a woman throughout her life, it seems obvious that keeping herself healthy must be a priority. One woman may bear the responsibility for the mental and physical health of many others – children, husband, parents, siblings, friends, patients, colleagues.

But don't let me give the impression that the demands of women's caring roles are necessarily unreasonable or painful. Many women thoroughly enjoy the process of nurturing another human being, of whatever age, and find it a fulfilling, enjoyable experience.

One very important proviso: don't forget to take time for yourself. Common sense will tell you that all these people who rely on you will really miss you if you are incapacitated because you ran yourself into the ground, mentally and physically.

PERSONAL HEALTH

For personal reasons too, such as improving your quality of life and mental attitude, good health is so vital. I have shown throughout the book how improving your diet and taking some exercise can help in all sorts of fields, from PMT to arthritis, from depression to heart disease. I am hoping that anyone suffering from a curable disease or emotional problems will be inspired to make the small and gradual changes necessary for a better quality of physical and mental health. After all, a healthy woman can make a better contribution to society, as well as enjoying her own life more, free from the pain and restriction of illness.

So get out there and take a walk to your local park, with or without children or dogs. Don't buy any shopping this time; just appreciate the sun and rain, and the feeling of using your muscles. Be careful what you eat tonight. Try something new – don't get stuck in a rut. And take time to think about your life.

ARM YOURSELF WITH INFORMATION

There are occasions when a little ignorance can be a good thing – when your daughter, away at university, decides to do a parachute jump. Sometimes it's best not to know what is going on, at least beforehand. It just causes worry.

Medical knowledge, however, is another matter. There are many situations in our lives where being warned of risks means we can avoid a stumbling block ahead. Think of the dangers of sexually transmitted infections in a teenage girl. There she goes, having exciting sex with her new boyfriend, never thinking that she might be making herself infertile. A few years later, she settles down with her husband and tries to start a family, and it is only then that she realizes what damage she has done to her body. My aim is to make sure that every woman is aware of the warning signs and finds the remedy while there is time, or – even better – knows how to avoid the problem altogether.

Each time our body changes throughout life we need to be aware of the possible consequences, and how to cope with them. We need to know what help is available, and where to get it. This book aims to guide women through all those physical changes, from puberty, through the fertile years to menopause and beyond. And when old age comes, we need to be forearmed with knowledge and a good attitude so that our last years can be productive, fulfilling and, most of all, enjoyable.

I hope that the information in this book will prove illuminating and inspiring for women of all ages, and will be a useful resource for you, your daughter and your mother as the years go by.

RESOURCES

This is a selection of places where you can go for trusted information and advice. For general health advice regarding guidance on your local health services, I suggest the first port of call should be NHS Direct, telephone 0845 4647 / www.nhsdirect.nhs.uk. Also, see below:

DENTAL HEALTH

British Dental Health Foundation: for information and advice on all aspects of dental health, from childhood onwards. Smile House, 2 East Union Street, Rugby, Warwickshire CV22 6AJ. 0870 770 4000 / www.dentalhealth.org.uk

DIETARY INFORMATION

Food Standards Agency: www.eatwell.gov.uk
Vegetarian diets: Vegetarian Society: 0161 925 2000 / www.vegsoc.org

INFECTIOUS DISEASES

Health Protection Agency: for information on infectious diseases and health hazards in the community (such as chemicals, poisons and radiation). 7th Floor Holborn Gate, 330 High Holborn, London WC1V 7PP / www.hpa.org.uk

WOMEN'S HEALTH PROBLEMS

Wellbeing of women: 020 7772 6400 / www.wellbeingofwomen.org.uk

Women's health concern: 0845 123 2319 / www.womens-health-concern.org

CHAPTER ONE

ALLERGIES

Allergy UK: 01322 619898 / www.allergyuk.org

CHILDREN'S HEALTH

Institute of Child Health: www.ich.ucl.ac.uk

Your Child's Health: www.yourchildshealth.nhs.uk

Health For All Children: www.healthforallchildren.co.uk

For information on immunizations: www.nhs.immunization.nhs.uk

GENES AND GENETIC TESTING

The British Society for Human Genetics: www.bshg.org.uk

Genetics Centre, Guy's Hospital: www.guysandstthomas.nhs.uk

MENTAL HEALTH

Young Minds: 0207 336 8445 / www. youngminds.org.uk

www.sunsmart.org.uk

CHAPTER TWO

ACNE

Acne Support Group: 0870 870 2263 / www.stopspots.org
British Association of Dermatologists: (has a leaflet on acne that you can download) www.bad.org.uk

DRUGS, ALCOHOL AND SMOKING

Talk to Frank: Helpline 0800 776600 / frank@talktofrank.com
Drugscope: www.drugscope.org.uk
Addaction: www.addaction.org.uk
Turning Point: 020 7702 2300 / www.turning-point.co.uk
Alcohol Concern: 020 7395 400 / www.alcoholconcern.org.uk
ASH (Action on Smoking and Health): www.ash.org.uk
QUIT: 0800 002200 / stopsmoking@quit.org.uk

EATING DISORDERS

Eating Disorders Association: Youthline (up to age 18) 0845 634 7650
Adult helpline: 0845 634 1414 / www.edauk.com

SAFE SEX, FAMILY PLANNING, SEXUALLY TRANSMITTED INFECTIONS

Family Planning Association: 0845 310 1334 / www.fpa.org.uk

Brook Advisory Centres: 020 7284 6040 / www.brook.org.uk

Playing Safely: 0800 567 123 / www.playingsafely.co.uk

The Herpes Association: 0845 123 2305 / www.herpes.org.uk

National AIDS Trust: 020 7814 6767 / www.nat.org.uk

TEENAGE HEALTH

For general information on teenage health:

www.teenagehealthfreak.org

www.thesite.org.uk

CHAPTER THREE

CERVICAL CANCER AND SCREENING

Cervical Cancer: Jo's Trust / www.jotrust.co.uk

Cervical Screening: www.cancerscreening.nhs.uk

DEPRESSION AND MENTAL HEALTH

MIND: 0845 766 0163 / www.mind.org.uk

Royal College of Psychiatrists (factsheets on line): www.rcpsych.ac.uk

Mental Health Foundation: 020 7803 1100 / www.mentalhealth.org.uk

Depression Alliance: 0845 123 2320 / www.depressionalliance.org

Association for Post Natal Illness: 020 7386 0868 / www.apni.org

British Association of Counsellors and Psychotherapists:
www.bacp.co.uk

ENDOMETRIOSIS

National Endometriosis Society: www.endo.org.uk

FERTILITY PROBLEMS

British Infertility Counselling Association: 0114 263 1448 /
www.bica.net

Ectopic Pregnancy Trust: 01895 238025 / www.ectopic.org

Fertility UK: www.fertilityuk.org

Human Fertilization and Embryology Authority: 020 7291 8200 /
www.hfea.gov.uk

Infertility Network UK: 08701 188088 / www.infertilitynetworkuk.com

More to Life: 08701 188 088

IRRITABLE BOWEL SYNDROME AND PILES

IBS Network 0114 272 3253 / www.ibsnetwork.org.uk

POLYCYSTIC OVARIAN SYNDROME (PCOS)

Verity: www.verity-pcos.org.uk

PREGNANCY

Benefits advice: Department of Work and Pensions: www.dwp.gov.uk

National Childbirth Trust: 0870 444 8707

Tommy's Baby Charity: 08707 70 70 70 / www.tommys.org

RELATIONSHIP PROBLEMS

Relate: 0845 130 4016 / www.relate.org.uk

British Association for Sexual and Relationship Therapy: 020 8543 2707 / www.basrt.org.uk

British Association for Counselling and Psychotherapy: 0870 443 5161 / www.bacp.co.uk

CHAPTER FOUR

ANGER

British Association of Anger Management (BAAM): 0845 1300 286 / www.angermanage.co.uk

ARTHRITIS

Arthritis Research Campaign: 0870 850 5000 / www.arc.org.uk

Arthritis Care: 0808 800 4050 / www.arthritiscare.org.uk

DOMESTIC VIOLENCE

Respect: National Association for Domestic Violence Perpetrator Programmes and Associated Support Services: 020 8563 8523 / www.respect.uk.net

EXERCISE

Keep Fit Association: 020 8692 9566 / www.keepfit.org.uk
Sport UK: 020 7211 5100 / www.uksport.gov.uk
Dancesport (including list of dance schools in the UK): 020 8568 0083 / www.dancesport.uk.com
English Federation of Disability Sport: 0161 247 5294 / www.efds.net

FIBROIDS

Fibroid network: www.fibroidnetworkonline.com

HAIR LOSS

Hairline International: 01564 775281 / www.hairlineinternational.co.uk
Institute of Trichologists: 0870 607 0602 / www.trichologists.org.uk

HEADACHES AND MIGRAINES

Headache UK: 020 7436 1336 / www.headacheuk.org
Migraine Action Association: 01536 461333 / www.migraine.org.uk
Migraine Trust: 020 7436 1336 / www.migrainetrust.org

HYSTERECTOMIES

The Hysterectomy Association: 0871 781 1141 / www.hysterectomy-association.org.uk

LUPUS

St Thomas' Lupus Trust: 020 7188 3562 / www.lupus.org.uk

PRE-MENSTRUAL SYNDROME

National association for Pre-menstrual Syndrome: 0870 777 2177 / www.pms.org.uk

STRESS

International Stress Management Association: 0700 0780 430 / www.isma.org.uk
UK Council for Psychotherapy (UKCP): 020 7436 3002 / www.psychotherapy.org.uk

THYROID DISEASE

Thyroid UK: 01255 820407 / www.thyroiduk.org

CHAPTER FIVE

BREAST DISEASE

Breakthrough Breast Cancer: 08080 100 200 / www.breakthrough.org.uk

Breast Cancer Care: 020 7384 2984 / www.breastcancercare.org.uk

Breast Cancer Haven: 020 7384 0099 / 01432 361 061 /
www.breastcancerhaven.org.uk

CARERS

Carers UK: 020 7490 8818 / www.carersuk.org

Help the Aged – senior line: 0808 800 6565 /www.helptheaged.org.uk

Citizens Advice Bureau: 08451 264 264 / www.citizensadvice.org.uk /
www.adviceguide.org.uk

COSMETIC SURGERY

The Department of Health has an excellent website: www.dh.gov.uk
(search for cosmetic surgery)

Healthcare Commission, for checks on clinics:
www.healthcarecommission.org.uk

Royal College of Surgeons: www.rceng.ac.uk

British Association of Aesthetic and Plastic Surgeons:
www.baaps.org.uk

British Association of Beauty Therapy and Cosmetology:
www.babtac.com

MENOPAUSE

The Amarant Trust: 01293 413000 /
www.amarantmenopausetrust.org.uk
Daisy Network: www.daisynetwork.org.uk

OSTEOPOROSIS

National Osteoporosis Society: 0845 130 3076 / www.nos.org.uk

CHAPTER SIX

BLADDER PROBLEMS

InContact: 0870 770 3246 / www.incontact.org

CANCER

Cancer Research UK: 020 7061 8355 / 0800 226 237 /
www.cancerhelp.org.uk or www.cancerresearchuk.org
Cancer Backup: 0800 800 1234 / www.cancerbackup.org.uk
Breast cancer: Breast Cancer Care: 0808 8006000 /
www.breastcancercare.org.uk
Breakthrough Breast Cancer: 08080 100 200 / breakthrough.org.uk
Ovarian cancer: Ovacome: 020 7380 9589 / www.ovacome.org.uk

Bowel cancer: Beating Bowel Cancer: 020 8892 5256 /
www.beatingbowelcancer.org.uk
Bowel Cancer UK: 08708 50 60 50 / www.bowelcancer.org.uk

DIABETES

Diabetes UK: 0845 120 2960 / www.diabetes.org.uk

EXERCISE

Extend: 01582 832760 / www.extend.org.uk
The Fitness League: 01932 564567 / www.thefitnessleague.com

HEART DISEASE

British Heart Foundation: 0845 120 2960 / www.bhf.org.uk

LICHEN SCLEROSIS

Lichen Sclerosis support group: www.lichensclerosis.org

RETIREMENT

Department for Work and Pensions: 0845 120 2960 / www.dwp.gov.uk
Pensions Service: 0845 60 60 265 / www.thepensionservice.gov.uk
Age Positive: www.agepositive.gov.uk

CHAPTER SEVEN

ACTIVITIES

Third Age Trust: 020 8466 6139 / www.u3a.org.uk

The Dark Horse Venture: 0115 256 8866 / www.darkhorse.rapid.co.uk

AGE CONCERN

Age Concern: Astral House, 1268 London Road, London SW16 4ER / 0800 009 966 / www.ageconcern.org.uk

Help the Aged: 0808 800 6565 / www.helptheaged.org.uk

ALZHEIMER'S AND DEMENTIA

Alzheimer's Society: 0845 300 0336 / www.alzheimers.org.uk

For Dementia: 020 7874 7210 / www.fordementia.org.uk

Dementia Care Trust: 0870 443 5325 / www.dct.org.uk

ARTHRITIS AND BACK PAIN

Arthritis Research Campaign: 0870 850 500 / www.arc.org.uk

Arthritis Care: 0808 800 4050 / www.arthritiscare.org.uk

Back Care: 0845 130 2704 / www.backpain.org

BEREAVEMENT

Cruse Bereavement Care: 0870 167 1677 /
www.crusebereavementcare.org.uk

EYESIGHT

Royal National Institute for the Blind: 0845 766 9999

HEARING

Royal National Institute for the Deaf: 0808 808 0123

INSURANCE AND TRAVEL

Insurance: BIBA: 020 7626 9676 / www.biba.org.uk

DVLA: 0870 240 0009 / www.dvla.gov.uk

Institute of Advanced Motorists: 020 8996 9600 / www.iam.org.uk

Tourism For All: 0845 124 9971 / www.tourismforall.org.uk

INDEX